Kitty Bartholomew's

DECORATING STYLE

RODALE
LIVE YOUR WHOLE LIFE™

Every day our brands
connect with and inspire
millions of people to live
a life of the mind, body,
spirit — a whole life.

Kitty Bartholomew's
DECORATING STYLE

A Hands-On Approach to Creating Affordable, Beautiful, and Comfortable Rooms

Kitty Bartholomew and Kathy Price-Robinson

RODALE

Notice

The writers and editors who compiled this book have tried to make all the contents as accurate and correct as possible. Photographs and text have been carefully checked and cross-checked. However, due to the variability of personal skill, tools, materials, and so on, neither the writers nor Rodale Inc. assumes any responsibility for any injuries suffered or for damages or other losses that result from the material presented herein. All instructions should be carefully studied and clearly understood before beginning any project. Mention of specific companies, organizations, or authorities in this book does not imply endorsement by the publisher, nor does mention of specific companies, organizations, or authorities imply that they endorse this book. Internet addresses and telephone numbers given in this book were accurate at the time it went to press.

Printed in the United States of America
Rodale Inc. makes every effort to use acid-free ∞, recycled paper ♺.

Book design by Patricia Field

Library of Congress Cataloging-in-Publication Data

Bartholomew, Kitty.
   Kitty Bartholomew's decorating style : a hands-on approach to creating affordable, beautiful, and comfortable rooms / Kitty Bartholomew and Kathy Price-Robinson.
        p.   cm.
   Includes index.
   ISBN-13 978–1–59486–071–3 hardcover
   ISBN-10 1–59486–071–8 hardcover
   1. Handicraft.   2. House furnishings.   3. Interior decoration.   I. Price-Robinson, Kathy.   II. Title.
TT157.B345   2005
747—dc22   2004029469

Distributed to the trade by Holtzbrinck Publishers

2   4   6   8   10   9   7   5   3   hardcover

RODALE
LIVE YOUR WHOLE LIFE™

We inspire and enable people to improve their lives and the world around them
For more of our products visit **rodalestore.com** or call 800-848-4735

I dedicate this book to Buzzy, my first love and the father of
our three children, whose emotional and spiritual generosity
gave me freedom without guilt to pursue my creativity,
and to Brooke, Bo, and Birdie, who are my greatest
creative projects and my finest creations.

—Kitty Bartholomew

I dedicate this book to my husband, Bill Robinson,
who has gently pushed me toward greatness,
both by encouragement and by example.

—Kathy Price-Robinson

Contents

Introduction

How do you make your home affordable, beautiful, and cozy—in your very real life with your very real budget? You're going to make a lot of choices, and I'm going to show you how.

The word *decorating* sounds so daunting, like it would take a special degree, months of precious time, and a whole lot of money to do it. That's why this isn't a book about decorating your home.

Instead, this is a book about *furnishing* your home. So relax. Take it easy. The key is that decorating is elective—you don't *have* to do it. But think about it: You're going to be furnishing your home anyway. All you have to do is make some choices. It's as simple as getting dressed in the morning.

Furnishing instead of decorating takes a huge amount of pressure off. You're going to do it anyway, so what's the big deal? The biggest question is: How do you make it work best for you?

The thing that is so amazing is that even small choices can make a big difference in your mental state. Not just *your* mental state, but your family's mental state. I think a lot of people are unaware of the impact your choices in furnishing your home can make. It could be as simple as adding a light near a chair. Or being able to pull an ottoman up rather than just dangling your feet. After making those two small choices, you might suddenly find yourself reading more, or enjoying the newspaper more, or

How do you make your home **affordable, beautiful, and cozy—** in your **very real life** with your **very real budget?** You're going to make a lot of **choices,** and I'm going to show you how.

Every day you furnish your body with clothes. You're going to put shoes on. Chances are you're going to put socks on. You might choose to put white socks with your black shoes, or black socks with your black shoes. But you're going to dress yourself. You're going to make choices. The same goes for your home.

actually finishing magazine articles. The furnishings in your home can really affect you, your lifestyle, your spouse, your children, and your friends and visitors. It's all about making cost-effective choices that work for you. This book helps you to make those choices.

I'd like to suggest that the essence of this book could be

summed up in photograph. You see two finials, which are designed to screw onto the ends of a curtain rod. They give the rod a finished look and prevent it from slipping off its brackets. So in both finials, we've got form and we've got function. But which one would you choose for your home?

Notice the finial on the left. It's new, clean, and unfinished, unburdened with color or depth. Some fashion trends call for just this look: spare and simple, uncluttered and unfettered. Perfect, really. The finial on the right, however, is what this book is about. I transformed it from a stark and barren object into a lush and gleaming addition to my home. I whacked the finial with a chain belt and a garden cultivator (see the nicks?), poured strong coffee over it, ground dirt and gravel into it, and, finally, polished it to a deliciously warm glow. *That's* what this book is about: beauty and imperfection.

Now I'm not suggesting you go out and buy a knob-finishing kit. I'm suggesting you learn to look at something wonderful in a house, magazine, or store and then ponder, "Hmmm, how was that done?" And then think, "I can do that!"

I also took the same kind of finials, but larger, and used them in a different way. I screwed them into the top corners of my dining room bay window and then draped beautiful silk fabric over the top to create a unique valance. That's *also* what this book is about: finding new ways to use common things.

In my bedroom, I cut and painted some old table legs I found in the attic to make new finials for the posts on my four-poster bed. I turned the needlepoint seat cushions of my grandmother's chairs into pillows, and I converted her crocheted tablecloth into a shower curtain. I framed a picture of my dad with buttons from his military uniforms, and I made a colorful floor canvas with paint left over from various rooms and projects. That's *also* what this book is about: finding new uses for things. And when I found out that

This book is about choices. Which curtain finial would you choose?

the wallpaper I wanted for my hallway was no longer available, I created a stencil based on a sample of the paper, and I stenciled the exact pattern right onto my walls. That, too, is what this book is about: empowering you to go forward.

If you've seen me on television or in person, you're familiar with my decorating philosophy: *It's not what you* don't *have, it's what you* do *with what you* do *have.* Look at what you already have—a chair, a couch, a wall, a window, a house—and find creative, clever, affordable ways to make it warm, to make it cozy, and to make it work for you.

My goal is to encourage you to embrace a hands-on approach to furnishing your home, an approach where money is not going to stand in the way of you getting the look and feel you want. Those curtain rod finials might be found in the most luxurious home, in the swankiest showroom, or in your very own living room. I want

Come On In!

Hello! Welcome to my book. Please step inside for a visit. Grab a mug of tea, put your feet up, and enjoy. Here's what you'll find . . .

OVERVIEW: At the beginning of each chapter, I share my thoughts on how to approach bedrooms, kitchens, dining rooms and so on, with clever ideas and affordable solutions.

GET YOUR HANDS DIRTY: Let me show you projects I've done that are fun, fun, fun. Try these, if you wish, and then create your own.

A PRIVATE TOUR: Join me as I "walk my talk," showing you how I've put these ideas and principles to work in "My Home."

IN MY OPINION: You know why I love giving advice? Because I get such great questions. In "Ask Kitty" I help solve real decorating dilemmas.

LET'S GO SHOPPING: I'm taking you along on my flea market outing. Best bring a basket, as you'll be amazed at what we'll find.

GOT A MINUTE? Here are some "Last-Minute Ideas" that might make your own home more beautiful, comfortable, and cozy.

Here I am at the **flea market,** seriously on the lookout for the next item to **put a smile on my face.** When that happens, I stop and **give it a look.**

to help you create a home with continuity, flow, and warmth, without spending a lot of money. You want to paint a floor canvas? I'll show you how. Dress a mantel? I've got some ideas. Wonder how to get started? I'll tell you how I figured it out for my own home.

Most of the chapters in this book are separated into three parts. The first part of each chapter gives you some basic thoughts on the topic, be it furniture, walls, bathrooms, or living rooms. In the second part of each chapter, I walk you through my own house and explain how I made my own choices. In the third section, I give directions for some projects that I really enjoyed doing in my home and that I think you might like to do in yours. Then I answer my favorite reader decorating questions. I hope these will solve some dilemmas that you have in your own home. And, finally, I give some last-minute ideas.

One of my favorite chapters in the book is Flea Market Shopping with Kitty. I thought it would be fun to take you flea market shopping with me to show you some of the neat things I found and explain some of the possibilities those things could have. Toward the end of the book, you'll find a chapter called Organizing, Tools, and Resources. Finally, I've put my life story down on paper in Kitty's Story so you can see how providence brought me to share my decorating knowledge with you.

You may have heard me point out that "if you're curious, you can do anything." I guess I'm lucky that I was born curious. I've always wanted to know how things worked, why they worked, and how I could take them apart and put them together again better than before. When my husband and I bought our first house, an appallingly ugly dwelling, I set out to redo it and discovered a happy thing about myself: I have no fear when it comes to decorating. Completing one project inspires me to try the next.

This is the real me, getting my hands dirty and getting involved to make my family's home beautiful and comfortable without spending a lot of money.

I don't know if I'd use the word *success* to describe what I've accomplished since that first house. The point is that I've had so much pleasure. And I want to share that great feeling with you. I want to give you information and inspire you so that you can get your house to work for you and your family and have it reflect what you're all about. Most of all, I want this book to show you how incredibly satisfying it is to create an affordable, beautiful, and comfortable home for you and your family. So relax, take it easy, take some risks, and enjoy the ride. Let's get started!

Treatments

I installed unfinished **tongue-and-groove bead board** two-thirds of the way up the wall and then gave it a **unique paint and glaze finish.**

color and wall treatments

People often ask me, "Where do you get your inspiration?" I get my inspiration everywhere! I've got my eyes wide open, and I notice things other people don't. You can teach yourself to do this. Notice the furnishings in a room that appeal to you. Notice the things that don't appeal to you. Notice light and dark. And most of all, notice color and how it makes you feel.

Color affects us on many levels. Color is more than style, more than beauty, more than a trend—it touches us at the core. Color can make us feel warm, calm, or safe. It can fill us with anxiety, or it can fill us with peace. Color can make food taste better, or color can make food taste worse.

People ask me a lot of questions about color. How do I create a color palette for my home? What color should I paint my living room? Will celadon green walls be too dark for my den? Are red walls okay for my dining room?

I like questions about color because they tell me that people are open to having color in their lives. I like color in my life. And if you know me, you know that red is my favorite color.

While people used to be timid about experimenting with color, that is changing. White, off-white, and very pale neutrals were by far the most common wall colors in houses across the country for decades. In the 1980s, a common question I got was, "How can I make my room look bigger?" Generally, the answer to that question is to paint the walls a light color, even white, to open up the space.

I rarely get asked that question anymore. People have learned that making a room look bigger doesn't always work for them. I think that today people want to have their homes as their refuge, their shelter. They don't care about big so much as they do cozy. And an easy way to make a room feel cozier is to warm it up with color. Generally, the darker the color of the walls, the smaller—and cozier—a room will feel.

Of course, where you live in the country influences the colors you choose. Californians tend to be pacesetters and experimenters. On the East Coast, there is a lot more tradition and history and often there are historical areas where the exterior house color, for instance,

Decorate Kitty's Way

❑ **Identify** what you like in other people's homes, then re-create a similar look in yours. **Use colors** that make you feel **comfortable,** rather than colors that are trendy. ❑ Use **low-sheen paint** to hide imperfect walls. ❑ Add a touch of black in every room because it makes the colors around it **more vivid.** ❑ **Tie rooms together** by repeating one **main color** or one accent color from an adjacent room.

is dictated by architectural by-laws of the community. In the Midwest, jewel tones are big. People feel very comfortable with a rich, library palette of burgundy, navy blue, and forest green, and variations of that every which way.

In the heartland, folks are more cautious about exploring color. Things that are different are not easily accepted. Let's say that I went jogging in San Diego wearing a chartreuse jogging suit. People wouldn't

People feel comfortable with jewel tones—burgundy, navy blue, and forest green.

look twice at me. But if I were jogging in a chartreuse jogging suit in Des Moines, Iowa, people might say, "Whoa, that's a little weird."

Throughout the country, color choices are influenced by climate and landscaping, too. For instance, in the Southwest sagebrush colors and sand colors are popular. Tropical plants and tropical colors are prevalent in the Southeast. The South, attempting to combat heat and humidity, tends to favor lighter colors.

In this chapter, I'll share my favorite ways to bring more color and textures into your life, starting with your walls. Once you've lived with color, you'll never go back. Color for your walls truly embodies the ideals of affordable, beautiful, and comfortable rooms. Paint isn't expensive, but the color that it adds to a room really increases its beauty and comfort.

That being said, if you don't want a lot of color in your rooms or if you don't want a lot of different colors throughout your home, you can add interest with textures, patterns, and shades of the same color, even if it's white or cream.

The **color on my kitchen walls** is called "elephant's breath," and it's a **nice departure from off-white.** If you have white or off-white moldings, a color on the walls **kicks up** the **impact of the moldings.**

Living Life in Color

When I talk about color, I'm not talking so much about trends, but rather about how color makes you feel. There's more to color than meets the eye. I think it's a lot more important to make color work for you than to be trendy. While it's interesting to know about color trends, it's more important to know how people respond when they are in the presence of color.

Color Trends

Just like clothes, colors have trends. Are you old enough to remember the pedal pushers that were popular in the '50s? Well, now they're back, and they're called capris. Colors are trendy as well and cycle back now and again. Who could have predicted that harvest gold and avocado green would be popular again? Of course, young adults wouldn't call this rich maize color harvest gold, but we know it is. And we know a lot of the greens that are out there today are really those avocado greens we swore we'd never use again.

As for color trends for the future, I don't think that can be predicted accurately. A lot of it depends on what is happening in the world at any given time, what kind of art is being created, what kinds of movies are popular, and what's going on with trade, climate, and scientific inventions. So many things influence color trends and fashion. What we do know is that everything that was old will be new again.

But I do have one prediction: I predict that wallpaper is coming back. For years and years, we've focused on using great blocks of color, and I think we're ready for a change, perhaps something prettier. For quite some time, high fashion made "understated elegance" the rage and frowned on "pretty." But I think patterns and prettiness will come back—to the delight of many of us.

Red walls make my **office feel cozy,** especially at night.

Color 101

Here's a primer on a few color terms you might not have heard before.

CHROMA: The chroma of a color is how saturated that color is. For example, the yellow of a child's rain slicker is a very high chroma yellow.

VALUE: The value of a color has to do with its lightness or darkness. For example, the red of a Red Delicious apple is a high value of red.

COLOR WHEEL: The color wheel is a tool that shows how the major colors relate to each other. For example, on a color wheel you see that the color orange is opposite the color blue, and opposite colors complement each other.

Color Choices

The main thing about any color is whether or not it works for you and your family, not whether or not it's trendy or popular. And to know if a color will work for you, it helps to know more about how color affects us.

I've studied books on color for many years, and there's a lot of research that proves that certain physiological things happen to you when you're in the presence of color. Much of my information comes from the Wagner Institute for Color Research in Santa Barbara, California, which studied color for more than 30 years. Knowing how color impacts people's moods will help you to make choices, such as how to furnish your home, which car to buy, or even what to wear when going to the bank for a loan.

Let's talk about each of the major colors in turn: red, pink, orange, yellow, green, blue, purple, brown, gray, black, and white.

RED

I'll start with my favorite. Red is the most dynamic, warmest, and most energizing color of the spectrum.

As you know, not all reds are alike. In fact, red is the great separator between men and women. Men and women respond to reds in very different ways. When babies are born, the first thing they focus on is shapes—both black and white. Then they start focusing on color, in particular the color red. But here's the difference: Little boy babies will see yellow-based red first. This would be a tomato red, or what we think of as lipstick red. Little girl babies will see blue-based reds first. An example of a blue-based red is burgundy.

Looking at the color red can actually make us feel hot. It can accelerate heart rate and breathing and raise blood pressure. Red can stimulate the pituitary gland. Red also makes food look more appealing. Restaurants know this, which explains red-checked tablecloths. Studies have shown that men in particular eat more, drink more, and spend more money when there's red in their line of vision. So red is a good color choice for the dining room or kitchen.

Another reason red is a good choice for the dining room is that it looks especially good in rooms in the nighttime, which makes it a wonderful color to use in rooms that are used primarily in the evening. Red can also be very flattering to any kind of complexion, especially by candlelight or low-voltage lighting. Even if red makes the dining room look smaller, so what? You'll be dining most often at night, and the coziness can add much to your life.

Red has been shown to stimulate the creation of positive neurons in the brain. So it makes a lot of sense to have it somewhere in the nursery. I'm not advocating red walls in the nursery; that

Red in the kitchen helps stimulate the appetite.

Pay Attention to Light

When you're thinking about color for your walls, I suggest that you really pay attention to the lighting in a room and the exposure to natural light. How many windows do you have? How much sunlight does the room get? What direction does the room face? Are you using the room primarily in the daytime or the nighttime?

Here's an example. Even though the color blue is a very calming, restful color, and many people like the choice for a bedroom for its relaxing qualities, there are times when blue may not work. I painted a bedroom blue, which was calming and which would generally be a good choice for me. With my high energy level, I thought, "Oh boy, this is just what I need after a busy day." But guess what? It didn't work for me, and I'll tell you why. It was a northern-facing room that didn't get much sun. I found that I always felt cold in that room. I may have been calm, but I was cold and calm, so it didn't work for me. I'd rather be warm than calm any day. I could have repainted the room, but instead I in-stalled small, round skylights, called So-latubes, that brought natural light from above and turned out to be a wonderful solution.

On the other hand, if you live in Arizona and you have a room with large windows that gets a lot of sunlight, you probably don't want to paint the room red or orange, which are very warm colors. The combination of the heat from the atmosphere, the sun in the windows, and the warm colors on your walls will just be too much. You'd be better off painting your walls a neutral color or a cool blue or green.

---

might be a bit much. But red toys, mobiles, or area rugs would make a lot of sense.

The intensity of red can be overwhelming, though. It can be very stimulating. Let's say you have an adolescent who's very hyperactive, and you need to calm him down. You wouldn't want to have a primary shade of red in his bedroom because it would add to his overstimulation.

You can tone down red with the shades of green and blue-green that are its opposite on the color wheel. You can temper it with beiges and off-whites. Artwork in these colors or plants in a red room will provide necessary visual balance and relief. Or, you can just add red for accents instead of painting the whole room red. Spray-paint a wicker table red for accent in a living room or dining room. Or add some red to a kitchen with a red-and-white-checked floor or throw rugs.

PINK

Pink is wonderful. It's actually been proven to enhance the personal value of things. If you have a weight room, you can lift stronger weights if the room is painted pink because it enhances your perception of strength.

Pink has also been found to combat anger. The stronger the color pink, the better it will do this. This is surprising because pink isn't that far away from red, so you would think that pink would also stimulate the pituitary gland. But instead the color pink stimulates another hormone that can calm down anger.

Let's say you're going to have a confrontation with someone or you have to fire someone. Having pink around will help defuse the anger.

Here's another interesting quality about the color pink. It makes sweets taste sweeter. Bakeries know this. Oftentimes, baked goods come in pink boxes. So let's say you're on a diet and you go and buy a sugarless brownie. Put it on a pink plate, and I guarantee it's going to taste like it's got tons of sugar in it.

The color pink is also very flattering to our complexions. Here's a decorator tip you may not know about: Use pink light-bulbs. They used to be hard to find, but you can find them in many stores now. Try them out. They're very flattering to skin, but yet they're subtle. You don't walk in a room and say, "Oh, there's a pink light-bulb."

Pink would be a good choice in a laundry room (who couldn't use a little calm when faced by mountains of laundry?) or perhaps in a dining room.

Despite these many good attributes of the color pink, it can be hard to live with for a long period of time. A lot of men aren't wild about living in pink bedrooms or pink living rooms, but I think that when it's used in the proper place, pink can be a great decorator color.

ORANGE

The color orange is a very faddy color right now. You're seeing a lot more orange in interior design and clothing than you ever did before. Reality decorating shows use a lot of bright orange and lime green because they're hip, faddy colors. And that's fine, if you like to be on top of the latest trend. But orange is a tough choice to live

oneminutemakeovers

Old color ads from vintage magazines make interesting artwork. Cover them with Plexiglas, and screw the Plexiglas to kitchen cabinets, stairways, and other quirky places. Imagine how nostalgic an old cereal ad would look on your pantry door!

with, I think, for a long period of time—especially in its strongest values, like pumpkin orange.

Research indicates that the best use of orange is when you want people to think economy—low cost. Home Depot knows this, and they use orange in their signs and logo. They want to give you the perception that you will find good value there. Where would you want people to think value? What if you're having a garage sale? You might buy white poster board for your signs. But if you have a choice, buy orange instead. Subconsciously, people will think, "I'll bet there will be some good deals there." But orange probably wouldn't be a good choice if you were going to a very formal black tie party. If you found a dress that you loved for $600 but it was orange, nobody would believe you spent $600 for it.

But if you love the warmth of the color orange, consider a soft, brown-infused orange like coral. A pinkish kind of orange like salmon also goes in a lot of décors and is very flattering to most complexions. It's kind of a sexy color, great in a bedroom and great in a living room.

You also might like terra cotta; it's a rich and earthy color.

You'll see it in Mexican pavers and in painted furniture. This color adds a little spice, especially when we want to use neutrals such as browns and beiges in our homes.

YELLOW

Yellow is often considered a sunny, happy color. Remember this about yellow: It's the first color you notice. Give this a try: If you close your eyes and open them, your eye is always going to go to the yellow first. So it's easy to spot people or things that are in yellow.

For this reason, yellow is a really great color when it comes to safety. More and more fire hydrants and safety vehicles are being painted yellow. It makes perfect sense that a child's raincoat would be bright yellow, too.

Because it is so powerful, bright yellow is best when it's used in a temporary situation. Studies have shown that really bright yellow can actually cause anxiety if you're spending a lot of time looking at it. The stronger the yellow, the more tension it can create.

There seems to be confusion about using yellow. I often hear statements like, "Kitty said I can't use yellow because it's going to

When I caution people not to surround themselves with lots of bright yellow, which can cause anxiety, they often think I don't like yellow. But here a soft yellow on my house trim is very attractive.

The Big Paint Question: Flat or Glossy?

Paint comes in several different finishes, which range from very shiny to not shiny at all. The shiniest type is called high gloss, followed by semigloss, satin, eggshell, and finally, flat.

Generally speaking, I'm not a fan of walls that have any kind of a gloss to them. The higher the gloss, the more imperfections you can see in the wall. I always try to avoid the combination of sheen on a wall and an overhead lighting fixture; the light reflecting on the wall is distracting and glaring. Even in kitchens, where people tend to want a semigloss paint because of its washable properties, I would recommend low-sheen finishes such as eggshell or satin.

I like low-sheen finishes so much that I almost never use a satin finish. I have found that even if furniture scratches up against a wall that then needs to be scrubbed, I can remove any kind of mark with the abrasive side of a sponge and a little white cleanser.

cause anxiety." That's not what I mean. It's only when you're exposed to bright yellow for a long period of time that it can cause stress. For instance, bright yellow might not be good for the walls in a kitchen. If there's going to be any kind of a confrontation within the family, chances are it's going to take place in the kitchen because we spend so much time in there with our families. Having a lot of yellow in a busy room can add to the fast pace and tension. A kitchen with bright yellow walls might look fresh, especially when filled with attractive antiques, but if it seems to add chaos to an already-busy family life, you should choose another color.

Bright yellow is not a great choice for nursery walls either. Studies have shown that babies cry more in a bright yellow room. Choose a softer yellow, like buttermilk yellow, for a calmer environment.

If high-chroma yellow is your very favorite color, where can you use it? It would be great in an entryway or hallway, where you're just passing through and not spending a lot of time. Or, how about your laundry room? It might get you revved up to finish those loads in no time. Once you leave the laundry room, though, you'll find that you can settle back into a slower pace for the rest of the day's tasks.

Where else can you use yellow "temporarily"? Try accenting with flowers. A

bunch of yellow flowers can be a very powerful decorating tool, whether they're on the inside or on the outside of your house. You can actually train people's eyes to go wherever you want them to go with the color yellow. Maybe you have a dark corner in your house with a black baby grand piano and that area always seems really dark, almost invisible. Place a bowl of yellow lemons or a vase of yellow flowers on the piano. You'll add instant brightness, and you'll find that visitors will pay attention to those areas where you've placed the yellow accents.

GREEN

Green is actually the easiest color for the eye to see. That's because we focus the color green directly on the retina. There are three kinds of light-sensitive receptors, called cones, in the retina. Each kind is tuned to absorb light from a different portion of the spectrum of visible light. Some cones absorb long-wavelength light, which we see as the color red. Other cones absorb short-wavelength light, which we see as blue. And still other cones reflect middle-wavelength light, which we see as green. The center of the retina is primarily green cones, surrounded by red-yellow cones, with blue cones being mainly on the periphery.

You've probably noticed the color green gaining in popularity over the years. This past decade, green has been the most popular color. The most popular green has a lot of yellow in it, like chartreuse. A decade ago, we saw more gray-greens, such as olive and sage.

colorsolutions

When painting a room, dip a few popsicle sticks in the paint and let them dry. Take these color sticks shopping with you to help you coordinate fabrics, furniture, and accessories with your new room color.

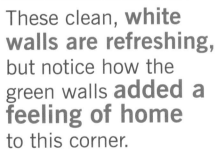

These clean, **white walls are refreshing,** but notice how the green walls **added a feeling of home** to this corner.

But no matter how much you like them, these new greens may not be great colors for your kitchen or dining room. Some studies have shown that pea green or chartreuse green can actually be nausea enhancing. So if you're pregnant or have a weak stomach, green may be a color that you want to avoid.

This is a perfect example of why I don't really like to focus too much on trends. Madison Avenue might have all their ads in a certain color, and you might be brainwashed into thinking this is the color to have. But if it doesn't work for you and your family, then it's not the right choice.

Not all shades of green have the above effect, though. More primary shades of green, without so much yellow in them, are actually proven to *enhance* the taste of food. We're used to seeing that little sprig of parsley on our plates. And we know it makes the plate look a little bit nicer and the food look more appetizing. You might consider green plates or place mats.

Green can be a great choice in other rooms, too, because it's a color that men and women can generally agree upon. Green has been a traditional favorite for years, and I consider it to be as neutral as brown. Because it's so neutral, green is the best color to use in a study or library, helping you to read, relax, and concentrate.

The color green is also connected with feelings of security and stability. Studies have shown that green, particularly a rich, deep forest green, can help ease homesickness. For that reason it's a great color choice for furnishings and accessories for kids going away to college, boarding school, or camp for the first time or for parents downsizing or moving in with you. Surround them with green area rugs, green towels, and green bedspreads. It's subtle, but it can really make a difference.

One place you might want to avoid green is near the mirror in the bathroom. Greens with a lot of yellow in them, such as pea green, are not flattering to most complexions. They have a tendency to draw the color out of our faces. So women tend to overcompensate when they're applying makeup in a room that has a lot of green, especially when the walls near the mirror are green.

Green-blue, or teal, was a favorite accent in the late '80s. It replaced popular Wedgwood or country blue, which was the favorite color for bathrooms, bedrooms, and living rooms in the previous decades. Aqua or turquoise is another great separator of men and women. If you're wearing the color turquoise, everyone's going to notice you. However, men will find you somewhat unapproachable, while women will find you approachable. So a turquoise outfit might not be a great choice to wear to a singles party.

BLUE

Blue is an American favorite in every shade. Eighty percent of Americans say medium blue is their favorite color, or at least one of their favorite colors. Much of our wardrobes is blue, from denim to oxford. It's a very safe and easy color.

Navy blue is a very powerful color when you want other people to trust you. And who wouldn't want the people coming in contact with us to trust us? That would be really important in a job interview, or if you're going to the bank for a loan. So if you're a woman going to a job interview with a man, wear a navy blue suit with a tomato-red accent, such as a pin or blouse.

colorsolutions
To dramatize a colored wall, hang beautiful, empty frames on the wall. You'll notice the negative space in and around the frames, as well as the unique qualities of the frames themselves.

Blue is an American favorite. **Touches of red and white for accents** seem just right.

The color blue slows respiration and heartbeat, making you feel calmer. One shade of blue, often called sky blue, has been shown to stimulate 11 calming, tranquilizing chemicals in the brain. This is particularly important to know if you have a high metabolism or if you have a child who's overactive. Blue will calm him or her down. It's great for bedrooms to help create a soothing, nurturing atmosphere. You'll often see sky blue in hospitals because of its calming effect.

But while green can add to the taste of food, studies have shown that blue actually detracts from the taste of food. I saw an ad in *Architectural Digest* for a very expensive-looking, contemporary kitchen with very deep cobalt blue appliances, cabinets, and countertops. It was a striking photograph, but I guarantee that food would not be appetizing in an all-blue room.

But you can use this to your advantage. Here's a great diet tip: Replace the white lightbulb in your refrigerator with a blue lightbulb. When you open the refrigerator door and you're looking for something to snack on, nothing's going to look very appetizing.

I'm not suggesting you put away your blue and white dishes, which everyone loves. I have a collection of those, too. The key to using blue in a kitchen or dining room is moderation. If country blue is your favorite color for your kitchen, go ahead and use it, but easy does it. Temper the blue with bits of red and green, particularly when it comes to serving food.

Blue is a cool color, and it can make you actually feel cold, which is not such a good thing if you have a room without a lot of natural light. But again you can use this to your advantage. Let's say you work in an office where you can't control the temperature. You can actually raise or lower your body's temperature by facing a particular color. If you always feel cold, hang a painting or some-

A Word on Marring New Walls

A lot of my projects involve stapling and nailing into walls, and that might make you nervous. I could understand that if you have a brand-new house. Once you put the first hole in it, you'll realize that it's like spilling the first glass of red wine on your new carpet. You're paranoid until it happens. But after it happens, it frees you. You realize, what the heck, paint is cheap, and walls don't have feelings. I say that's why God created spackle—to fill nail holes. It's not such a big deal. A hole is nothing. It can be fixed.

In many cases it's easier when you've got an old house. You know it's been lovingly messed with and has accommodated different families and different needs. Older houses are less intimidating than brand-new homes with fresh, new white walls.

Because necessity is the mother of invention, you can often come up with a clever solution to cover up a blemish in an older wall. For instance, I just put a little ribbon creation over two framed botanicals in my bedroom because I wanted more color on that wall. But when I put my creation up there above the prints with ribbon hanging down behind them, I thought the two paintings looked too far apart. So I took off the top picture and used that nail hole to hold the ribbon, and I just made another nail hole to hang the picture lower. But if I wanted to I could have just filled the hole and painted over it or I could have covered it with decorative cording. Perceived blemishes are not blocks to creativity—they can be the spark of creativity.

thing in your line of vision that is a warm color—a warm red color or an orange—and you'll feel warmer. Conversely, if your body is always running hot, then hang a seaside scene or something with a lot of blue, and you could actually cool down your body's temperature.

PURPLE

Purple is an amazing color because it can relax and stimulate us at the same time. The older we get, the more we're drawn to the color purple (and the less we're drawn to yellow). And the older we get, the better we look in the color purple.

Violet, which is a darker purple, is relaxing, making it a good choice for a bedroom. But it's a tough color to use in interior design, though it does work well in its darkest values for accessories here and there. Touches of deep, rich purple can be very dramatic.

Young adolescent girls love lavender, which is a much lighter purple. Studies show that it stimulates the imagination. Perhaps that's why purple is often favored by artists, designers, and musicians. Daydreams are more likely when you're surrounded by purple. Lavender can be tricky to combine with other colors, however, with the exception of green and some values of brown. Purple can be challenging to combine with other colors, but with practice you'll find that purple is best with green or white. Think of violets.

BROWN

Brown makes us feel secure and nurtured. If you think about it, the majority of the color in our homes tends to be some value of brown, from Berber or beige carpeting to hardwood floors, neutral walls, and wood furniture. We feel very safe choosing this

If you have a lot of brown in a room, you get variety with different textures and materials. Here, we have shades of brown wicker, wood, metal, fabric, paper, and wax.

color because most furniture is brown or some shade of brown. We think, "Well, it's not going to show the dirt. Everybody's going to like it. We don't have to paint it often. It's nice and safe." And this is all true.

But you know what? Brown can be very boring. If you have a brown and beige monochromatic room, the best way to make it interesting is to vary the textures within that color family. Vary your furniture with woven wicker, wrought iron, and old wooden pieces with the paint chipping off and with different patterns. You can contrast the richness of dark brown with strong whites to add interest and make the room seem lighter.

I don't really recommend using brown as the main color for a room because most rooms already have lots of brown furniture, and even hardwood floors, in them. Brown walls in addition to brown furniture don't provide enough contrast.

colorsolutions

When you have leftover paint from a project, keep it in a coffee can with the color marked on the plastic top, rather than in big, paint-splashed paint cans. Tape the paint can label to the side of your coffee can for future reference.

GRAY

Gray is the easiest color for the eye to digest. It's very calming to your eye. That's because every color except for gray has an after-image, which means the eye has to recover from it and adjust itself. Here's how to test that. Stare at a brightly colored object, such as a red dictionary, for 15 seconds. Then quickly shift your gaze to a blank wall. You'll see the same shape there in the complementary color, in this case, a green rectangle. That is how your eye recovers and balances itself. Gray is the only color that doesn't require this process.

Studies show that people will create more and be more creative in a gray room. We forget about gray when it comes to our homes, but I think that gray is an interesting color that we could consider more. It doesn't have to be a boring battleship gray. Grays can be warm, or they can be cold, depending on how much brown, yellow, or blue is in them. Most of us wouldn't think to use gray in a traditional home or in a country home, but it could be a new classic color. Imagine a cool gray wall, one with a lot of blue in it, contrasted with a white country bed. It could be very calming and peaceful.

Think of how popular concrete has become. Whereas once we used to cover up concrete floors, now we score, stain, and polish

them. You see concrete countertops, even in country kitchens. So consider gray for some room, if not for the walls, then for the floors. I encourage you to think about gray, particularly if you work around a lot of color. Say you're an artist, or you're a gourmet cook and you're working with a lot of colors. Gray can give your eyes a break from all of that saturated color.

BLACK

Although we think of it as a color, black is actually the absence of color.

Black is the ultimate power color when it comes to clothing. It's sophisticated and sexy. We tend to have a lot of respect for people who wear black, whether they are priests, rabbis, or others in authority. The thing about black, though, is that a lot of people choose it when they're not sure how they want to be seen. A lot of times shy people will "hide" by wearing black because you can't really tell anything about a person wearing black. They tend to fade away.

This **apartment fireplace** was ~~painted~~ white and as boring as ~~possibl~~e. **Simply adding black** paint has made the fireplace a ~~dra~~matic focal point.

When it comes to using black inside your home, rarely would you see four walls painted black. Sometimes you'll see one wall painted black. A lot of designers believe, and I agree, that every room can have black somewhere. It adds sophistication and weight, whether it's a black lacquer table, a coffee table, an iron candelabra, an Asian piece, a screen, or a black lampshade.

Here's a very interesting thing about black: It makes whatever's right next to it more vivid. Imagine a brick home with a beige front door. Now imagine a brick house with a black front door. You will actually notice the brick more on the house with the black door. This is a good thing if you like the brick, and you want it to be noticed more. A lot of men like to go out and buy a nice black leather sofa. And a lot of women complain, "What am I going to do with this $5,000 black leather sofa?" Well, put a favorite red pillow on it. You'll notice the pillow more than the sofa. Your eye goes to the color or the texture next to black, so use black to your advantage.

WHITE

We think of white as a color, but actually white is all of the colors together. Most people have very positive responses to the color white. It indicates cleanliness, delicacy, and chastity. Also, it creates an environment of trust. Studies show that people trust nurses and dentists who wear white more than nurses and dentists who wear colored clothing.

White is great to use in decorating because it's easily used with other colors. But I find it to be cold. It's very reflective and hard on the eyes. I avoid using white as the base color in my rooms, and I reserve it instead for accents, such as white plates on a wall.

Pattern and Texture for Your Walls

Even without a lot of color, walls can be interesting. Walls can have pattern and texture. Paint is great, but there's so much more you can do to bring life to a room.

WALLPAPER

Wallpaper is one of my favorite ways to bring warmth to walls. Actually, wallpapers are a very underused decorating tool, but mark my words, wall coverings are poised to make a comeback. For inspiration, head down to your local paint store and pore over the mile-thick wall-covering books. Even though wall coverings have taken a backseat to painted faux finishes in the past decade, the wall covering companies are still creating beautiful products and photographing them in interesting and clever settings. I always enjoy time spent sitting at a table in a paint store, turning the pages of wallpaper books.

WALLPAPER BORDERS

If you don't care to cover the entire room or wall with a pattern, wallpaper borders are fun to use. I have a shelf of books near the ceiling of my dining room, but the same warm,

Once you start exploring wallpaper, you might find paint a little less exciting.

The bead board on the wall adds to the country look I was after. Notice the stencil I did for my daughter Brooke, "A Babbling Brooke."

library look can be achieved with a bookshelf-looking border made just for that purpose.

Did you know there are removable borders? I love the idea of using removable borders for a child's room, so the borders can be changed every few years as the child matures.

PAINTED FAUX FINISHES

Faux finishes are painting techniques where you use paint to look like something else, such as stone, leather, or parchment paper. You can use paint to cleverly create interest, texture, and design. I faux-finished the wood around my fireplace to look like marble and the ceiling in my bedroom to look like clouds.

The faux-painted clouds on my bedroom ceiling help me have sweet dreams.

STENCILS

Stencils are always an option, either as vines "growing" along the ceiling line or around a window or in more overall patterns that can suggest leather or other natural materials. Stencils are fun and easy. I personalized my daughters' rooms in a previous house by stenciling "A Babbling Brooke" and "Birdie's Nest" on the walls. And later I'll show you how to use the transfer method to transfer almost any image you want onto your walls. (See "Hands-On Project: Transfers" on page 33.)

TROMPE L'OEIL

This style of faux painting is so detailed that it looks like a photograph. Although it usually takes an artist's touch, the trompe l'oeil technique can create the look and feeling of a window or outdoor landscape where none exists.

Trompe l'oeil is a type of mural that brings instant excitement. When I remodeled my kitchen, I added a mural to the wall above my sink. What a striking addition it made to the room!

Your local high school is an incredible place to find artists for trompe l'oeil. You could call the local high school art teacher and find out if there are any promising students who would want some part-time work. I had a student paint a trompe l'oeil on a door for me when I was redoing a room on a "Win Your Dream Kitchen" segment on *The Home Show*. I was in an unfamiliar city, and I called the local school and talked to the art teacher. A talented student took the door home to work on it. I designed it, he painted it, and he got credit for college.

This rabbit trompe l'oeil gave my stove hood unexpected zest.

CHAIR RAIL

Chair rails were initially added to walls to keep people from scratching the walls or wallpaper with their chairs. Now they're used more decoratively. A chair rail adds dimension to a room, and it can break up a huge expanse of wall, especially if you have high ceilings. Anytime you take four square white walls and add some personality to them, it's great. I'm all for it. It's like adding a scarf to a dress.

A chair rail divides a room visually in half. In some cases if you really like a wallpaper but don't want to put it on a whole wall, just having it above the chair rail gives you visual interest that's not overwhelming. The chair rail gives you a natural place to stop.

BEAD BOARD

Bead board is most often used in ceilings of old-looking homes or on old-style cabinets, but I used it in the guesthouse I remodeled for my daughters in a previous house. (See "Hands-On Project: Aged Bead Board" on page 30.) I aged the new bead board with two shades of blue, and it brought interest and texture to the room. Bead board is also good in a kitchen or a bathroom. If your walls are a bit rough and you don't happen to be an expert at drywall or plaster repair, bead board will cover a lot of imperfections.

QUILTS

Another underused technique for adding interest and beauty to walls is hanging quilts. If you have quilts on three walls of a guest room, you'll create a cozy nest. Quilts are great wall art, they can be used to cover damaged walls, and they're easy to change.

kitty's style and spirit

Make Your Home a Haven Your home is your haven, your retreat. You want to spend quality time there, but you can't have quality time in a room that's cold, where people don't want to spend time, or where guests feel unwelcome.

The more senses you engage in a room, the more quality time people will spend there, and in many ways, the better provider you will be. How can you engage people's senses? Set a bowl of fragrant flowers on a piano, place a mirror to reflect a magnolia tree in full bloom, and keep cozy knitted throws at arm's reach.

Providing for people is more than putting food on the table, more than buying new clothes. It's providing an environment that is conducive to quality time, whether it's private time, family time, animal time, teenage time, baby crawling and exploring time, bridal shower time, barbecue with the neighbors time, or whatever.

Here's an important tip: Many of us hang our textile art the wrong way, with a few pushpins holding the piece to the wall. This eventually damages and tears the fabric. The proper way to hang a quilt is to first hand-sew a fabric pocket along the top back edge of the quilt, thread a wooden rod through it, then hang it from hooks attached to the wall. Another method is to install a wooden strip on the wall and attach the quilt with Velcro strips.

The pillow in the center could have been **the starting point** for both this **pale yellow room and the red room** beyond.

When you **stand in the entryway,** you see into the **living room, dining room, kitchen, and hallway.** The mural in my entryway **sets the tone** for the rest of my house.

My Home

Even though I'm viewed as an expert on color, I'm not without angst in choosing my own colors. When I bought my 1939 bungalow not too long ago, it had been painted completely white on the inside—every room, everywhere. So I literally had a blank slate, and I had to start from scratch. Where do we start? That's a big question I'm asked often, and I have my own struggles. I'd like to walk you through my home and tell you about the choices I made.

ENTRYWAY: I did in my own home what I suggest to my viewers, which is to set your color palette in the entryway, and let all rooms flow from that. The inspiration for my entryway came from a large painting in my dining room of a woman on a ladder reaching up into an apple tree. I'll talk more about creating a cohesive look and feel for your home later in this book, but I want to mention here that I almost always use paintings as inspiration for the colors in a room. You might have a favorite pillow, a fabric on a sofa, or another prized possession that would be your starting point. I decided the painting would be mine.

Once I realized the painting in my dining room would be the inspiration for the entryway, I asked my artist friend Jane Benson, who's from Scotland, to paint a mural in my entryway that loosely mimics the painting. I'm talented, but I'm not really an artist, and I have no trouble paying some-

one to paint art on my walls. Hiring a muralist can be less expensive than you would think, if you're clever about it. The mural has a similar vibe to the painting's—similar colors and similar images of cypress trees. Because I don't like things to be too perfect, I asked Jane to add a telephone pole to the mural, and that makes me laugh. So, when you're in my entryway and you look into the dining room, there's a feeling that the rooms are separate yet connected.

DINING ROOM: When it came to painting the walls in the dining room, it was a tough decision. I really had to labor over what colors were going to work because I needed to tie together three rooms—the entryway, the dining room, and the kitchen. I wanted the dining room color to work with the mural in my entryway and the red-themed kitchen. And the dining room paint had to work with the painting of a woman on a ladder that I used as inspiration for the whole project.

I settled on a dark green for the woodwork on the bottom of the walls, a light khaki (called "elephant's breath") on the upper walls, and white trim. Even after I decided on the colors, getting the green right took a lot of experimenting, and I had to go back to the paint store several times. But paint is cheap, and the experimenting was well worth it. Don't be afraid to make mistakes; think of them as experiments in progress.

kitty's style and spirit

Find Your Inspiration Just as I find my inspiration from the things around me that I love, I hope that you will find your inspiration from the things that you love. You may be inspired by an Elvis Presley painting on velvet that is your pride and joy. Or you might have a soft blue, pink, and lavender quilt from your grandmother from which the colors of your room will flow. Your style is unique to you. Find your own starting place.

LIVING ROOM: I wanted the walls in this room to be light because I didn't want the room to feel closed in. The color had to be fairly neutral because I have two sets of slipcovers for my sofa and chairs: a red paisley for winter and a blue toile for summer. So I chose an off-white color, then I gave the walls a very soft texture by carefully sponging on a raw umber golden glaze.

Every room has something going for it, and this room had an entire wall of woodwork around the fireplace. And it had been painted many, many times. I was able to strip the paint off, distress the wood, and wax it to a golden sheen. (See "Hands-On Project: Distressed Fireplace Wall" on page 190.)

I also wanted to give my fireplace surround an Old World, marbleized look. So I painted the entire area around the fireplace a dramatic black, including the hearth and brick part, and my artist friend Jane painted on the faux marble.

HALLWAY: Beyond the entryway is my home's central hallway. I had my heart set on covering the walls with a green-and-gold wallpaper that I loved. I had a sample of the wallpaper, but I was dismayed to discover it was no longer produced. So I came up with a great solution. I stenciled my walls to look like the wallpaper. It was a lot of work, but it was a labor of love. (See "Hands-On Project: Handmade Stencils" on page 28.)

KITCHEN: I painted my kitchen the same "elephant's breath" beige as the dining room to help

As you can see, I have a **good bit of color** in my own home—with an **abundance of red** in the **living room and kitchen,** and **soft greens and pinks** in the **bedrooms and baths.**

the rooms relate well to each other, but I added a lot of my favorite color—yes, it's red—with red-checked curtains, a red table, a braided rug with red in it, a red shelf over my stove, and my ever-growing collection of red-handled cooking utensils.

Frankly, this kitchen is not the best one I've ever had. But it's the one I have, so I'm making the best of it. Remember: It's not what I don't have that counts—it's what I do with what I do have. I took the doors off the upper cabinets. Why look at cheesy doors when I can look at my lively yellow and red dishes?

You could also put wallpaper on the back of the cabinet walls, even tacking it up with pushpins or tape. I wanted something snappier on the back wall of my open pantry, so I sponged on a checkerboard pattern. (See "Hands-On Project: Checkerboard Pantry" on page 243.) For a final touch, I applied some stick-on letters over the sink that repeat one of my favorite sayings, "A balanced diet is a cookie in each hand."

MASTER BATH: Ever feel so good in a room that you didn't want to leave? So cozy and nurtured that you linger just to enjoy its furnishings? That's how I feel in my bathroom. The original pink tile was still intact when we moved in, and it was in very good shape for being around more than 60 years. I'm grateful to the previous owners for their care of this house. I might not have chosen pink tile if I were starting from scratch—in fact I know I wouldn't have chosen pink. But tearing out the tile was not in my budget, nor did I want to destroy this piece of history. So I made the best of it. I put up green-and-pink-striped wallpaper above the tile, and that paper became the inspiration for the palette in the room.

Then I added Laura Ashley curtains, hung plates, and made a shower curtain from my grandmother's tablecloth. I hung a large mirror over the tub, which makes the small room appear to be more spacious.

Hands-On Projects

In this section, I'd like to show you step by step how to use five beautiful techniques in your home: handmade stencils, aged bead board, sponge painting, transfers, and stenciled lettering.

Hallways never need to be boring.

HANDS-ON PROJECT: Handmade Stencils

I had a sample of this wallpaper, but when I wanted to use the pattern in my central hallway, I found it was no longer made.

As I mentioned earlier, I had my heart set on a certain wallpaper pattern for my hallway. But when I discovered it was no longer made, I decided to create my own stencil based on the sample I had and stencil the hall to look like the paper. Because I had the sample and I could clearly see the look I was after, I was ready to take on this fun challenge.

Creating a stencil from the wallpaper sample seemed doable. In this case, the pattern of ivy leaves and wispy gold stripes seemed like it could be done with three stencils—one stencil for the light green ivy leaves, a second stencil for the wispy gold lines, and a third stencil for the dark green centers in the ivy.

Stencils can get very complicated, so you'll want to find a fairly simple pattern to trace, and not something like the ceiling in the Sistine Chapel. For this project, I used a large sheet of stencil paper. I could have used a smaller piece of stencil paper, but then I would have had to move it more times as I was stenciling the walls.

Please note that I didn't try to be perfect or persnickety in my tracing or cutting. You can take liberties. It's not like I'm trying to counterfeit $100 bills or anything. It's a loose approximation of the original.

I can't express how much enjoyment I got out of seeing those plain white walls come to life. I framed the original wallpaper sample and hung it on the wall in the hallway, and that gives me a chuckle.

WHAT YOU'LL NEED

* PATTERN YOU LIKE
* SHEETS OF BLANK STENCIL PAPER (I USED LARGE PIECES, ABOUT 16 TO 20 INCHES)
* WAX PENCIL, CRAYON, OR MARKER
* STENCIL-CUTTING GUN
* PAINTER'S TAPE
* STENCIL BRUSH
* PAINTS

WHAT YOU'LL DO

1. Place the stencil paper over the image you want to re-create.

2. If your image has several colors, you'll need to create several stencils; just focus on one at a time. Decide which element you want to stencil first, and trace just that element with the wax pencil or crayon onto the stencil paper. Repeat this process by tracing each new element onto a new stencil sheet. **A**

3. Next cut the image out of the stencil paper with the stencil-cutting gun, which plugs in like a solder gun and is ready to use in about 5 minutes. Do the stencil cutting on a metal, concrete, or stone surface because the gun will burn a wood table. Grip the stencil-cutting gun by the handle only. You might want to practice first on a scrap piece of stencil paper. To cut, move the gun, not the pattern, at a moderate and comfortable rate. I think you'll have more control if you move the gun toward you, rather than moving it sideways. **B**

4. Once you have all of your stencils cut, put the first stencil on your desired surface, using painter's tape to secure it. It's a good idea to start in the least noticeable corner of a room. **C**

5. Dip the tip of your stencil brush into your paint. The key for dabbing paint onto stencils is to make sure the brush is not carrying too much paint, which is a common mistake. So "pounce" it on a blotter until the brush is almost dry.

6. Holding the brush like a pencil, perpendicular to the wall, brush over the cutout areas of the stencil with a circular motion, working over the stencil edges for a clean outline. **D**

7. Carefully remove the stencil from the wall. When the first color of paint dries enough, place the stencil for the second color over that area, and dab on the second color. Then do the third, if applicable, and so forth. **E** ❖

HANDS-ON PROJECT: Aged Bead Board

I wanted a Swedish farmhouse look, which I achieved by aging bead board with paint and glaze, but this white room wasn't inspiring.

Look at what a striking impact the bead board made! It's hard to believe this is the same room.

When deciding how to furnish a guesthouse where my daughters shared a room, I decided on a Swedish country look. I got my inspiration from the Old World paintings of Carl Larsson. He and his wife, Karin, are often referred to as the creators of the Swedish style. Larsson's sketches and paintings of his family life show lots of bead board, plates on the wall, the color blue, and wall transfers. In those paintings, I see a happy family life.

To get that look, I decided to enhance the bland walls of the guesthouse with bead board, finished to look like it had been time-worn in a Swedish farmhouse and not pulled right off the shelf at a big-box store. I needed to age it artificially, because I didn't have 100 years to wait for the natural process to occur.

If you're not familiar with bead board, which is sometimes called beaded board, it's got grooves in it, and you might find it on the ceiling or on the cabinets of an old house. I figured I could achieve an aged look was if the grooves were darker than the bead board surface. The darker grooves would make it seem like the surface of the board had faded. By putting a darker blue in the grooves and a lighter blue glaze over the top, I got exactly what I wanted.

WHAT YOU'LL NEED

* BEAD BOARD (I USED A VICTORIAN-TYPE CEILING BOARD, WHICH IS SOLD IN LARGE SHEETS)
* 2 CANS OF THE SAME COLOR OF PAINT, PREFERABLY IN AN EGGSHELL FINISH, ONE A FEW SHADES LIGHTER THAN THE OTHER
* INEXPENSIVE FOAM BRUSH WITH WEDGED TIP
* PAINT ROLLER
* 4-INCH BRISTLE BRUSH
* COLOR WASH (GLAZE TINTED WITH UNIVERSAL COLOR IN THE SAME COLOR AS THE LIGHTER PAINT COLOR)

WHAT YOU'LL DO

1. Glue and nail the bead board to the walls as you would paneling.

2. Mix the darker shade of paint with a bit of water, so the paint will glide down the grooves of the bead board easily.

3. Brush the darker paint down the grooves of the boards, using the foam brush. Let the paint dry.

4. Roll the roller into the lighter paint color and roll the paint over the bead board.

5. Let the paint dry, and then apply a coat of color wash with the 4-inch bristle brush. Run the brush up and down over the boards for a bit of a striated effect. ❖

The idea of sponge painting, which is commonly called sponging, is to give a very soft surface interest to your walls with paint, sort of a billowy effect. There are two ways to go. You can sponge on paint or you can sponge off paint, which means putting paint on a surface and then sponging it off with a dry sponge. Sponging on is much, much easier, and that's what we'll discuss here.

In choosing your paint colors, you can start with a light background and sponge on a darker color (or colors). Or, you can start with a dark background, and sponge on a lighter color (or colors). Whatever you like.

The most important thing to know about sponging is to stay loose, loose, loose when you apply the paint with the sponge. I recommend you put on some music with a beat, like a rumba. And then pounce, pounce, pounce to the beat. I highly recommend practicing on cardboard first to get your rhythm down.

People make three common mistakes when they're sponging. The first mistake people make is they start in one corner with sponging and do it too tight, so the wall looks uptight and forced rather than loose and dreamy.

The second mistake people make is using a cheap synthetic sponge. You must have a natural marine sponge. Synthetic sponges have an artificially patterned surface that will register on your wall as such. The idea with sponging is to not recognize the pattern of the sponge. You should not look at the wall and think: sponge. A natural marine sponge has a much more irregularly patterned surface, and you can rotate the sponge to make sure no particular pattern registers on the wall.

Yes, marine sponges are expensive. Mine was $20, and, yes, I almost choked over the price. But you've got to pop for it. Also, buy a small sponge—one that fits in the palm of your hand. You want to be able to control it. Or tear a larger sponge in half if you need to.

The third mistake people make when sponging is slopping on too much paint. Your sponge should be almost dry by the time it gets to the wall. Don't worry about wasting paint if you have to blot most of it off on newspaper to release some of the paint. You want a subtle, attractive sponging job that will last a long time and bring great benefit to you and your family. As you're sponging, you'll quickly discover that too much paint on the sponge will result in a solid paint job rather than an airy, open one.

(continued)

The sponging I did in my daughters' room, along with the painted transfer, really sets off my grandmother's fine blue and yellow china.

* PAINT OR GLAZING MEDIUM FOR SPONGING, DILUTED TO YOUR LIKING (TRY 2 CUPS OF PAINT AND ½ TO 1 CUP OF WATER)
* BACKGROUND PAINT (READY IN CASE YOU NEED IT)
* MARINE SPONGE
* NEWSPAPER

WHAT YOU'LL DO

1. Dip your sponge into the paint or glaze. Wring out the sponge so there's not a lot of paint left in there. Tap it on newspaper to get it almost dry.

2. Pounce your sponge on the wall in a wide and rhythmic motion. Keep your arm loose and easy, and pounce each stroke far apart on the wall. **A**

3. After you've got your sponge marks wide and loose, start filling in. **B** Rotate the sponge often in your hand. The idea is to not glob too much paint on there, and to not smear it. But if you do, don't panic. You can use some of your background paint to tone it down.

4. At the ceiling line, or in corners, be especially careful not to apply too much paint. Do your regular sponging effect to within a few inches of the ceiling, and then take a smaller piece of sponge to lightly fill it in. Be careful; it's very easy to smudge any excess paint. You want an overall, even look. **C**

5. If your dog is a little rascal like my Spot is, keep your sponge off the floor or plan on chasing it down. **D**

6. Always have some of the base coat standing by. If you sponge on too much color, simply sponge some of your base coat on top to tone it down. **E**

7. Keep pouncing. The paint will dry quickly, so if you need to wipe off paint, do it before it dries. To give the wall more dimension, you can sponge on a light layer of the background color, or add another color. ❖

A

B

C

D

E

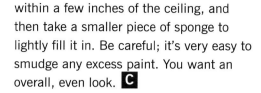

After you've sponged the wall, you might want to add a transfer to create more interest. I did both in my daughters' guesthouse. The transfer technique allows you to transfer virtually any design to your wall and then paint it in, like I did with the blue garland. You'd think you would have to be a great artist to reproduce a lovely flower or shape onto your wall. But all you need is transfer paper, an image, and courage.

You place the transfer paper on a wall, making sure the dark side is toward the wall, and then place your image on top of the paper. By tracing along the lines of the image, pressing down on the image and the transfer paper underneath, you will transfer the image to the wall. Then, you paint it in with whatever kind of paint or markers you like. I happen to love oil paint pens, so that's what I used for the sweet garland above my grandmother's blue and yellow china. You can use a photocopy machine to make the image bigger or smaller to meet your creative needs.

WHAT YOU'LL NEED

* DESIGN YOU LIKE
* TRANSFER PAPER
* PAINTER'S TAPE
* PENCIL
* PAINT PENS, MARKERS, OR BRUSHES AND PAINTS

WHAT YOU'LL DO

1. Place the image on top of the transfer paper, and then place the dark side of the transfer paper against the wall. Use painter's tape to hold the image to the paper and to secure the transfer paper to the wall. **A**

2. Trace the image with a pencil, using enough pressure so that the image transfers to the wall. **B**

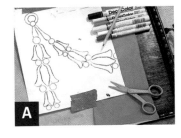  

3. Paint the design. In this case, I found it easier to outline the design with oil paint pens and then to fill in with markers. **C** ❖

HANDS-ON PROJECT: Stenciled Lettering

Stenciled letters give a room a personal touch over a sponged wall. In my daughters' guesthouse, I used standard stencil letters, like you can get at a hardware store, to write "Birdie's Nest" to honor my youngest daughter, and "A Babbling Brooke" to honor my oldest daughter. Above a bed, I wrote "Happiness Is Homemade."

WHAT YOU'LL NEED

* PENCIL
* STRAIGHTEDGE
* STENCIL LETTERS
* PAINTER'S TAPE
* STENCIL BRUSH
* PAINT (POUR A SMALL AMOUNT ONTO A PLATE)
* NEWSPAPER

WHAT YOU'LL DO

1. Decide where you want your lettering and draw a pencil line using a straightedge.

2. Figure out your letter and word spacing, based on how many letters you plan on stenciling and how long your word or line will be. Mark the location where you'll start your first letter.

3. Hold the stencil up to your surface, and notice that there are little holes in the cardboard before and after each letter. These are called registration marks, and you'll use these to make sure your letters are evenly spaced. Few things look worse than a stenciled line where some letters are spread out and some are scrunched together.

4. Place the stencil so the registration mark to the left of the first letter you want to stencil is on the left end of your pencil line. With your pencil, darken in the registration mark to the right of the first letter you're stenciling. This is where the left registration mark of your next letter will line up. Use painter's tape to hold the stencil in place.

5. Dab your stencil brush into the paint, and then dab it on the newspaper to blot any extra paint. Tap it onto the stencil, lightly filling in the letter. In my case, I didn't want really solid lettering, but something loose and easy.

6. Let the letter dry a bit before you remove the stencil, or you might smear the wet paint. It won't take long. Then, line up your next letter with its left registration mark on the spot you made after the previous letter. Also mark the right registration mark so you'll have that ready to line up the next letter.

7. Repeat until the word or line is completed. ❖

My living room and dining room are combined in one room with sage green furniture and little natural light. The trim in the room is white. I'm having trouble picking a paint color. What do you suggest?

Kitty: Because of the lack of natural light in both rooms, I feel you must choose a color in a light value. Perhaps a very, very light version of the sage color of your furniture. This would give a rich look to both rooms. Or maybe, for a more formal look, you would like a beige infused with yellow.

To enhance what light you have, perhaps you could hang a mirror (the larger the better) opposite a window. Keep the window treatments and floor coverings light.

I want to help my parents redecorate their house. I feel like the rooms lack style and the lack of style comes from the all-white walls. They say all-white walls open up the house (even though it's a large house that doesn't need to feel larger), but I disagree. How can I change their minds?

Kitty: The best way to change their mind is to show them by example. Buy magazines that show rooms painted with the colors that you feel would look right in their home. Also, have them visit homes of friends so that they can be convinced (if possible) that wall color can be subtle, yet decorative.

It's important to realize, though, that feeling of openness and cleanliness may be more important to some people than the cozy feeling that color can bring. If your parents have lived with white walls their whole lives, it's possible that they may feel uncomfortable with anything other than a light neutral on the walls.

I don't know if I paint the walls first and then make my furniture match, or if I get my furniture first and then paint the walls. Which do you recommend?

Kitty: A lot of it depends on where you start. If you have a brand-new house and no furniture, then you can start anywhere. But generally speaking there's going to be something that you're bringing to the party, whether it is a painting or a chair with a fabric that you love and don't want to change and is in good shape. Generally, it's good to choose something that's going to be in the room—a painting, a pillow, a tapestry, or an upholstered piece—and take color cues from that.

Moldings and woodwork are labor intensive to paint; **keep these neutral** and change your wall and ceiling colors **as often as you like.**

I'd like to make my living room more interesting (to me at least) by painting the walls pale mauve and the crown molding and window frames dark maroon, or even some kind of green. But I've noticed in magazines that moldings and trims are almost always white. Do they have to be?

Kitty: No, moldings and trim do not have to be white. I'm not a big fan of the thinking that there's a color your trim

"should" be. Your house should work for you and your family. But speaking practically, it makes sense to paint the woodwork a neutral color because it's a pain in the neck to repaint when you change the color of your walls.

Think about it. It's easy to slap a new paint color on your walls with a roller. But with trim, you've got to mask the trim and moldings off, and you have to be careful painting the details. But if you keep them a neutral color, you don't have to paint the woodwork every time you paint a room.

Also, keeping the trim the same neutral color throughout the home helps create a flow through the house. It can be very jarring to have different colors of trim from room to room. Now there are exceptions, of course. You may have one room where you want to have an interesting color palette, maybe a powder room or a fun little room. In that case, go for it, because it's not that big of a deal to repaint it.

I saw a room recently that had soft green walls and a little bit darker green woodwork. And it was very, very colorful. Colorful trim tends to draw attention. A lot of it depends on the architecture and the flow of the house.

I have just purchased a new dark blue love seat and couch. I already have a mauve recliner. I want to paint my walls burgundy and the ceiling sand. I have oak trim and floors. My room is 20 feet by 15 feet with lots of windows. Will this be too dark?

Kitty: I'd say that burgundy walls probably won't be too dark, because of the windows. Remember, the darker the color value, the smaller the room feels, but it will be cozier! "Too dark" is a matter of personal taste, and only you can say if it's too dark.

Here's a neat trick to help you decide: Buy a small can of the color and paint two coats on a long strip of heavy-duty shelf paper or the solid side of an unused roll of wallpaper. Tape it up and live with it for a few days and nights to see how it makes you feel. I ask you to live with it a few days to see it in the daytime and at night. Just looking at it for a few minutes won't work.

You didn't mention where you live, so I don't have a sense of your climate. If you live in Seattle versus Florida, the dark color could matter because of the average amount of sunny days compared with overcast days.

I'm trying to pick a color for my living room and want faux texture. My curtains are cream and red toile, and my furniture is mainly green. My living room leads directly to the hall. I want a formal, warm statement color because you walk directly into my living room upon entering my house; there is no foyer. My husband likes blue-green. I like neutrals. Is there any way to combine these in a faux treatment?

Kitty: My instincts are that blue-green would not be a wise choice. It would make the room feel small. And if the blue-green didn't blend well with the green furniture, it wouldn't work at all. I would consider going with the cream background color of the toile drapes. Use cream as a base and glaze over that with a rich umber (an earthy brown) color. Refer to Jocasta Innes's book *Paint Magic* (which is my personal favorite) for glazing techniques.

Could you consider a light blue ceiling? This would add a soft dimension and a special design touch. It works especially well if you have crown molding because the molding creates a natural separation between the wall and ceiling colors.

Our Orlando-area family room has high ceilings with wooden walls and beams; there is only 4 to 5 feet of wall between the chair rail and the ceiling. We have bright skylights also. The previous owner painted the walls peach. Yuck! We need help with a new paint color. We love jewel tones.

Kitty: One of the points to consider is that Orlando's in Florida. When you live in the South and you already have skylights, the heat is going to be a big factor. Heat rises, so the combination of high ceilings and skylights means the room will hold heat and bright sunlight. Peach is in the orange family, and even though it can be soft, it is a really warm color. So that's another factor that's adding to the heat.

If you love the William Morris jewel tones and the Arts and Crafts period, you want a cool color. I would suggest a cool, soft blue, which could actually go up the drywall above the chair rail and continue up the ceiling in between the beams, which would make it all feel higher. The blue would feel as though it would wash up into the sky, so it would be an extension of the walls. Or, try a very pale green, which is typical of the Arts and Crafts era. Either one of those should blend well with the jewel tones.

1 You don't need **expensive molding to make a chair rail.** You can **paint a faux chair rail** by masking off and painting a 3- to 4-inch strip on the wall, or **use a prepasted wallpaper border.**

2 For a child's room, paint a chair-rail strip around the room and then use rubber stamps as tall as the strip (3 to 4 inches) to print the child's name over and over all around the room. And, please, let your kid get in on the fun of this project.

3 Do you have a favorite collection? Maybe maps? Or clocks? Or teapots? To highlight your collection, you can write related sayings over a wall in the room where you keep the collection. Use a ruler and light pencil to make lines, then use a felt marker to write themed sayings in longhand. Afterward, stencil gold stars between the sayings for a more sophisticated look.

4 For a neat look, upholster the walls of a man's office with pleated linen. You start at one end, at the ceiling line, and staple the linen to the wall (you don't use batting underneath for this treatment). Fold under to make a pleat every few inches, and staple. Do this all across the top, then along the bottom, stapling it tight. Cover the staples with grosgrain ribbon, then iron the pleats flat against the wall for a tailored look.

Adding clouds to a light blue ceiling is, in my opinion, beyond wonderful.

ceilings and floors

With all the talk about walls and color, it's easy to forget about ceilings and floors. But I encourage you to give these areas more thought. I often say the ceiling is like a fifth wall, and I guess you could say the floor is like a sixth wall. What could be better than to be surrounded on all sides, as well as top and bottom, with a thoughtfully furnished space?

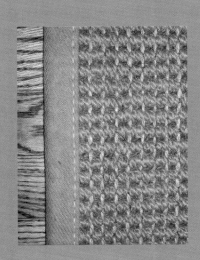  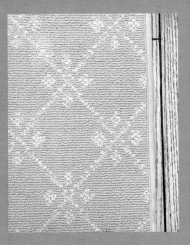

What's Up with Ceilings?

It's true that you probably aren't going to do anything too unusual with your ceilings. It's just not convenient to change a ceiling on a whim. But because people are so used to seeing white on ceilings, even subtle changes can make a big impact.

I happen to be a huge fan of light blue ceilings. Some people are shocked by that. But think about it. We're so used to seeing blue overhead outdoors that we almost don't notice a soft blue ceiling.

It's important to note that a blue ceiling really works best if you have molding between the wall and ceiling or if you have a really good painter who can get the line between the walls and ceiling perfectly straight. If you don't have molding between the wall and the ceiling, it's trickier to pull off the light blue ceiling.

At any rate, I'm talking about a really soft blue. This color actually gives a richness to whatever is on the walls. Beige walls will look more interesting against a blue ceiling than they would look against a white ceiling.

I also like a very, very soft pink ceiling, maybe even a neutral color infused with pink. That can be very flattering to your skin. Even though the ceiling is far from your skin, color reflects down.

Decorate Kitty's Way

❑ **Paint ceilings** a soft, soft blue or a neutral pink to give the wall color **more richness.** ❑ **Layer area rugs** over wall-to-wall carpeting for **a cozier look.** ❑ **Don't be afraid to hire help** if the decorating job is too big to go it alone. ❑ You'll always have decorating dilemmas. **Be patient.** Eventually you'll find **just what you're looking for.**

My preference is to always see a very light color on a ceiling, or at least a color lighter than the walls. If you want to paint your ceiling a darker color than the walls, be aware that it will make the ceiling feel like it's coming down. If you're a tall person and your home has standard-height ceilings, dark ceilings should be avoided.

I've featured a lot of interesting ceilings on my television shows. Here are some of my favorites:

INSTALL A STARRY SKY. Once I painted the ceiling of a 17-year-old boy's room deep blue. Then I installed 240 fiber-optic lights in the configuration of constellations. The star theme was reflected in the upholstery, on pillows, and in a saltwater aquarium.

STENCIL IT. I once featured a TV segment on stenciling a ceiling. It's an inexpensive way to add interest to a ceiling, though it might be a bit uncomfortable for the stencil artist. In fact, the artist on the show recommended wearing a cervical neck collar and goggles for the job. She painted the ceiling to look like a trellis atop a stone wall.

For all stencil work it's critical that you don't load too much paint in the brush, but it's especially important when stenciling a ceiling. Otherwise the excess paint will drip right on your head!

ADD SKYLIGHTS. Of course, skylights are wonderful for adding interest to a ceiling and light to a room. When skylights are not practical, try a Solatube, which has a small domed turret on the roof, aimed to the south, that transmits light into a room down a reflector tube. A 10-inch tube can light 100 square feet and is relatively easy and inexpensive to install. A handy homeowner who's familiar with power tools should be able to install one herself.

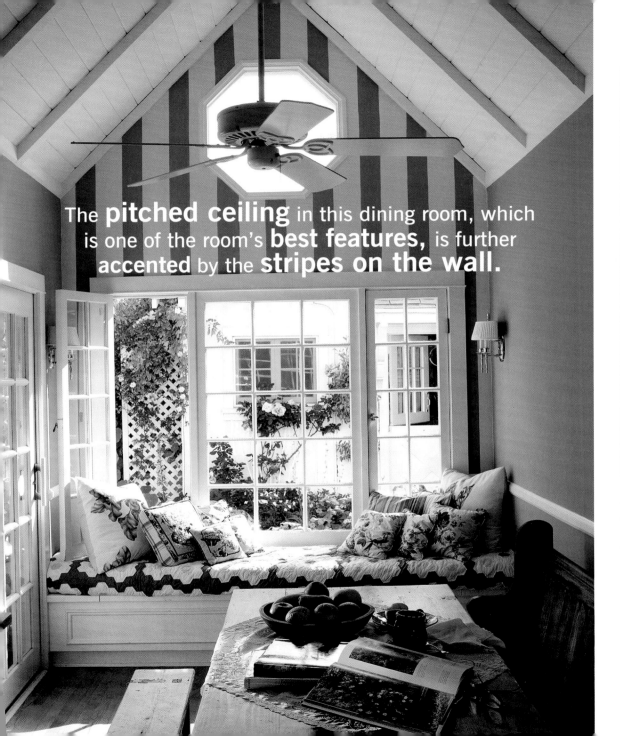

The **pitched ceiling** in this dining room, which is one of the room's **best features,** is further **accented** by the **stripes on the wall.**

In one of my kitchens, I put a beautiful mural above my garden window, and then continued some of the vines onto the ceiling with paint. See how this turns the ceiling into a fifth wall to decorate?

WALLPAPER IT. It wouldn't occur to most people to wallpaper a ceiling. Sometimes you'll see it in little cottages that have dormer windows. But any ceiling could be treated as another wall and wallpapered. Ceilings are huge, generally unbroken expanses.

I successfully wallpapered a kitchen ceiling for *The Home Show*. It was for a "Win Your Dream Kitchen" contest, and I had $10,000 and a month to redo the kitchen. The wallpapered ceiling was really quite charming. What made it work was that the kitchen walls were broken up with five doors—to various rooms, the outside, and the garage. The ceiling was the only large unbroken space, and the wallpaper helped to pull the room together.

In recent showcase houses, I've seen gold leaf–looking wallpapers on ceilings that shimmer at night. I think that is a really glamorous effect that costs very little.

ADD BEAMS. Beams are very appropriate on ceilings, especially in country-style homes. I did a show once on using Styrofoam

makes$ense

You can make your own area rug with a carpet remnant and a sharp utility knife. Make a template out of newspaper in the shape you want—a heart, a circle, or a leaf—then tape the template to the back of the carpet. Using the utility knife, cut around the template, cutting through just the carpet backing. Carefully separate the carpet fibers to reveal your new rug.

beams that look like real wood. And why not? They're light and add interest. A company called Gingerbread Trim Company sells them. (See page 315 for their contact information.)

PUT UP A TENT. You can also tent a ceiling by stapling fabric along one side of a room where the wall and ceiling meet. Then staple the fabric along the adjacent wall, and so on around the room. The last step is to push the center up and attach it to the ceiling. You can hot-glue ribbon to the fabric to cover the staples. This is very dramatic in a powder room, and I've seen breakfast rooms done, too. Sheets are very good to use because they're big and the edges are finished. But tacking them up on the ceiling is a pain in the neck, literally.

Tricks to Lower Your Ceiling

Most times people want their ceilings to feel regular height, or even higher than they are. But every now and again, you want the effect of a lowered ceiling, particularly if you live in a house with very tall walls and a cathedral ceiling. Some people have wanted cathedral ceilings their whole lives. They dream of it . . . until they live with it. Rooms with cathedral ceilings can feel cavernous.

If you want to make your ceiling feel warmer and lower, try painting it a color slightly (one or two shades) darker than the walls. This will bring the ceiling down visually and make the room cozier.

You can also install track lighting. Even if you don't need the extra light, track lighting will help the ceiling appear lower by focusing the light down from the ceiling.

Unforgettable Floors

A lot of people tend to forget about their floors. But think about it this way: It's really a fifth wall—just as a ceiling can be a fifth wall. Your floors give you another decorating opportunity to bring interest and texture into a room. Today's flooring options are as varied as individual tasks, but there are a few standouts that work in most homes—carpets, area rugs, hardwood, linoleum, tile and vinyl.

Carpet

Wall-to-wall carpet is easy to care for and offers a soft foundation in your room. As I like to say, the toes know. Can you imagine your child taking her first steps on a tile floor? Or cuddling up in front of a fire on a vinyl floor? Generally speaking, most people like to have something soft and resilient underfoot. But because it's so common, wall-to-wall carpeting can be uninteresting.

Area Rugs

To shake things up, consider adding area rugs. If you want to remove the carpet, by all means go ahead. But you don't have to. It's perfectly fine to put an area rug over carpeting. It gives a cozy layered look. You may not set out to have rugs over carpeting, but if your carpeting is not that attractive or if you just inherited a bunch of fine area rugs, by all means use your rugs.

If you are in the market for area rugs, know that they don't have to be expensive. One place to shop for area rugs is a carpet retailer. Carpet stores will cut an area rug or a runner for you from stock carpeting or from remnants. You can buy whatever length you want—12 × 6, 12 × 8, 12 × 16 feet—and the retailer will bind it for you, or even add fringe.

Getting area rugs made at a carpet retailer is practical for a lot of people. If the rug matches your upholstered pieces, you can take it with you when you move. And let's say you move again and your living room is smaller or you want to put that rug in a den or library. It's easy to have the rug cut down, whereas you can't have a Persian or a needlepoint rug cut down.

My favorite shopping strategy is to shop at the top. Go to the carpet retailer in your area with the best reputation, not the one with the cheapest prices. Ask if they have some ends from a very fine job or remnants. They just might have the right size to make an area rug. Even if it's from a very expensive carpet, you'll get a good deal on it because they're eager to get it out of the warehouse.

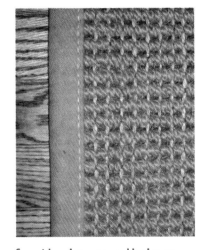

This **sisal rug** fits perfectly in my living room, but it was previously used in a different room in a different house. Because **red is my favorite color,** I knew the subtle red in this rug would **always fit** into any house of mine.

I prefer wood floors to tile floors because they're warmer and more forgiving.

Hardwood Floors

A lot of people don't realize that a floor treatment can tie rooms together. Here I made a painted floor canvas using leftover paint from my various rooms and projects. (See "Hands-On Project: Painted Floor Canvas" on page 54.)

Another great alternative to carpet is hardwood. I love hardwood floors, especially in kitchens. Most people choose linoleum, tile, or vinyl in kitchens, thinking of practicality. "What's going to be the easiest material for me to clean that will take a beating?" People don't even entertain the idea of wood because they think of the old days when cleaning your kitchen meant taking a mop and bucket and splashing water all over the floor. They just can't see that happening with hardwood.

What you might not know is that the polyurethane you can buy these days protects floors better. Plus electric brooms and damp sponge mops are far easier to clean with than mops and buckets.

One reason why I think hardwood is a good choice for kitchen floors is it's really easy on your legs, especially if you're standing on it for a long time because it does have movement and give as you walk across it. Some surfaces—such as brick, concrete, and tile—are actually hard on your legs because they're not pliable.

Another reason why I like hardwood in kitchens is that it flows with the rest of the house. If your kitchen opens up to other rooms that have hardwood, it helps to make your home look bigger because it's a continuous look. If your other rooms are carpeted, hardwood usually complements carpet well, too.

If you like hardwood *and* area rugs, you can always compromise by placing area rugs over your hardwood floors to cozy up the floor in front of the sink and under the table.

Linoleum, Tile, and Vinyl Floors

These three types of flooring are very practical choices for many people and homes. Like everything, each has its plusses and minuses. Linoleum, for instance, is easy to clean, although it can be more expensive than vinyl.

Vinyl is probably one of the easiest materials to maintain and it holds up well in bathrooms and laundry rooms where water is a factor, but it's not really a rich-looking floor treatment.

Tile can be very beautiful and rich looking, but it sure is cold. I would tend to compromise if I had a tile floor and cover it with a cozy, woven rug.

I put a brick floor in this kitchen, and I lived to regret it. It looked great, but it was hard on my legs.

My Home

As you might imagine because all of the walls in my home were painted white when I bought it, the ceilings were all painted white also. A lot of the floors were hardwood. I had to start from there—a decorating blank slate. Let's go through my home so I can share with you the stories behind the choices I made for my ceilings and floors.

My Ceilings

ENTRYWAY, LIVING ROOM, AND DINING ROOM CEILINGS:
The ceilings in my living room, dining room, and entryway are painted very light blue, which I'm very fond of. They're not so blue that a guest walks in and says, "Oh, how blue your ceilings are." In fact, nobody notices. My guests just feel good in these rooms and want to spend time there. And my family and I feel good in these rooms, too.

I was lucky that this house had dentiled molding in the dining room and living room, which makes pulling blue ceilings off even easier. I treasure that, and it was

colorsolutions

Here's a way to make a ceiling look taller: Extend the wall color onto the ceiling, painting a 3-inch band around the perimeter of the ceiling. Separate the wall and ceiling colors with a thin black line. The eye will subconsciously extend the height of the wall another 3 inches.

probably quite an extravagance almost 70 years ago when this house was built. The crown molding helps create a natural separation between the blue of the ceilings and the color of the walls.

If you're going to do something special to your ceilings, it's nice to call attention to them and to encourage the eye to go there. In my entryway and dining room, I added elements near the ceiling that draw your eye up, such as the tree mural and the trees near the ceiling. Giving your ceiling a special color or treatment offers you more to look at and enjoy than just the walls. A lot of people tend to keep their furnishings low, in a horizontal band around the room, so it's nice to look up and see something interesting.

WORKSHOP CEILING: My workshop started out its life as a garage, and when the previous owner turned it into his architecture studio, he finished it with a low suspended ceiling that I found wasn't very interesting. A few of my previous houses have had pitched, natural wood ceilings, and I wanted that for this room as well. All it required was taking off the old flat ceiling and applying tongue-and-groove wood to the pitched ceiling that was already there.

To give the wood some color without covering it with paint, I decided to stain it. But the stain turned out to be darker than I thought. Did I cry? Did I feel like a failure? Not at all. I decided to whitewash

The shelves in my dining room **encourage** the eye up to the blue ceiling.

When I bought my property, the workshop had a normal-height ceiling, but I wanted something with a "higher calling." By removing the old ceiling and adding raw wood on the rafters, I got the open feeling I was after.

it to lighten it up. So I diluted the paint color that's on the walls, called "elephant's breath" beige, and I applied the paint wash over the wood with a very large sponge.

Wood is very absorbent, so I needed to apply the wash over it several times. I particularly liked putting the wash in the grooves, because the wash really helps bring attention to the bevels. And you know what? I like the ceiling much better now than I would have if the stain had been just right from the start.

OFFICE CEILING: If you visited me in my office, you might notice the molding along the ceiling. There is a strip of modest crown molding, and then a nice detail of bamboo that makes an interesting relief against the rich red walls. But unless I told you, you probably wouldn't have guessed that the bamboo came from my garden and supported the vines of the previous season's tomato plants. Why not? I like the look of aged materials, especially if they are waxed with a product called Briwax to give them a warm glow.

If you want to add bamboo to your molding, you can buy it at garden supply stores. It's very cheap. And if you want, go ahead and wax it. But consider using it outside for a few seasons first. Nothing creates true beauty better than nature. I hung the bamboo with small nails called brads. I tapped them into the bamboo partway before hanging them, then put the bamboo in place and hammered the brads the rest of the way in.

BEDROOM CEILING: My bedroom ceiling has some angles that a lot of people would find interesting. The ceiling isn't something you would traditionally find in a house of this age, and so that leads me to think that the master bedroom may have been added on or altered in some way after the original house was completed.

Though it's interesting, the ceiling bothered me a lot. I thought

My office has modest crown molding, which I enhanced by adding waxed bamboo stakes salvaged from last season's tomato plants.

The odd angles in my bedroom led me to create this conservatory look with the help of an artist. The room turned out better than if I hadn't had that problem to solve.

The day we decided to paint morning glories on my ceiling, I planted the real thing outside my window.

it looked a little contemporary, and I didn't like the fact that it didn't have any crown molding.

But adversity often sparks creativity, and it did so here. I needed to do something to make the shape of this ceiling work for me. Beams wouldn't have worked with all of the angles, so I knew I wanted to paint something on it. I wanted to capture the look of a solarium, a conservatory, or an outdoor room, and I realized that lattice was the answer.

I hired an artist to paint the angled ceiling for me. The ceiling mural gave the room structure, and it gave me a reason to have a blue ceiling, which you know I love. In this case, the green walls coordinate nicely with the blue ceiling, and the mural creates a division between the two.

I like to be creative so I knew that painting green ivy on the lattice just wasn't the look I was after. I decided that morning glories would look terrific! So on the day we decided to paint the morning glories, I bought a morning glory and planted it outside my bedroom window to reinforce the theme.

My Floors

KITCHEN FLOOR: The previous owner of this house had installed a very inexpensive white rolled vinyl floor to cover up the many layers of old flooring. There was nothing really wrong with the white vinyl—it went well with the all-white walls and ceilings in the rest of the house—but the floor didn't work for me.

As it turned out, there was a house being torn down at the end of my street. And I thought it certainly wouldn't take a lot of wood to cover the kitchen floor. The rest of the house was hardwood, so I figured why not? I asked the workers if I could have the old wood flooring and they said, "Take it." So

I hauled it off in the back of my PT Cruiser.

My first task was to pry up the layers of old flooring. I took off the new white vinyl and two layers of linoleum under that. I also found some square tiles. I pried them off with a hammer, a screwdriver, and a chisel. It was hard work because the mastic used to secure floors is meant to last.

Finally, I just decided that it was enough hard work, and I asked my handyman to install the salvaged flooring. I decided not to remove any more layers before we installed the hardwood because it was so involved. Looking back, I realized then that if I had taken off more old layers, the wood floor would have been more level with the other floors in my house. So by the time I added the hardwood, the kitchen floor was higher than the other floors. We just installed a strip to provide a transition between the kitchen floor and the dining room floor, and that was that!

In retrospect, I probably should have done the extra work to pry up more layers, but I was eager to get to the next project.

DINING ROOM FLOOR: My dining room came with hardwood floor. And while the floor

kitty's style and spirit

Enjoy the Experience Believe it or not, I don't really do a lot of my projects for the final result. Take knitting, for instance, which is one of my favorite hobbies. I don't knit because I'm going to end up with a sweater. I knit for the pleasure of doing it. It's the doing that's so much fun. For me, it's almost a way of meditating; I get so focused on knitting that everything else disappears. When a project is finished, I say, "That was fun. What's next?"

The salvaged wood floor in my kitchen gives me the rustic look I wanted, and it goes well with my old-fashioned step stool.

is in good shape, I'd like to find a rug to go under the table. This is a place where I spend a lot of time because of the good overhead light, and because it's next to the kitchen. My daughter studies here, and I like the idea of placing something soft underfoot.

So it's on my to-do list to find a rug. I'm keeping my eyes open for one, but I haven't found the right rug yet. The lesson here is that sometimes we have to learn to live happily with unresolved issues. The rug for my dining room is one of those yet-to-be-resolved issues. But the truth is, I'd never want to be finished with my house. I like the idea of it being "in process."

ENTRYWAY, HALL, LIVING ROOM, BEDROOMS, AND OFFICE: These areas of my home all have hardwood floors. In the bedrooms I placed area rugs. I'm not fond of stepping onto a cold floor first thing in the morning. For my daughter's room, I found a carpeting I really liked and had the edges bound to create an area rug to soften the hardwood floor. In my living room and office I have sisal rugs. The one in my living room was actually in my dining room in another house.

Hands-On Projects

I'd like to show you step by step how to create three unique floor rugs: painted floor canvas, yarn rug, and Amish dust-catcher rug.

Using my leftover paint on this hallway floor canvas ties my whole house together.

HANDS-ON PROJECT: Painted Floor Canvas

Floor canvases have been used for centuries. Back in the day when everything was used until it was threadbare and nothing was thrown out, floor canvases were made from old, worn-out ship sails.

I needed something for my hallway, and I decided this would be the perfect place for a painted floor canvas to add color and to help tie the house together. The first thing I did was gather together all the leftover paint colors I'd used in my house—the red from my office, the "elephant's breath" beige from my kitchen, the green from my dining room, and so on—to use on the canvas. At the craft store, I picked up a roll of pre-primed artist's canvas and a container of gesso. Gesso is a paste that stiffens canvas to make it more substantial. For the base paint, I chose a flat paint for a rich and subtle effect. There is drying time with this project, so you'll probably need 2 days to finish the rug.

I used different widths of sponge brushes—2-inch, 3-inch, and 4-inch—to make stripes of different widths. I didn't want precise stripes with perfectly straight edges on this canvas. I wanted it to look more natural, like a woven rug. So I drew the stripes by hand. It was a fun project, and I get to enjoy the results of it every day.

WHAT YOU'LL NEED

* LEFTOVER PAINT FROM VARIOUS ROOMS AND PROJECTS
* ROLL OF PRE-PRIMED ARTIST'S CANVAS
* SCISSORS
* IRON
* WHITE GLUE
* PAINTER'S TAPE
* ASSORTMENT OF SPONGE BRUSHES
* GESSO
* BASE PAINT (FLAT IS BEST)†

* T-SQUARE
* PENCIL
* OIL PAINT PENS
* QUARTERS OR GLUE STICKS
* OFF-WHITE PAINT
* TWO NATURAL SEA SPONGES
* NONYELLOWING POLYURETHANE

†*NOTE:* CHOOSE A BASE PAINT ONE SHADE DARKER THAN YOUR INTENDED FINAL COLOR.

1. Gather together all the leftover paint from different projects and rooms in your house. **A**

2. Lay your canvas on the floor, wrong side up. Calculate the size you want the finished canvas to be, add about 2 inches to the length and the width to accommodate the hem, and cut it with scissors. **B**

3. With the wrong side of the canvas facing you, fold in a hem on all sides, about 1 inch wide. The exact dimension does not matter, but it should be consistent along both sides and on the ends. Iron the canvas down along the fold. You want to make it as flat, flat, flat as possible. **C**

4. Apply white glue under the hem and use painter's tape to keep it flat. Keep the tape in place throughout the whole process. You can press the hem before the glue totally dries. Take care not to squeeze out any of the glue. **D**

5. Mix 4 parts of your base coat or primer with 1 part gesso.

6. Turn the canvas over to the right side. Using a sponge brush, paint it with the gesso and base coat mixture. **E** Because gesso is white, it will lighten up your base coat. Using a sponge brush, put on at least three coats of base paint and gesso, letting the canvas dry between coats.

7. Using a T-square and a pencil, draw stripes of random widths onto the canvas. Some might be 5 inches wide, some 3 inches, some 4 inches, and so on. The idea is to make it look like a woven, hand-loomed rug. **F**

8. With sponge brushes, paint the stripes freehand, alternating the colors along the canvas in any order. **G**

(continued)

9. To prevent the oil pens from leaking under the T-square or leaving paint on the edge of the T-square, tape quarters or another object (I used glue sticks) to the bottom side of the ruler part of the T-square. This elevates the T-square's edge slightly above the canvas. **H**

10. When the stripes are drawn and dry, use your T-square and oil paint pens to draw various thin lines alongside and in between the larger stripes. Make some close, some farther apart. The goal is to make the stripes look like woven fabric and the lines like threads. **I**

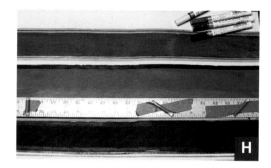

11. For the color wash that will soften the colors, mix two parts off-white paint (or your base paint if it's in that family of colors) to one part water. **J**

12. Apply the wash over the canvas with a natural sea sponge. **K** If you find you have too much wash on the canvas, have a dry sponge ready to blot it up and blend it in. Keep adding wash until the canvas has a nice, soft look. Let the canvas dry between coats of wash.

13. Once the paint is perfectly dry, apply several layers of nonyellowing polyurethane with a sponge brush. Let the layers dry between coats. Note that the polyurethane goes on cloudy and clears up as it dries. **L** ❖

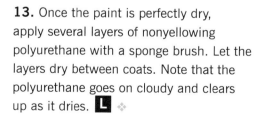

This is a very easy area rug to make using whatever materials you have at hand, such as yarn, T-shirts, or denim. I made one out of used T-shirts for a dorm room for a segment on *The Home Show* where I had a budget of only $100. When I talked to the students who lived in the room, they said they didn't like getting out of bed in the morning and putting their bare feet on the institutional carpeting. So I decided to make them a rug. But it had to be inexpensive. I decided to use wide-mesh rug canvas, which is the canvas used for latch-hook rugs, and then I looked for materials that were already there.

So I thought, what do college kids have endless amounts of that they don't need? T-shirts! So we went up and down the halls and collected dozens of solid-colored T-shirts from the students. If you're going to use strips of materials, the front and back of the material should be the same, like T-shirts without printing on them. Denim looks good, as does terry cloth. I've even made rugs out of old towels.

For the rug for this Hands-On Project, I used leftover yarn that I had hanging around. I combined four or five strands of different yarns I'd used in various projects, along with some pretty ribbon, to make a ball of yarn. (I took various balls of yarn and placed them next to each other. I took the ends of each of them and started rolling them into a new ball. When one ball of yarn ran out, I got another ball and tied the new yarn to the one that was ending and kept rolling.) When I had my ball made, I cut the yarn into 7-inch lengths, each of which I pulled through the mesh with a needle, and then tied a knot. It couldn't be easier.

When I work with yarn or twine, I'm able to pull four to seven strands through at time, depending on how large the eye of the needle is. The bigger the eye of the needle, the more you can pull through, the more density you're going to create with each stitch, and the faster you're going to go. I cut my yarn to 7-inch lengths, which gave me a floppy, casual look. If you cut the strands shorter, they'll stand up more.

(continued)

Nothing could be **easier** to make than this **yarn rug.**

WHAT YOU'LL NEED

* WIDE-MESH RUG CANVAS USED FOR RUG MAKING
* YARN, RIBBON, TWINE, OR FABRIC
* NEEDLE WITH LARGE EYE (IF YOU'RE USING YARN OR TWINE)

WHAT YOU'LL DO

1. If you're using fabric, cut it into strips about 7 inches long and 1 inch wide. I wound balls of different yarns and ribbons, then cut 7-inch lengths. **A** and **B**

2. Pull the ends of the fabric through the mesh from the back, with each of the two ends coming up through the mesh in different holes. Use a needle for yarn or twine.

3. Tie the fabric or yarn in a knot on the top of the rug to secure it in place. **C**

4. Keep pulling strips of fabric or lengths of yarn through the mesh in every fourth or fifth hole, maybe going diagonally sometimes. Pull the fabric or yarn through evenly throughout the rug, so the mesh doesn't show.

5. If your strands are too long, you can cut them, either during the process or when the rug is completed. Short lengths will stand up better, but they will tend to show more of the mesh underneath. **D** ❖

I found out about this type of rug from my friend Vicki Clabaugh. What I like about this rug is that it uses materials that I already have on hand. It's perfect for my philosophy that it's not what you don't have, it's what you do with what you do have. You could make an Amish rug from old pants or shirts that have worn out, that you're tired of, or that have a stain or tear. I like making new use of something that has outgrown its original purpose. Of course, you can also buy new fabric, combining a lot of different colors that you have in your room or house to help unify your whole color scheme.

This rug is basically made of fabric rectangles, stacked four deep, and sewn in rows to a piece of canvas or heavy denim. Each row is pushed up to sew the next row, which ends up making all the rows stand up rather than lay flat against the canvas. I used $2\frac{1}{2} \times 5$-inch pieces of fabric, and I sewed them in rows 2 inches apart. But you could have 3×6-inch pieces and sew them in rows 3 inches apart. The idea is that when all the pieces are sewn on, you don't really see the base material. When you're done, you'll have a very fun and attractive throw rug, a real conversation piece.

You'll need a lot of fabric for this. If you hope to make a rug that's a square yard, you'll need about 8 yards of fabric. It's best to choose a fabric that has a lot of sizing in it. Choose a duck or canvas, for instance, rather than a washed-out denim because it will prevent the edges from curling. To cut the fabric, use scissors or a rotary cutter. (A rotary cutter with a pinking blade is ideal.)

What these rugs do best is catch dust, thus the name. When your rug gets full of dirt and dust, just pick it up and shake it out. You want to avoid vacuuming it, at least with a rolling brush, because the loose threads of the fabric pieces will unravel and wrap around the brush. You could vacuum your rug with a hose attachment, but it's really easier to take it outside and shake it clean.

To wash a dust-catcher rug, mix a Woolite-and-water solution and work it into the fabric, then rinse it off with a hose. Drape the rug over lawn furniture to allow it to dry, shaking and turning it to fluff up the fabric pieces.

(continued)

This easygoing rug uses whatever you have hanging around.

WHAT YOU'LL NEED

* HEAVY DENIM OR CANVAS FOR BASE OF RUG

* PENCIL

* TOP FABRIC (YOU'LL NEED ABOUT 8 TIMES THE AREA OF THE BASE)

* SCISSORS OR ROTARY CUTTER (A ROTARY CUTTER WITH A PINKING BLADE WOULD BE IDEAL)†

* STRAIGHT PINS (USE ONES WITH LARGE, COLORFUL HEADS SO THEY'RE EASY TO FIND LATER)

* SEWING MACHINE (THIS ISN'T STRICTLY AMISH, BUT WHAT THE HECK)

† *NOTE:* ROTARY CUTTERS REQUIRE SPE-CIAL SELF-HEALING CUTTING MATS. DO NOT USE A ROTARY CUTTER ON A TABLETOP OR SOFT SURFACE.

WHAT YOU'LL DO

1. Hem the canvas base around the edges.

2. Starting about 1 inch from the edge, draw lines on the canvas with a pencil about 2 to 3 inches apart, depending on how close you want your fabric pieces to be. **A**

3. Cut the top fabric into rectangular pieces with a scissors or rotary cutter. I cut $2\frac{1}{2} \times 5$-inch pieces. **B**

4. Take four pieces of $2\frac{1}{2} \times 5$-inch fabric pieces and make a stack, with the pieces slightly off-kilter, not stacked perfectly one under the other, and pin them with a straight pin in the center. **C**

5. Align the center of a pinned fabric stack with the first drawn line and pin it to the rug base. Continue pinning the first row of stacks side by side along the first line on your canvas.

6. Sew the row of stacked pieces onto the canvas, through the center of the pieces, removing the pins as you go along. **D**

7. You'll see that the row of fabric now covers the next line on the canvas. Lift up the fabric to expose the next line, and pin and sew your second row of stacked pieces. **E**

8. Continue stacking, pinning, and sewing rows until the canvas is covered. Take off your shoes and wiggle your toes in your new rug. ❖

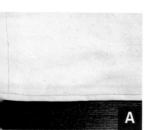

I'm considering dark mustard yellow carpets for my home. I've heard you say that yellow is very stimulating, so should this color be all over my house?

Kitty: A dark mustard yellow is really a golden color, almost like what we used to refer to as a harvest gold. One of the reasons it was so popular for so long is that it goes with so many different colors. It went with a lot of those muted, grayed-down rusts and browns that were popular back then. So I say, go for it.

It's really the brighter, high-chroma yellow that can create anxiety after a while.

I have seen some really nice drop ceilings in magazines, but the only ones I find at local stores have the plain white tracks and traditional tiles. Where is a good place to look for brass tracks and a wider selection of tiles?

Kitty: A large home center, like Lowe's or Home Depot, usually has many options. If you can't find what you like, browse through ads in decorating magazines or ask your local retailers for the names of ceiling tile manufacturers. Not every retailer can display and stock the many styles offered by

a manufacturer, so you may find that there are more choices available. You can always check online sources, too.

Check model homes in your area. Builders often opt for special looks, and I'm sure they would share the manufacturer's name with you.

I once saw a show you did using faux beams. I am interested in getting some, but I have not been able to find them. Any suggestions?

Kitty: Beams and molding made of foam are becoming more popular. Wood is expensive these days, so wooden beams and moldings may not be the quality you desire if the price is low.

Manufacturers are coming up with affordable alternatives for homeowners.

Using Styrofoam for interior beams and moldings is a good idea. It's lightweight (which is good for earthquake country, where I live), easy to cut, and very inexpensive. The company I featured on my show is called Gingerbread Trim Company, and it is in Port Charlotte, Florida. The phone number is (941) 743-8556, and their Web site is www.gingerbreadonline.com.

I've got wall-to-wall carpeting, and I just inherited a collection of fine area rugs. Is it tacky to put the area rugs on top of the carpeting?

Kitty: It's not tacky at all. What can be better than to have treasured rugs? Hardwood floors are the ideal undersurface when you have area rugs, but not everyone is lucky enough to have them. If there are hardwood floors under your carpeting, refinishing them is one of the most cost-effective things you can do to increase your home's resale value.

But if you don't have hardwood floors, or if you don't have the money to redo them, by all means, use your rugs right over your carpets. In fact, I've seen some of the best designers layering area rugs, with one on top of another. If you have an inordinate number of rugs, don't feel like you should limit yourself to just one.

But, here's another thought. Do you have cement or concrete slab floors under your carpeting? There's never been a time in history when cement or concrete slab floors have been as revered as they are now. Years ago, people would never have considered staining, waxing, and polishing cement floors. But now cement floors are being uncovered. It may not be the look for the typical Colonial home, but you might consider it for certain rooms in the house. Lay your area rugs right on top of the cement. The rugs will help warm up the cold nature of cement.

I'm thinking about painting my master bedroom walls a medium to dark cocoa color. The room is large and gets lots of light. I want to paint the ceiling the cocoa color also, rather than the traditional white. The room has lots of pretty white moldings. What do you think?

Kitty: Although I don't mind painting a library or den ceiling a dark color, I'm not crazy about that idea in a bedroom. It's going to make the room feel too dark, perhaps even claustrophobic. It's obvious that you love the cocoa color, but I think you'll be happy with just painting the four walls.

Remember, when the walls are painted, each wall is going to reflect the opposite wall, and the overall effect is going to be darker than your paint sample. You can still capture the look you want by sticking with the white moldings and painting the ceiling white or perhaps very soft, light blue. I think you'll feel better about waking up on a rainy day if you keep the ceiling light.

The color palette of my small California ranch home is Easter egg colors, and I am very happy with it. I need to replace the flooring and would like suggestions for something that would provide continuity from room to room, including the hallway.

Kitty: You didn't mention a budget, so I'll make a few suggestions. Hardwood would be my first choice, for warmth and comfort, in a natural to medium stain. You could also go with a laminate like Pergo or a wood-look plank. Or, 12 × 12-inch Spanish tile in a light bleached tone would work in your house.

I have a dark taupe bedroom with white trim. What color rug would you suggest— light or dark? The windows have tortoise-shell blinds, and the floors are hardwood.

Kitty: It sounds like you're on the verge of a British Colonial look. You could go with sisal on the floor, a contemporary pattern, an Oriental rug, or needlepoint. You're off to a great start with the items you've chosen, but don't feel restricted by any particular color.

First, determine how much floor you want to be seen. Then start looking around for a rug you like. If you can't find an area rug that you really, really like, you can create a custom rug out of carpeting. I suggest you go to your local carpet dealer to see if there is some kind of carpeting that really sings to you. Have the store cut a piece to the size you want (it usually comes in widths of 12 to 14 feet), and have them bind the edges.

Do you like Berber carpeting in a cottage-style living room or do you think it's too informal?

Kitty: The idea of cottage style is by definition informal and so Berber feels just fine in that environment. Have you considered sisal instead? Both sisal and Berber are looped broadloom. Currently, I see a lot more sisal being used than Berber. Sisal is a natural material, but it's not as easy to care for or as comfortable and soft as a Berber. Berber is most often made of synthetic fibers, like nylon, olefin, or blends.

My recommendation is to shop around. Take some samples home of a Berber that is a nylon/olefin blend in a maize or golden tan color. You'll get the look of sisal but the easy-care qualities of Berber.

The idea of **cottage style** is by definition **informal** and so Berber feels **just fine** in that environment.

How do you paint ceiling fan blades?

Kitty: The good news is that most ceiling fan blades can be removed. Take the blades off, and then paint them with high-gloss paint, or if they're wood, you could strip and stain them. Get creative—you can have fun with faux finishes, stenciling, or wall decals. You can have whatever look you desire!

If for some reason the fan blades don't come off for painting, get a tall ladder, mask the blades off carefully, then paint them. If the fan is controlled by a switch on the wall, I suggest you turn it to the off position and then put tape over it to prevent someone in your household from accidentally turning on the fan while you're working on it.

My entryway is hardwood, and the three adjoining rooms have tile and Berber carpet. I want to replace the tile and Berber carpet with wood laminate to give the whole area a continuous look. I have two small boys, so we need something durable. How would a wood laminate look next to hardwood floors? Would it help to use a contrasting shade?

Kitty: Unless it matches almost perfectly (which is next to impossible), simulated wood next to natural wood might look a little cheap. So using a contrasting shade would be preferable. I would go at least four shades lighter. My advice is to get a number of samples, and then place them right next to the natural wood for a couple of days before you make your choice.

1 If you have a **wooden stairway** that is a little bland, **paint the risers** (the part of the stair that is vertical) black. This gives the whole stairway a **subtly sophisticated look.**

2 Make a rug for a porch with heavy-weight striped canvas (sprayed with waterproofing sealer), and set it over a nonskid pad. You can create fringe on the rug ends by pulling horizontal threads for 2 or 3 inches. Make chair pads with matching canvas.

3 Here's a neat decorator trick to make your ceilings look taller: Hang your curtains all the way up to the ceiling, not just to the top of the window. You will be amazed at the look this creates.

4 Did you know that a wallpaper ceiling can brighten a dark room? It's best to choose a sunny floral pattern, not a heavy-oppressive pattern. Or try blue-and-white-cloud wallpaper. Many wallpaper companies make cloud-themed wallpaper, and the ceiling is the perfect spot to feature it.

5 A mirror can add light to a dark room, especially when you use it for a tray table. Place a small lamp or candles on the tray to reflect light onto the ceiling. Place a vase of flowers on the mirror as well for a feminine look, and add holly during the holidays.

I added this **window and Dutch door** to a bedroom wall. Is this **too costly?** If I decide to part with this house, I guarantee that this will be **a selling point.**

windows and doors

Many of us overlook windows, and especially doors, as decorating opportunities. We see them and use them, but we often don't give them the attention they deserve. As you'll see in this chapter, I like to take doors away if they don't work for me, and I'll add doors and windows where they do work for me. Privacy is an issue for most of us, but we don't want heavy draperies in every room. As you'll see, I'm a big fan of using roll-shades for privacy, with softer window treatments to frame the window and the views of nature beyond.

Warm Up Your Windows

In contemplating your window coverings, a lot of your decisions will be based on whether or not privacy is an issue. In my last house, I didn't have a stitch of curtains on my windows. Privacy wasn't an issue because the house had a courtyard and tall fences around it. Also, the style of the home was Santa Fe, with thick adobe walls. That adobe-style thickness is revealed around the windows, so I didn't want to cover that up with window treatments. But because windows are cold, hard surfaces and most windows are angular squares or rectangles, it helps to add window treatments to soften them.

It's especially helpful to hang curtains in windows if the rest of your room is filled with hard surfaces. The window treatments balance the hard and cold surfaces with warmth. A lot of modern houses have concrete floors, stone countertops, and stainless steel appliances. That wouldn't work for me without a lot of softening. I may overdo the softness, but I find a lot of people want a cozy house.

Luckily there are myriad options from which to choose, including blinds, curtains, draperies, shades, sheers, shutters, and valances. Here are some factors to consider when dressing your windows.

Decorate Kitty's Way

❑ **Install** the same blinds in every room as a starting point; this gives you time to make decisions about window treatments. ❑ Play up a door with color, or **add accents** to it to create interest. ❑ Minimize doors if they break up a room by wallpapering over them or **painting a trompe l'oeil.** ❑ Use a room's **best feature** as its focal point. ❑ **Poof** up a flat valance with Bubble Wrap!

LET THEM UNITE. If your room has more than one window or more than one size of window, having the same window treatment on each window can help to pull the room together. You can also use the same window treatment in different rooms to carry the same vibe from room to room.

CHECK IT OUT FROM INSIDE AND OUT. When choosing window treatments, keep in mind what your house is going to look like from the outside. If you have a different type of window treatment in each window, it looks like a mishmash. This is especially true if you have a two-story house, which tends to have more windows on the front of the house.

One solution is to install the same roll-up blinds or mini-blinds in all rooms, no matter what the curtains or draperies are. Because the blinds are installed behind the curtains or draperies, only the blinds will be visible from the street.

Another idea is to have neutral-colored lining in all your draperies, so that one consistent color shows in the front. A lot of people think you can only have white or off-white linings. But I'm a big fan of having a very subtle print for a lining, which reveals itself inside your room if you pull the draperies back. To make drapes like this, buy curtains that are the same size and sew them together, with the wrong sides facing.

CONSIDER THE VIEW, TOO. When I think about windows, I also think about the view outside the windows. Some of this is

In this room, I wanted to play up the beefy moldings around the windows, and I didn't want to hide them with thick draperies. **But I did want privacy.** So I used mini-blinds, which also helped unite the windows with the French door.

beyond your control, of course, such as your neighbor's yard or the business across the street. But there are things you can do to *your* property to enhance the view from your windows.

For example, if you live in a boxy, rectangular apartment with a boxy, rectangular sliding glass door, placing a large, potted tree outside the door will soften the view. My daughter and her husband have a citrus tree on their apartment balcony. Or you can add container gardens that overflow with blooms to soften hard edges. You could also "frame" the inside of the door with artificial greenery.

MAKE THE MOST OF LIGHT. I think most of us like a lot of natural light. We're solar-powered! But if houses were walls of glass, they would be neither as energy efficient nor as cozy as we might like. But you can double the impact of your windows by putting large mirrors on the walls opposite the windows. A lot of apartments and bedrooms in newer houses have windows on one side only. Double that natural light with a well-placed mirror.

kitty's style and spirit

Build a Prototype If you're worried about how a project is going to work out, making a prototype is a good idea. For example, if you're deciding on window treatments, sketch them out or make a small-scale one from scraps of fabric. To see how a paint color will look in a room, paint a piece of cardboard and hang the cardboard on the wall for at least a day and a night.

So if you have an idea, don't just go out and do it. Take some time to chew on it.

This large plant softens the harsh lines of the large sliding glass doors. A citrus tree on the balcony also softens the impact of all that glass and adds color when the fruit forms.

Privacy was not much of an issue in my daughter's **study nook,** but these **wispy little curtains** offered just the **right amount of softness.**

Don't Ignore Your Doors

Doors are the final frontier of decorating. Think about it—how many people do anything interesting at all with their doors? But like the ceilings we talked about in chapter 2, doors are an underused canvas for adding color and interest to a room. Here are a few interesting things I've done with doors.

PAINT THEM. If you have a small room, consider painting the door (and possibly the door trim) the same color as the wall so the door doesn't "break up" the room. In my daughters' guesthouse I used an idea I found in a book about Swedish style. In the book, the door's moldings were painted blue, and a decorative transfer was painted on the door. I adapted that technique for their door. People ask me where I get my inspiration. Here's a perfect example of seeing an idea in a book and figuring out how to create the look in my home.

I saw a door painted like this in a book, and then I made it happen in my own house.

WALLPAPER THEM. You couldn't really wallpaper a paneled door, but you could wallpaper the panels. I wallpapered the panels of the bathroom door in my guesthouse.

EMPHASIZE THE FRONT DOOR. The front door of your home holds a special importance. Your color choice is important here. It often works well to have three different colors on the outside of your home: one color for the walls (brick counts!), another color for the trim, and a third color for the door. Black front doors can be very sophisticated. But it could look like a black hole if the door is recessed back into the house. If that's the case, choose a lighter color. Very fine townhouses in London and New York often have black or dark green doors. My best advice is to drive around different neighborhoods and notice the colors of the front doors. Some colors pop; others seem dated and tired. A door is super easy to paint, so don't be afraid to experiment—you can always repaint it if you don't like it.

On a house I owned previously, I wanted to create more of a country feel for what was pretty much a standard Cal-

makes$ense

Do you like the look of a lattice screen door? Instead of replacing your current screen door, you can draw a lattice design right on the screen by using white oil paint pens. Just tape off the areas in a diagonal fashion and fill in with paint.

ifornia ranch-style home. I added plank-style shutters, planted climbing roses over the porch, and painted my front door a fascinating graying pink. On another exterior door leading to the porch, I had an artist paint a trompe l'oeil of three adorable pigs. Those pigs made me smile every time I went in the door.

RETHINK YOUR DOORS. In my opinion, most houses, especially older homes, have too many interior doors. I suppose the habit of putting a door from the kitchen to the laundry room, and from the kitchen to the dining room, and from the dining room to the living room, and from the living room to the hallway came about at a time when houses were not very well insulated, when heating costs were high, and when people needed to shut off parts of their houses during cold winters. Or, maybe house designers were trying to mimic large mansions where there were a lot of doors so that the servants could be separated from the masters of the house. Obviously, that need is no longer there for most of us!

I removed the door between my kitchen (in the foreground) and service porch and **use it on my potting shed** instead. And now, **my kitchen seems larger.**

colorsolutions

If you have a piece of glass in your front door, consider replacing it with a vintage-look stained glass or leaded window. It's a simple change that will have big paybacks, especially when the sun shines through. At night, with the lights on inside, visitors and passersby will be treated to the sight of a pretty glow and you'll be treated to a color show all year-round.

I added this door from my bedroom to the backyard. I thought, "Why is that solid wall standing between me and my garden?"

makes$ense

Hollow-core doors hinged together make a very lightweight and flexible room divider. You can paint or wallpaper the doors to match your décor.

I find that some interior doors can be removed, and the doorways even widened, to create more user-friendly homes with better flow. There's no need to let a door stand in your way just because some architect drew it on the plans! You decide what works for you.

MINIMIZE THEM. Sometimes, it's not possible to remove a door. I decorated a kitchen for *The Home Show* that had five doors coming into it. One door led to the garage, another led to the basement, a third led to a bathroom, and so on. The doors were all necessary, so I was stuck with them. But all those doors made the kitchen feel confusing, so I really wanted to cut down on the visual impact of them.

I simply wallpapered over one door, to match the wallpaper I put in the rest of the kitchen. Magically, the door "disappeared." On another door, I had a local art student make a trompe l'oeil of a corner cabinet. If you can't find an art student or afford an artist, see if you can buy a wallpaper mural to mimic the hand-painted look.

Although some homes have too many interior doors, I sometimes think there are not enough exterior doors. This is what happened in my bedroom, where I wanted access to my backyard. The previous owner didn't need this, apparently, but I did. It was not that big of a deal to get a door installed. I chose a Dutch door that splits horizontally in two so I could open the top, the bottom, or both. It keeps my dog, Spot, in the house and at the same time opens the door to the fragrances in my garden.

ADD THE OUTSIDE. If you have a solid front door, consider having a decorative glass panel or two installed. Many hardware stores will take your existing door and install decorative glass peek-throughs (sometimes long and rectangular or equal-sized squares) to let the light shine in. You'd be amazed at how much it can lighten up a dark foyer or hallway, and it's much cheaper than buying a whole new door.

A student painted a **trompe l'oeil** of a corner cabinet onto this door. **See the doorknob?** The **"books"** on the shelves **reflect the family history** of the homeowners.

My Home

As you probably could have guessed, when I moved into this house there was nothing at all on the windows and the doors were just regular old plain doors. Of course, they didn't stay that way for long!

One of the first things I did when I bought my home, before I even moved in, was to order matchstick shades for every window in the house. I knew that privacy would be a factor, especially in the front of the house because it faces the street, but I didn't know yet what types of decorating decisions I was going to make for the rooms. How could I commit myself to window coverings when I didn't even know what color the rooms would be, or what furniture and accessories I would put in those rooms? These things take time, at least for me. Matchstick shades are a good first purchase for any new (or seasoned) homeowner.

I love the natural color and look of matchstick shades. The shades helped to warm up the windows and gave me instant privacy. You can buy them in many catalogs, which tend to carry more sizes than a retail store. And you can buy them lined or unlined. In this case, I chose to get them unlined so you can still see the light through. As you'll see, while I went on to make my decisions on curtains and draperies, the matchbook shades stayed in place, and they actually help unify my whole house.

DINING ROOM: Whenever I approach a decorating situation, I always ask myself: What does this room have going for it? Then I usually use the room's best feature as its focal point. Then most of the rest of my decorating decisions flow from this starting point. Decide what the focal point of your room is—whether it's an architectural feature, a window, or a still-blank wall.

Even after I chose my bedroom curtains, the matchstick shades that I hung previously for privacy stayed in place.

The focal point of my dining room is the bay window with a window seat. So that is where I began decorating this room.

To play up the usefulness of the window seat, I pushed my dining-room table to that end of the room so that I can sit on the window seat, work at the table, and enjoy the sun on my back.

This **unique window treatment** is simply **yards of silk** hung over **two large finials.**

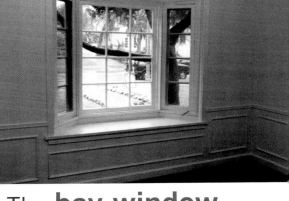

The **bay window** was a good start, but it **needed to be softened.**

This is great, too, for dinner parties because I can squeeze a couple of kids on the window seat. And of course, my wonderful dog, Spot, sits on the window seat, watches the other dogs passing by, and barks at the mailman.

After I painted the room, I had a cushion made with a trapunto-type quilted fabric that blends with the color of the walls. But then I wanted to have a bit of fun with the window seat and the bay window.

Because Spot likes to spend a lot of time on the window seat, I decided to do something for her. One day I was looking out at the grass in the front lawn, and I thought, hmmm, why not have a cushion just for Spot? And so I bought a piece of indoor-outdoor carpeting, and I asked my local upholsterer to make a window-seat cover out of it. Some of my friends think I'm crazy, but Spot thinks it's great. And it makes people laugh.

Finally, to soften the bay window, I found a wonderful silk crewel at my favorite fabric store and decided to make a draped valance. So I got two round finials, with screws on the ends, which are actually meant to put at the ends of curtain rods. But rather than using them in that way, I stained them dark and screwed them straight into either side of the trim around the window. To make the valance, I measured the width across the window, added the length down on both sides, and hemmed the fabric long enough to puddle on the floor. Then I draped the fabric across the finials. It

oneminutemakeovers

Want a unique and fun look for a party? If you have jalousie windows, the kinds with slats of glass, open them all the way until they are horizontal. Then they make a perfect place to put votive candles in small glass holders; just put a little drip of melted wax on the window to secure the glass holder in place.

Spot is very diligent about sitting in the window seat and watching out for the mailman. And with great success: Not once has the mailman broken into our house.

looks more spectacular than fabric draped over curtain rod ends, but that's exactly what it is. At Christmastime, I layer garland over the top of the fabric.

LIVING ROOM: Because I had the matchstick shades in my living room already, I was in no great hurry to decide on my draperies. I knew I wanted wooden rods and lined silk draperies. But I wanted something just a bit more personal than that. It all came together for me when I found two different trims at my fabric store. One trim was a good companion to my living room's red winter slipcovers, and the other coordinated nicely with my blue summer slipcovers. I discovered that if I sewed both trims onto drapes for the window—one on top of the other—my curtains would perfectly match my furniture all year around. (Take a look at "Hands-On Project: Custom-Trimmed Draperies" on page 82.)

I figure that these silk draperies, with this beautiful fringe, would probably have cost $400 to $500 a panel, if they were custom made. It cost me less than a third of that. I saved all kinds of money, and I still have a custom look.

This simple valance, hung in the center from a cup hook and ring, unites the two windows.

You can see how the two trims—one blue and gold, the other a red and green fringe—were combined on my silk draperies.

BIRDIE'S ROOM: For my daughter's room, I wanted to create a valance to soften and unite the windows and add color to the room. After all, I already had the matchstick shades for privacy.

I wanted this to be simple and use a minimal amount of fabric. I bought 2 yards of fabric at Shabby Chic, and I hemmed it. I'm not really handy with the sewing machine, but I can hem. Then I tied a piece of fabric in a very soft knot in the center. Next I needed to secure it above the window. I simply screwed a cup hook into the wall and hung a curtain ring on it. Then I strung the fabric through the ring, adjusting the soft knot so that it hides the ring and hook.

The valance fashioned from a Kashmir shawl and a French coatrack helps soften the window, and it brings attention to the bamboo I had added to the crown molding.

This tie valance is hung off the same type of curtain-rod finials as is my dining room valance. So simple.

You'll never guess what I stuffed the valance with to make it poofy instead of hanging limp—Bubble Wrap! If I had all the money in the world, I might have bought double the fabric so it wouldn't look so skinny. But the Bubble Wrap solved that problem, and now the valance gives some curves and grace to what would be a very angular window.

OFFICE: I tried two unique ideas with my office windows. I decorated the window above my computer desk with a combination you might not have seen before: a French coatrack and a red Kashmir paisley shawl, which I bought in London. Of course, it's a crime to cut a shawl like this, so I needed to come up with a way to hang it without cutting it. The solution? I hung it on the coatrack!

On my other office window, I made a valance out of ties. This technique would be perfect for a man's office. I purchased silk ties from thrift stores and yard sales. You could use a collection of ties that you already have, maybe from your dad, grandfather, or a favorite uncle who passed away.

MY BEDROOM: I painted the walls in my bedroom a very odd color: a light celadon green. I already had my matchstick shades, and I also had some sheer white draperies made for my windows. But I wanted to find some green fabric to put behind the white, to make my draperies look like a little girl's pinafore dress. My goal was to add color without blocking any light. Then one day, I found it: the *exact* color green. My patience—and persistence—paid off.

I waited until I found the **exact shade of green** I needed to create **the pinafore look** I imagined.

Hands-On Projects

I'd like to show you step by step how to create three of my favorite window treatments: custom-trimmed draperies; distressed curtain rods, finials, and brackets; and custom kitchen curtains.

HANDS-ON PROJECT: Custom-Trimmed Draperies

The look I was after for my living room—lined silk drapes trimmed to match the colors of my living room in various seasons—would cost a lot to achieve unless I took matters into my own hands.

So I bought lined silk draperies from Restoration Hardware for $149 a panel. They're a beautiful flax-colored fabric in a soft striped silk, and I love them. They blend beautifully with the walls. Of course, the texture of the fabric is really much more formal than anything else in the room. But I like the addition of silk. It flows and drapes really beautifully, and it adds an element of sophistication to the room.

But the draperies weren't really finished enough; I wanted them to be a little more detailed to complement my two sets of slipcovers—a blue toile for summer and a red paisley for winter. I could not find one trim that worked for both slipcovers, and I wasn't about to change my draperies every time I changed my slipcovers! By keeping my eyes open, I found two different trims that I could put together.

The fringe trim I found was quite expensive—about $30 a yard. But I realized that it was doubled moss fringe, which means two rows of fringe stitched together. So I ripped it in half to have double the amount of trim.

But I still had a problem: Getting the trim sewn on the draperies. I don't have a lot of patience with a sewing machine, and this was going to be fairly thick for my simple-minded sewing machine to handle. I negotiated with a seamstress at my local

This blue and gold trim relates to my blue summer slipcovers . . .

. . . while this red, green, and multicolored fringe coordinates with my red winter slipcovers.

With the two trims combined on my silk draperies, I have draperies that work for me all year around.

dry cleaners to sew the trim on for $8 a panel. The deal required that I cut the trim to the right size and pin it in place on each panel. That, I could do!

I wanted to leave a little of the original drapery fabric showing, so I indented the trim ¼ to ½ inch inside the drapery edge. Because you can't machine-sew through the red pocket, you need to hand-sew on the trim in that area. I saved money by not having the seamstress hand-sew it on the top, where it went around the rod; I did that myself at home. I also pressed the drapes myself. In retrospect, I should have paid extra to have them steamed at the dry cleaners because they have the right machinery to do that.

I wanted luscious silk draperies trimmed to blend well with both my blue summer slipcovers and my red winter slipcovers.

WHAT YOU'LL NEED

* DRAPERY PANELS
* TRIM (1 STYLE OR 2 COMPLEMENTARY TRIMS)
* FABRIC SCISSORS
* STRAIGHT PINS
* SEWING MACHINE (OR A COST-EFFECTIVE LOCAL SEAMSTRESS)
* THREAD
* HAND-SEWING NEEDLE

WHAT YOU'LL DO

1. Lay out the drapery panels and measure them from top to bottom. Also measure the height of the rod pocket on top and the hem on the bottom and add that to your total for each piece. (The trim will need to wrap around the top and bottom of the drapes.) Cut the trim to fit.

2. Pin the trim to the drapery panels with straight pins, setting it back ½ inch from the edge so that some of the drapery fabric still shows. Fold the trim over the height of the rod pocket.

3. Using the sewing machine or hand-sewing needle, sew the trim on the panel, starting below the rod pocket; be careful not to sew across the pocket so you can insert the rod later on. **A** If you're using rings, hooks, or something that doesn't go through the rod pocket, go ahead and sew all the way through the rod pocket. If your draperies are going through a rod, be careful not to sew through the rod pocket at the top when applying the trim. Sew it on by hand at the end.

4. Press your draperies and enjoy your custom life. If you've taken them to the cleaners to be sewn, get them pressed there.

HANDS-ON PROJECT:
Distressed Curtain Rods, Finials, and Brackets

Once I had the custom-trimmed draperies for my living room, I needed some way to hang them. These draperies are not necessarily meant to be put through a rod. They came with clips at the top and rings to hang them with. But I didn't want to see rings in that room. I wanted a cleaner look.

And so I decided to put the draperies on 2-inch rods. I didn't want anything too fancy like brass, so I decided on wood. I bought unfinished rods, unfinished finials for the ends of the rods, and very basic unfinished brackets to hold the rods. They were new, but I wanted them to look like they had been around for a long time.

Often brand-new things lack character. Something that's been around a while may not be pristine, but it is much more interesting (like people of a certain age!). So I wanted to add some sort of patina to the rods, finials, and brackets.

Actually, I used almost the exact technique that I had on my fireplace. (See "Hands-On Project: Distressed Fireplace Wall" on page 190.)

WHAT YOU'LL NEED

* NEW WOODEN CURTAIN RODS, FINIALS, AND/OR BRACKETS (CHOOSE THE KIND OF FINIALS WITH A SCREW ALREADY ON THE BOTTOM—YOU CAN SCREW THEM INTO A PIECE OF WOOD TO STABILIZE THEM AND ALLOW YOU TO WORK WITH THEM BETTER)
* GARDEN CULTIVATOR
* CHAIN (OR A CHANEL CHAIN BELT, IF YOU PREFER, JUST TO BE SASSY)
* STRONG COFFEE
* GRAVEL AND DIRT
* BRIWAX PASTE WAX (I USED LIGHT BROWN)
* SOFT CLOTH

WHAT YOU'LL DO

1. First you want to create nicks, gouges, and indentations in the wood as if it has been around for decades. You could start by striking it with a garden cultivator or other tool to create what looks like wormholes. **A**, **B**, and **C** Don't just hit the pieces straight on; hit them at an angle to create gouges.

2. For another kind of indentation, whip the wood with a chain. **D** Most of us worry about marring a soft wood like pine. But here you can use the soft wood to ad-vantage. It's easy to nick and mar. To make even deeper marks, I also hit the pieces against a sharp metal post.

3. To add another dimension to the distressed wood, pour strong coffee over the pieces and watch them soak it up. This is especially helpful if your pieces are made from different types of wood that might take the wax slightly differently. (My rod was pine and the brackets were birch, I believe.) The coffee helps equalize the tones of different woods. It will dry quickly. **E** and **F**

4. Next, roll your pieces in gravel and dirt. You don't need a box of gravel like I show here—just some dirt and gravel. Roll the items in the gravel and really grind the dirt into the wood. The dirt gives the wood added color and texture. **G** and **H**

5. Let this whole concoction dry, and then wipe off any loose dirt or gravel.

6. Finally, polish the pieces with Briwax. I used a light brown Briwax, rubbing it in with a soft cloth. Apply two or three coats, letting the wax dry for 20 minutes between each coat. Then buff the pieces to a glorious patina. You want the darkness of the wax to be obvious. Why make faux wormholes if they're not noticeable? **I** ❖

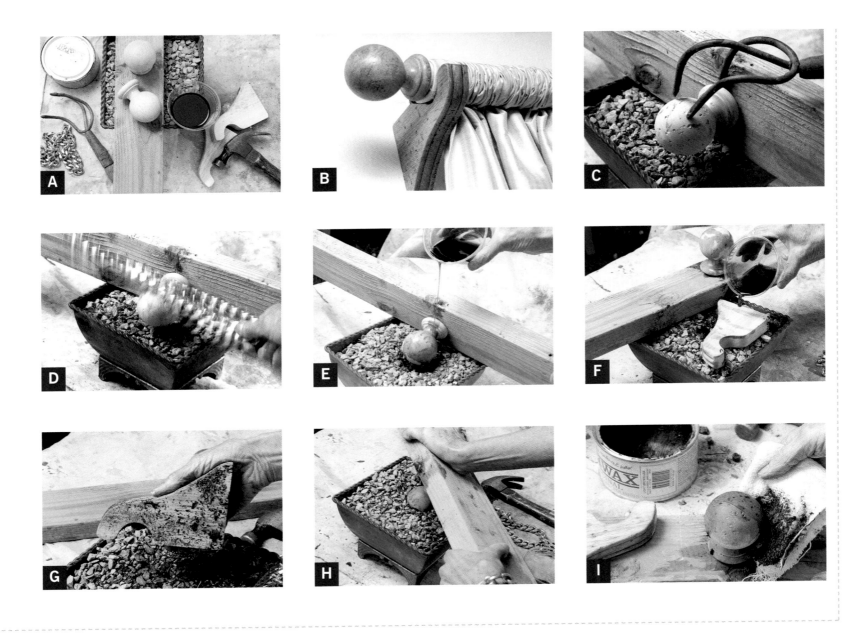

The window curtain over the sink in my kitchen is red and white country check. So is the curtain below my sink. For the other window in my kitchen, though, I wanted something different, to avoid that cookie-cutter look. I achieved that by combining standard elements—a curtain and a valance—in an unusual way.

I got my inspiration at least 10 years ago when I cut out a magazine photo of a pair of draperies I loved; I knew that someday I'd be able to use the idea. This look was perfect for my kitchen. I bought simple white cotton curtains from the Country Curtains catalog. They are very basic and very reasonably priced. I also ordered an extra checked valance.

I cut the checked valance horizontally into pieces that were one-third and two-thirds of the total length. Then I sewed the larger piece to the bottom of the white curtains and the smaller piece to the top of the curtains to create a border effect. Now I have crisp, white curtains that are a little bit more sophisticated for that large window.

I hung my curtain creation on the same type of rod and brackets that I used in my living room. But I painted them white to match the vibe in my kitchen.

I cut this picture out of a magazine at least 10 years ago with the thought that I might do something like this someday. I finally did.

WHAT YOU'LL NEED

* BASIC CURTAINS
* VALANCE (CHECKED OR PATTERNED WOULD LOOK GREAT)
* SEWING MACHINE
* FABRIC THREAD
* SCISSORS

WHAT YOU'LL DO

1. Cut the valance into two pieces, one that is one-third of the total length, and the other two-thirds of the total length.

2. Sew the bigger strip along the bottom of your basic curtain.

3. Sew the narrower strip along the top of your curtain. You can sew it right over the pocket and ruffle above the pocket, which will give the top of your curtain more substance than it had originally. Take care not to sew through the pocket so you can insert the rod when you're done.

A few weeks after I hung these curtains, I started thinking that I wanted to tie the curtains together more with the red, white, and black tablecloth on my tall kitchen table. So I glued some black rickrack along the hemline. I'm always open to future inspiration. ❖

I glued the black trim on later. Fun, huh?

My dining room has a cathedral ceiling, with a large picture window on the second floor. We can see the mountains from our bridge upstairs, and I don't want to cover the view, but I have no clue how to decorate the window. Do you have any ideas?

Kitty: If privacy isn't a factor, maybe you just want to soften the window on either side. You could bring the outside in by placing two very, very large potted trees on the inside of the house to frame the window and soften the angularity of it. If you don't have the space—or the budget— for trees, you could hire a painter to paint a trompe l'oeil on the walls of your dining room, extending up to and winding along the side of the picture window. That's a little pricey, too, though. So last but not least, you could place some naturally finished, decorative wooden shutters on either side of the window to soften the glare and the coldness of all that glass.

I have eight sets of windows throughout my house, meaning two windows side by side. All of the windows have mini-blinds. My question is, should I put two sets of curtains on each window or just two big panels, making one set per two windows?

I don't want to spend a lot of money on this house because we are just renting it and are hoping to buy a house in the near future. I am thinking about making my own curtains, because I think it might be cheaper going that way. But I'm not really good at sewing so I want something simple. Can you give me a little advice on this?

Kitty: You've already got blinds for privacy, so what you want to do is soften the look. I would treat each set of windows as one large window, and I would install a long valance above each set of windows. I suspect the windows don't go all the way to the ceiling, so I would suggest a deep valance. The higher you hang a valance toward the ceiling, the larger your windows will appear. It's cheating because you're literally hanging the valance over bare wall. But I promise no one will know! Once the valances are in place, if you feel you need something else, you can add a panel to each side of the window.

By using one long valance, you may be able to use the curtains again in another home—just cut it down to fit smaller windows.

Should my curtains be the same color as my walls, or the opposite?

Kitty: It depends on the size of your room. If your curtains are remarkably different in color from your walls, your eye stops where the curtains begin. Imagine a room with light walls and dark curtains. Your eye travels along the wall and then stops at the curtains.

This is fine in a large room. But if your room is small, it would probably work better to have the drapery material be more neutral, or more in line with the wall color.

I have a Mediterranean home. Three large arched windows in the foyer overlook the garden. How can I decorate the windows so that they make the biggest impact?

Kitty: Hopefully you're not going to need window treatments for privacy, because you don't want to diminish the drama of those windows. I would add simple, draped valances above the windows. Look for rich color to play up the Mediterranean look of your décor.

I also encourage you to think about what you see out the windows at night. That's very important. You probably see the trees in the garden from the back, or maybe you have a sculpture or a fountain in your garden that you illuminate at night. These outdoor features help to draw the eye to the windows, and also beyond them.

I live in El Salvador in a very small, dark house. What can you suggest for a window treatment that won't block all the light?

Kitty: I've been to El Salvador and have been so happy to see the courage that many people there have to infuse their homes with many different colors. You didn't mention if privacy is an issue here or what colors you've chosen for the inside of your house. However, may I assume that with your climate your windows will be open most of the time?

How about a lace of some kind that will give you privacy, natural light, and ventilation all at the same time? Few things are prettier than the combination of soft lace and colorful walls in a small house. I hope this works for you. Or, if you need occasional privacy, roll-up shades come in handy.

I found this **lace** at a flea market. It would make **wonderful curtains** for a house in an area with **lots of sunshine.**

I want some really nice lace curtains, but the ones I find at my local stores are poor quality. I live in a small town without upscale stores. What do you suggest?

Kitty: I am a huge fan of the Rue de France catalog. Check out their Web site at www.ruedefrance.com or call (800) 777-0998 to order a catalog. They sell a large selection of beautiful lace by the yard as well as ready-made curtains and drapes.

I have a nice new apartment, but I am having trouble decorating the windows in my living room. There are a patio door and a small window side by side. Can I cover both with curtains and still get to my patio?

Kitty: The best window treatment on a door is one that is secured to the door frame itself, such as a sheer curtain hung on a rod above and below the window. You don't need to have the same treatment on the window, however, but you may want to use the same fabric.

Consider catalogs to buy your curtains and drapes. You can shop at home, either online or with actual catalogs. You can measure your windows yourself and get ad-

vice from knowledgeable salespeople on the phone. They will send you swatches of fabric, and they are more likely than a retail store to have exactly what you want.

One of my favorite resources is Country Curtains. They have a wonderful catalog with many options and super customer service people. They have a wide variety of styles and fabrics at reasonable prices. Country Curtains is located in Stockbridge, Massachusetts, and their Web site is www.countrycurtains.com.

Due to an addition on the back of our house, I will be losing the only window in my kitchen, which is over the sink. Do you have any ideas how I can still have light without putting a mirror there? I don't want to watch myself doing dishes.

Kitty: I wouldn't like to watch myself doing dishes either! We've got to figure out a way to bring in some natural light. Would you consider a skylight or a Solatube? If there's no possible way to bring in natural light, you could have a mural of an outdoor sunlit scene that makes you happy painted on one of the walls or even hang a colorful poster there.

1 To add a **touch of color** to casual cottage curtains, **make tiebacks** with wide grosgrain ribbon and sew on **multicolored buttons.** Finally there's a home for the **single buttons of the world.**

2 Frosted glass is expensive, but you can brush watered-down paint right over window glass to give it the same look and to give you some privacy. Choose a medium color in a matte finish.

3 You don't have to spend hundreds of dollars on a desk. A nice loft look is to place a hollow-core door over two sawhorses. Home improvement stores sell sawhorses in bright, fun colors.

4 When thinking about curtains for a garage, laundry room, or workshop, consider using chamois cloths. They hang nicely from café clips on a rod.

5 Create interest inside the house by attaching outside shutters on either side of a window.

6 For thick, rich curtains or drapes, make them out of matelasse bedspreads. They come in a variety of soft and sophisticated colors. *Matelasse* is a French word that means "cushioned" or "padded." How cozy is that?

Specifics

How do I spell **bliss?** A **cozy chair**, an **ottoman**, and a **project to knit**.

furniture

Two of my favorite pieces of furniture are my upholstered armchair and ottoman, which are pictured on the opposite page. The chair is down-filled with a sturdy frame, and I bought it 25 years ago for about $600. It looked beautiful the day that I bought it, and it still looks beautiful today. It's a classic style with a back cushion, which can be removed for a more contemporary look and a deeper seat. I've had it in seven different houses, and for a while it was on my HGTV set.

The ottoman was not original to the chair, but when I paired them up later, with matching slipcovers, they looked like they had always been together.

This story highlights the many reasons why your furniture choices are so important. It's a tall order, but furniture needs to be affordable, beautiful, comfortable, and also flexible.

The ABCs of Furniture

It's easy to spend a lot of money on furniture. But it's not *necessary* to spend a lot of money on furniture. *Affordable* is a relative term. If a couch lasts 25 years, as mine have, that's affordable, no matter how much it cost back then. The money is soon forgotten, but the quality lives on. But if I buy poorly made couches that wear out and look tired in 2 years, they might have been inexpensive, but they're not affordable. That's why I suggest "shopping at the top," going to the best stores and learning how to spot quality and good value, so that you will know good pieces when you see them. (See "Shop at the Top" on page 148.)

Along with affordable, you want your furniture to be beautiful and comfortable. Everything in my house must be pleasing—to look at, to touch, and to sit on. If you visit me, don't bother asking if you can put your feet on the coffee table. I'll say, "Pshaw! Put your feet wherever you want." I think it's unnatural to live in a museum. Before you buy a couch or new dining room chairs, sit in them for a while. Ask yourself if you'd enjoy sitting in those dining room chairs

Decorate Kitty's Way

❏ **Shop** at the top but don't necessarily buy at the top. ❏ Drive through upscale neighborhoods and notice **house details** you find attractive. ❏ **Buy furniture** that's flexible enough to be used in **various rooms** of your home. ❏ **Invest** in good quality slipcovers, and consider having them made professionally—the **results are worth it.** ❏ Look under **dining room chairs** before you buy to make sure the seats can be **re-covered easily** when you change your décor.

for a leisurely dinner and coffee with your best friends. Otherwise, you might end up with dining room chairs that are lovely to behold, but so uncomfortable that you and your family end up drifting through the house like waifs wishing for a comfy place to land. So make comfort your goal, rather than image or trendiness.

If you're starting with something uncomfortable, feel free to change it. Visit your local upholstery shop and buy good-quality cushion foam to replace limp, lumpy, or too-firm foam. If you're handy, try re-padding or puffing up sofa arms; just choose a fabric for the arm portion that coordinates with the sofa fabric (and make pillows, too, so the whole mix-and-match fabric presentation looks planned). You might even be lucky enough to have a vo-tech school near you that teaches students upholstering skills, and they may accept your furniture as their hands-on projects.

In addition to affordable, beautiful, and comfortable, you want your furniture to be flexible. You should be able to use it in different homes and rooms over the course of your lifetime. What is flexible? Let's start by looking at what is *not* flexible. A large lounger, for instance, is not flexible. It works in a den, but not in a formal living room or in a bedroom. A nightstand from a bedroom set is not flexible. You would use it next to a bed, and that's about it.

So what *is* flexible? Pieces that could be used in different rooms for different uses are pieces worth investing in. An armless upholstered chair, for instance, works in the living room, the dining room, and a bedroom. A side table could have many purposes. The idea is not to go out and buy new furniture every time you move or feel like a change. Instead, have furniture that you can move from room to room and from house to house. The goal is to acquire furniture that you can change as your life changes.

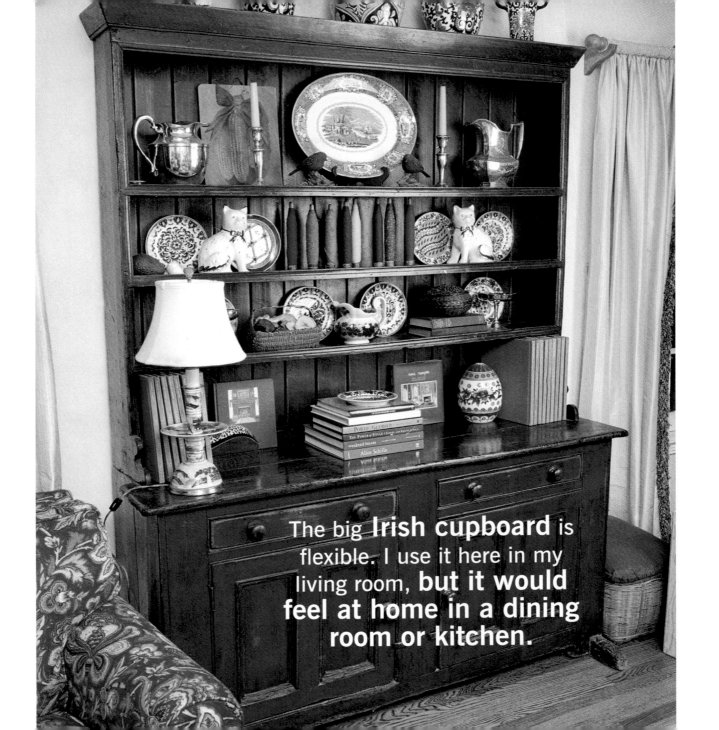

The big **Irish cupboard** is flexible. I use it here in my living room, **but it would feel at home in a dining room or kitchen.**

Good First Pieces

When you're starting out in life, you want to buy things that will be flexible enough to change and evolve as you do, or that will be treasured enough to delight you for decades.

First of all, of course, you want a comfortable place to sleep— a good bed—and a comfortable place to sit—perhaps a good sofa. I've had my comfy sofa and chairs for 25 years, so I am very familiar with the idea that good pieces can be with you for a long, long time.

A bed and the sofa will not outlive their usefulness. Other pieces, though, if they are not flexible enough to change with you, could end up at the Goodwill in a few years. But if you give it enough thought, you can buy items that will serve you now and will serve you later when you move up and move on in life. A perfect example of this is a trestle table. It's perfect for an apartment dining room because of its size. But when you move to a house where a more formal dining room is in order, you can move the trestle table to your patio.

That's the purpose of this chapter. To help you identify items that can serve you now and serve you later. If you pay attention to what you love, and not to what is trendy, you will not tire of the choices you make. I know this because over my lifetime, I've acquired pieces that I loved and that I have not gotten tired of. These pieces have moved from room to room, from house to house, and from use to use with great ease.

So consider this list of first buys that could be with you for life:

TRUNK: A trunk is the ultimate flexible piece. It can be a coffee table, a side table, or storage at the foot of the bed. It can be filled with kids' toys, Christmas decorations, craft supplies, or winter sweaters.

I've had one of my trunks for almost 30 years. When I first got married, I had it hand-painted to match a Schumacher fabric on a

I decoupaged this trunk; see how on page 112.

sofa and lined with a quilted material. Today, it still looks great. The trunk was in my living room, then it was in my den, and then it went in my daughter's bedroom. For a while it was in the garage, and now it's in my guesthouse. I've used it to store linens, papers, sweaters, and old blankets. I usually keep a couple of lavender wands in it, to keep moths and odors away.

TRESTLE TABLE WITH BENCH: This trestle table in my daughter's apartment is a copy of the one that is now in my workshop, where I use it for a worktable and a setting for my sewing machine. I had lent my table to my future son-in-law for his apartment a few years ago, and when I needed it back, Bryan had one made to match. This is a great first piece.

A combination of **chairs and a bench** gives this trestle table **ultimate flexibility.**

One of the many reasons why I love the table is that it works so well with a bench instead of chairs. With a bench, you can always squeeze in room for one more, especially if you've got kids. Benches are also great surfaces on which to stack books and organize your papers (think tax time). Sometimes when you have chair after chair after chair after chair lined up under a table, it looks like a refectory. A bench gives relief to the eye.

ARMLESS UPHOLSTERED CHAIRS: I've had the two armless chairs in my living room for many years. They're interesting and classic. They are actually from a set of dining room chairs from a decorating project. A girlfriend and I bought six of them: She kept two, I kept two, and we sold two to a client, the actress Cheryl Ladd. We loved them because of the curved shape of the back.

These chairs are very flexible. I dress them with red slipcovers for winter and blue for summer. These chairs have been in various places in my homes—a dining room, an entryway, a bedroom. Armless chairs are a good investment. They don't take up a lot of space, so they're good for people starting out in apartments.

OLD IRON CHILD'S BED: You might look at an old iron child's bed at a flea market or garage sale and think, "Well, I don't have any kids, so why would I buy that?" But these old beds have so many uses. Mine has functioned as an extra sofa in my workshop, and I use it now as a guest seat in my office. It's fun, it's easy to move because it has wheels under the skirt, and it's charming. It's also totally collapsible.

Someday, when grandkids start coming along, I will have a custom-sized mattress made. Many old iron beds are odd sizes, but I don't want you to be put off by the price of custom-size mattresses. They are not that much more expensive. This bed also has a side that folds up so the child doesn't roll off.

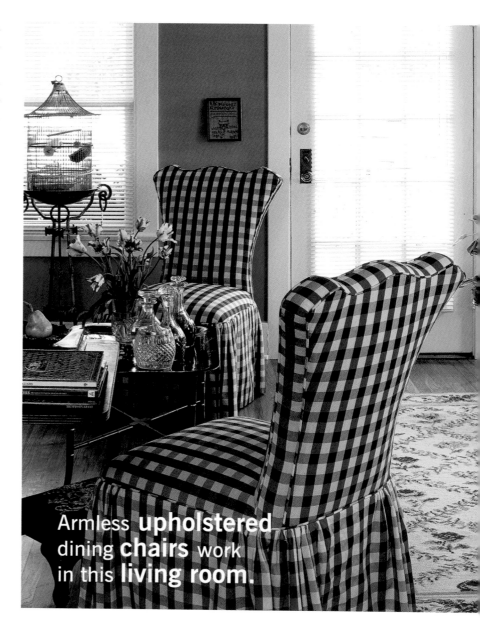

Armless **upholstered** dining **chairs** work in this **living room.**

CHILDREN'S CHAIRS: I love children's chairs. There's no reason why every room can't have a child's chair or two. You can have children's chairs even if you're newlyweds starting out; they're fun to have. You can sit on one (if you're small), you can put your plate on one, you can set your newspaper on it, or rest your feet. It's almost like a mini-ottoman with a back. They're easy to paint, and they're great on either side of a fireplace. And they're usually very inexpensive.

oneminutemakeovers

Give a small wooden tabletop a unique look by covering it with large upholstery tacks. Start on the outer rim and work in evenly spaced rows to the center. Cover with glass.

TABLE LAMP: Even though table lamp trends and styles come and go, I like the idea of always having a table lamp somewhere in the room (in case you're not familiar with table lamps, they're small side tables with lamps built right in). It's nice to have a table lamp positioned next to a reading chair, where it's easy to move closer when you need more light. They're so flexible. And they're a nice change of pace from matching large side tables.

Notice that the lampshade on mine is a dark red color. It's a traditional shape, but a nontraditional color. It could, however, have a very contemporary lampshade on it to suit a more contemporary room. You could use this table lamp near a chair that's in a bedroom, a library, or a living room. It's a classic first buy, a lifelong purchase.

I like places to set things down. Here you see a **coffee table, children's chairs, a covered chest, and a table lamp.** All serve that purpose.

Once upon a time, this wicker set was yellow and lived on a covered porch. Now it's painted black and lives in my workshop.

My Home

Now I would like to share with you some of my favorite affordable, beautiful, comfortable, and flexible furniture pieces.

WICKER SET: I've had this wicker set for many years, in several homes, and I've painted these pieces six or seven times. That's always something I think about when considering new pieces: Can this be painted? And notice how the pillows change the look. These pieces have been in the family for decades, and I see no reason why they won't be with us for decades to come.

PYRAMID SHELF: What originally attracted me to this piece was its flexibility. It's actually four different pieces, in a pyramid shape, which could be separated and put to new uses. I could take the top two pieces and stack them next to a sofa to make a side table and put the bottom two pieces next to a bed for a bedside table.

For my current house, I decided I would like a tall shelf unit in the entryway, but the original beige color would not add much to the scene. After the paint job, it's perfect for that corner.

I bought this **inexpensive shelf** for my daughters' guesthouse. It was beige and bland but **just right** for that corner. **In my current house,** I decided to add another point of interest to my entryway **by painting** the shelf unit dark, dark green.

kitty's style and spirit

Lose the Word *Should* Remove the word *should* from your vocabulary, as in, "What color *should* I use?" "What style *should* my room be?" This book and decorating in general are not exact sciences. It's not like a precise recipe for bread where if you don't put enough yeast into it, it's not going to rise. Instead think, "How can I make this work for me?"

SLIPCOVERED COUCH: Change is good, especially when it comes to slipcovers. I had mine professionally made to fit my couch and my cushions. I know you can buy generic slipcovers for much less money, but because they don't really fit the couch I think they can look a little sloppy. If you invest in or somehow acquire a nice couch or other upholstered pieces, which you could easily have for 20 years or more, it will make more sense to invest in slipcovers that fit.

A slipcover costs less than getting something reupholstered, and the piece doesn't have to leave the house. Rather, the person who will be making the slipcover comes to your home and measures the couch or chair, then returns to the shop to make the slipcover.

When you buy a **couch**, pay attention to the **quality, comfort, and shape.** Those are things you can't change. You can, though, **change the fabric** over the years.

The original chintz fabric is still on this couch, but I decided I needed a change, so I had these **red paisley slipcovers made to bring warmth** to wintertime and **blue toile slipcovers made to add coolness to summertime.**

This is one of my great finds, a comfy chair I found at a yard sale. I had it covered to go in my blue bedroom. When I moved the chair to my red office, I got it re-covered again. Of course, every room has to have one of my hand-knitted throws. What if someone got chilly?

Check out these dining room chairs re-covered from a green and red Spanish style . . .

. . . to a floral crewel Colonial.

UPHOLSTERED CHAIR: If you're lucky enough to buy or inherit a really comfortable chair, hang onto it. And when it needs a new look, invest in re-covering. Many people get stuck on the current color of the fabric and let that determine what room it can go in, rather than seeing how the chair can change to fit their needs in a new location.

By the way, see the red quilt on the blue chair? Well, one day my wonderful dog, Spot, got a little too rambunctious, and she ripped into the quilt. But I didn't toss it in the trash. I loved the fabric, so I had it made into pillows and seat cushions for my wicker set. If you see old quilts at garage sales that have holes in them, you can have pillows made from the good parts.

UPHOLSTERABLE CHAIR SEATS: When you shop for dining room chairs, always look for ones that can be re-covered easily. If you find a set you love, but they aren't re-coverable, I think it's best to look elsewhere. Better to get chairs that can be re-covered to increase your options later on. To see if it's possible to re-cover them, turn the chairs over and see if there are four screws holding the seats to the frames. If so, they can be re-covered later on when you're ready for a new look. You might even want to repaint the chair while you're at it.

Now don't let the fabrics and chair style I've chosen get in your way of embracing this concept of getting flexible chairs that you can re-cover. Maybe you'll want a black-vinyl-patent-leather look on a steel chair. Or velvet. Or washable ultrasuede. Go for it!

You could also upholster a chair with jeans. While jeans wear out in the knees, that leaves the biggest part of jeans—the butt—intact. If you cut that out, with pockets or not, you've got a big piece of fabric. Think how cool it would be to put that on the seat of your kitchen chair.

Hands-On Projects

I'd like to show you step by step how to create some great furniture pieces: a ladder-back chair, a painted octagonal table, a tie chair, a decoupage trunk, and a painted cane chair.

HANDS-ON PROJECT: Ladder-Back Chair

Here's one way to make a common chair look warm, fresh, and exciting. I liked the ladder-back on this chair, but the color was all wrong. I also didn't like the seat, and so I covered it with a tie collection. (See "Hands-On Project: Tie Chair" on page 110.) I've used red and black paint on my chair, but you don't have to use these two colors. I'm a nut for red. That's me. You might be a greenie. Or a purple person. Paint accordingly.

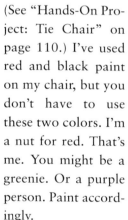

WHAT YOU'LL NEED

* DROP CLOTH OR OLD SHEETS
* LADDER-BACK CHAIR
* SCREWDRIVER
* LOW-TACK MASKING TAPE AND NEWS-PAPER OR PLASTIC (YOU'LL ONLY NEED THIS IF THE SEAT OF YOUR CHAIR DOESN'T COME OFF)
* SANDPAPER
* DAMP CLOTH
* 1 CAN LIGHT-COLORED GLOSS SPRAY PAINT (I USED APPLE RED)
* 1 CAN DARK-COLORED SPRAY PAINT (I USED BLACK)
* FINE SANDING SPONGE

WHAT YOU'LL DO

1. Assemble your materials outside and cover nearby items with a drop cloth or old sheets to protect them from spray mist.

2. Remove the seat from the chair, if you can, by removing the screws that hold the seat in place. If you can't remove the seat, mask it off with low-tack masking tape and cover it with newspaper or plastic.

3. Lightly sand the chair. This will take off any sheen that will prevent new paint from sticking well. Wipe the chair clean with a damp cloth and allow it to dry.

4. Spray the entire frame with two coats of light-colored gloss paint. Follow the directions on the paint can for dry times between coats.

5. Let the final coat dry for at least 48 hours.

6. Then, standing at least 3 feet away, spray over the frame with the dark-colored paint. Let it dry for an hour.

7. Next you'll take off some of the dark paint so the light base coat comes through. To do this, use a fine sanding sponge to sand horizontally on the horizontal crossbars and vertically on the vertical pieces (the legs and sides of the back). You'll want to remove about 20 percent of the dark paint to reveal the light. ❖

I found the octagonal table to the left of my sofa at a swap meet. I loved its shape and the starlike detail at the bottom. But I felt the details didn't get the proper respect. So I spray-painted it with a couple of cans of matte black spray paint and highlighted the details with one of my oil-based, gold paint pens.

The ideal place for this table would be in the center of an entryway.

Black paint and gold highlighting make this a fun project.

WHAT YOU'LL NEED

* WOODEN END TABLE
* DROP CLOTHS OR OLD SHEETS
* SANDPAPER
* FINE SANDING SPONGE
* DAMP CLOTH
* SPRAY PRIMER (YOU'LL ONLY NEED THIS IF YOUR TABLE IS BARE WOOD)
* 2 CANS BLACK SPRAY PAINT
* FINE SANDING SPONGE
* GOLD, FINE POINT, OPAQUE OIL PAINT PEN

WHAT YOU'LL DO

1. Move the table outside or to an area suitable for spray painting. Use drop cloths or old sheets to cover nearby items to protect them from spray mist. This is a perfect situation to use a big box as a painting chamber, especially if you live in an apartment where you have to do your spray painting on a small patio or if you live in an area where there's lots of wind and dust that makes spray painting a much-too-wild adventure for a do-it-yourselfer.

2. Lightly sand the table with the sandpaper and then the sanding sponge and wipe it clean with a damp cloth. Allow the table to dry.

3. If the table is bare wood, spray it with a spray primer and let it dry according to the directions.

4. Spray the table with the black spray paint. I turned my table upside down first and sprayed two coats, letting it dry between coats, before flipping it right side up and spraying the top. After the second coat, let the table dry for 48 hours. Patience is especially important when spray-painting furniture. Trying to save time by giving it one thick coat is not a good idea. Side effects of this may include drips, lumpiness, upset stomach, and trouble sleeping at night.

5. Lightly sand the table with a fine sanding sponge.

6. Now here comes the especially fun part: Using a gold, fine point, opaque oil paint pen, paint over decorative ridges and between turnings on legs. I chose to highlight sparingly because this table has a lot going for it designwise, and I wanted an understated look. Use your own eye to decide when you've got enough highlighting. ❖

Tie chairs, where ties are woven together to cover the seat, involve no cutting, sewing, or gluing. Tie chairs (and the belt chair shown on the opposite page) can be purely fun, and they can also be sentimental. To make this chair, you could use and display a loved one's ties, which may remind you of happy times. Maybe your father wore one tie when he took you to the father-daughter dance, or your grandfather wore one to your wedding.

You can also honor a person with the chair. Make a tie chair in your husband's college colors, for instance, or in the colors of his favorite sports team. Lakers blue and gold, anyone?

I've made a few tie chairs, and I always like doing them, especially choosing the ties and the colors. For this hands-on demonstration, I used a red chair I already had. The chair should have a seat on it, or the ties will sag over time with use. Believe me, I have firsthand experience of this.

I bought the ties for this chair for a dollar each at a thrift store. I wouldn't mind getting them for two for a dollar, but these were in pretty good shape. You can get cheap rayon ties, but in a thrift store where all the ties are mixed together, why not go for the silk ties? The cheap ones may have cost $5 each when new, but the silk ties I bought may have originally cost $50 or $75 each.

Rather than spending money on dry cleaning if there's a stain on a tie, you can always make sure the stain is hidden by its placement on the chair. I tried to find ties with a similar vibe—blues, reds, and paisleys. But even a mishmash of ties will become a conversation piece.

I made this chair to raffle off at a charity fundraiser. Even though I had to ship it off once it was done, I loved the process.

By weaving ties together, you can cover a chair seat in a lively way and have fun doing it.

WHAT YOU'LL NEED

* CHAIR WITH A SEAT
* 18 TO 30 TIES

WHAT YOU'LL DO

1. Lay out the ties in one direction over the top of the chair seat. **A** Keep in mind that ties are thin at one end and thicker at the other. So alternate thick and thin across the seat to keep the lines as parallel as possible. Consider the balance of colors also.

2. Lay out ties in the second direction, weaving in and out again alternating thick and thin to get as straight a line as possible. Adjust the ties back and forth to cover up the entire seat. **B**

3. When the composition is pleasing and balanced, tie the ends of each tie together in basic square knots underneath the seat. Stagger the knots across the bottom so you don't end up with too many knots all in one area. **C**

4. Tuck the ends of the knots under the seat. **D**

5. Now sit down and take a load off!

ANOTHER IDEA: An easy variation of the tie chair is the belt chair. You don't need a seat for a belt chair, as you do with the tie chair. The belts will not sag like the silk ties if they don't have a seat to support them. Making the belt chair is similar to making the tie chair. You lay out the belts horizontally, then vertically, and then you weave them. Instead of tying them in knots underneath the seat, you simply buckle the belts, staggering them underneath the chair.

The nice thing about belts is that when they wear out, they wear out near the buckle, which will end up unseen under the seat. I can't tell you exactly what size belts you need because it depends on the size of the chair seat you want to cover. You can punch new holes with an awl if you need to. ❖

The buckles and worn spots end up hidden from view on the bottom of the chair seat.

Covering a chair seat with belts makes for a warm and masculine piece.

HANDS-ON PROJECT: Decoupage Trunk

I'd had this old trunk for some time, and I wanted to spruce it up with a decoupage of old maps. As much as I love being home, I also love to travel. Get me on a plane, and I'm instantly happy. And while we don't travel with trunks anymore (and thank goodness for that), trunks still symbolize travel. So I thought a map decoupage would be appropriate. If you don't want to use maps, you could use fabric, wrapping paper, photographs, pictures from books, greeting cards, or even playing cards for your decoupage.

I bought the maps at a travel shop, which was a fun outing in itself. I like the vibes of the maps I chose. They're kind of Old World reproduction maps. I wanted maps that had red in them, but I didn't want too much bright-colored ocean. Even with their subdued colors, the maps looked too new for me, so I decided to tone them down and soften the fibers by soaking them in a bath of very, very thick coffee. I crinkled the maps a little first, to give them character, but not so much as to tear them. After the maps air-dried outside, I was very happy with the result.

To decoupage, you basically glue down your material and then protect it with polyurethane. Very simple.

This old trunk had a good feeling to it already. But I wanted to give it a makeover. The map decoupage turned out better than I expected.

* TRUNK
* MAPS
* STRONG COFFEE
* TISSUE PAPER
* PEN OR PENCIL
* SCISSORS
* WHITE GLUE
* FOAM BRUSH OR BRISTLE BRUSH
* PLATE
* X-ACTO KNIFE OR SINGLE RAZOR BLADE
* PAINT PENS
* WATER-BASED, NONYELLOWING POLYURETHANE
* SPONGE BRUSH

WHAT YOU'LL DO

1. Crinkle your maps slightly, then soak them in a bath of very strong coffee. **A**

2. Allow them to air-dry outside. **B**

3. Meanwhile, create templates out of tissue paper for each segment of your trunk. To do this, hold the tissue paper up to the trunk and trace the segment with a pen or pencil. Cut the template out with scissors and hold it up to the trunk to see if it fits, trimming as necessary. **C**

4. Use the template to cut the map sections for the trunk.

5. Squirt some white glue into a plate and mix in an equal amount of water. Brush the watered-down glue with a foam brush or bristle brush onto the area of the trunk you're going to decoupage first, and onto the back of your map section, and apply that map piece to the trunk. Smooth it down with your fingers. The paper should be saturated with glue.

6. After you've finished with one section of the trunk, allow the paper to dry. Then, using an X-acto knife or single razor blade, trim away any excess paper. Or if you have any gaps, use paint pens of a coordinating color to fill in.

7. Once you've finished decoupaging maps to the trunk and all the paper is dry, you'll want to protect the paper with water-based, nonyellowing polyurethane. Use a sponge brush to apply coats, letting them dry thoroughly in between. Apply at least four or five coats.

8. When the trunk is done, get out a new map and start planning your next trip. ❖

This is a very, very simple project, but one of many that give your home extra warmth and interest. For this project, I hoped to liven up the cane back of my grandmother's chair by mimicking the pattern in the upholstery.

Some people may be hesitant to alter something so precious that belonged to a beloved ancestor. But I figure that the chair worked well for my grandmother in her time, and now it has to work for me in my time. This way, I'm honoring both my grandmother and myself.

I made the chair even more special by highlighting the cane with a yellow oil paint pen. The crisscross pattern kicks up the pattern on the upholstery.

WHAT YOU'LL NEED

* CANE CHAIR
* PAINTER'S TAPE
* OIL PAINT PEN
* LIQUID SHOE POLISH

WHAT YOU'LL DO

1. Tape off the areas you want to high-light. I took my cues from the lines in the upholstery. **A**

2. Highlight the chosen area with oil paint pens. The tape allows you to achieve straight lines. Imagine how difficult this would be with a can of oil paint, a brush, and turpentine to clean the brush. These pens are a dream in comparison. **B**

3. Remove the tape and polish the cane with liquid shoe polish. I used brown, but if your cane is painted white and you've added red highlights, for instance, you would use white shoe polish to tone down the red and, again, to protect the cane. After all, shoe polish is not just for color, it's also for protection. **C**

ANOTHER IDEA: Shoe polish is good for any kind of leather, not just shoes. How about leather-bound books? If you find some old leather-bound books at a yard sale that would make great risers on a coffee table but are very worn on the spine, use some shoe polish to bring them back to life. ❖

Can you suggest a book on painting furniture? I want to update my French provincial dresser and vanity and am not sure how to paint it.

Kitty: There are so many books on the market. I consider Jocasta Innes the guru. My favorite book on painting techniques is her book *Paint Magic.* She also wrote *Painted Furniture Patterns,* which has some great ideas for painted furniture and *Paint Wise,* which contains helpful information about decorative effects on furniture.

I want to use a slipcover on my sofa, but it has a 3-inch wooden border on top. Is it possible to use slipcovers on this type of sofa?

Kitty: Sure it is! Many dining room chairs that are all wood except for the seat are slipcovered. You just have to use padding to cover the wood. If you're having the slipcovers made, this shouldn't be a problem. If you're making them yourself, just purchase batting or upholstery padding and sew it into the slipcovers to help pad the wooden areas.

I have a very small, narrow sitting room that I am interested in decorating. Is blue a good idea for the chairs?

Kitty: If you like the chairs and you like blue, then it's a good idea! The biggest challenge, it would seem to me, is not really the color of the chairs, but to create a conversation area in your seating, which is often a challenge in narrow rooms.

This is a porch I decorated for a TV show. Look how there are two seating areas in a very narrow space.

My couch is a sand-colored tweed fabric with rolled arms and nail-head trim. My rug is navy blue, burgundy, sage green, and sand. I have seen a brown leather chair and ottoman that I like very much. I prefer more traditional-looking furniture. Can you suggest colors or patterns for another chair?

Kitty: I love the idea of introducing leather, particularly if it's a good complement to the rug. You could choose another chair in a subtle pattern, perhaps a jacquard. Hopefully you will find and fall in love with a pattern that will also look great in throw pillows for the sofa. Or at the very least, use that pattern as a welt trim or ruffle accent on the throw pillow on the sofa.

Would Queen Anne–style furniture be the best choice for my 1913 Victorian home?

Kitty: Only if you really love it! After all, it's you and your family you want to please, not the home! And remember, even in classic houses, mixing different styles within the period makes it more interesting. But if you like Queen Anne or already own pieces, that style should complement the house.

Can you suggest some creative ways to hide a TV when it's not being used?

Kitty: A friend of mine had a slipcover made for her TV, kind of like a birdcage cover, when she had slipcovers made for her sofa. It was very nicely done with welt trim, and it had a tailored look. I've seen a TV put in a trunk where it opens up and the TV comes up with a lever. I've seen people put room dividers in front of TVs.

Here's an easier idea: Place a TV inside a bookcase and install shutters with hinges on either side to close. Sometimes just moving the TV to a corner, instead of making it the focal point at the center of the room, minimizes it and almost hides it from view.

May I also suggest you go to a high-end retail store that specializes in large-screen TVs and equipment and speak to the salesperson about projects where they have installed the equipment. Ask how the TVs were installed in a way where they could be hidden when not in use. They might even have pictures of finished projects you could look at or a catalog, of sorts, with furniture ideas. Then, go home and re-create that look on your own budget.

This piece was bought at Pier One and hides the TV in my daughter and son-in-law's apartment. It was made to be an armoire, so it wasn't really deep enough. We solved that problem by cutting a piece out of the back.

When you're thinking about antiques, think about more than just furniture. This antique shelf gives my kitchen the old-fashioned look I want and it didn't cost all that much.

I love antiques but can't afford expensive pieces. How can I get the old-fashioned look I'm after?

Kitty: A lot of people are intimidated by antiques because they think they are not affordable. A good place to start is with a mirror. They can be used in almost every room in the house. You can start out with a mirror you just love, rather than the perfect Queen Anne desk. You can even start with architectural fragments that don't have to be antiques but that come from old houses: cupboards that have been built in, a post or a pillar that could be put in an apartment, or two doors that are hinged together to be a room divider. Or two doors hinged together could be a very interesting headboard that you could take with you.

As your eye—and budget—grows, then you can expand into buying antique furniture.

I have recently finished stripping a lovely old armoire and wish to give it a crackle finish. How do I do this?

Kitty: To get a consistent crackle finish look is not that easy. Quite honestly, I'd only try it on a small piece of furniture, such as a chest.

You can buy crackle-finish kits, but they aren't very reliable. The results depend on a lot of factors, such as how much humidity is in the air and how thick you put the finish on. It's risky business; you can't really predict what's going to happen. For example, you might be trying to get a really delicate crackle, but if the circumstances aren't exactly right, you might end up with deep and wide cracks.

Don't get me wrong. Crackle is a wonderful finish. But you need to practice. It's an unpredictable, inexact science. One technique you could try instead, to get a similar result, is the painting technique I used on my ladder-back chair. (See "Hands-On Project: Ladder-Back Chair" on page 108.) In this technique, you paint one color, let it dry, then paint another color over that, let it dry, then sand some of the second layer off. Most natural wear occurs on edges and corners, so sanding there gives a natural look.

This is an aging technique that you can control. You're not dependent on the moisture of the air and the reaction of the crackle medium.

I have a new beige sofa, but the walls and accessories in the room are blue. How can I make the sofa fit in more?

Kitty: Add an accessory or two that contains both colors to tie them together. The best way to do that would be to add an area rug in front of the sofa in a blue-and-beige plaid or printed fabric. Or make or buy a folding screen or table runner with both colors. If you're a knitter, mix together blue and beige yarns and knit a cozy throw for your couch. In fact, a dilemma like this could be the very excuse you need to become a knitter. One reason I like knitting is that I can make throws, scarves, and sweaters that are just right for me and my tastes and needs. A beige and blue throw in just the colors and yarns that you love gives you the power to make your home more "you."

I am re-covering two chairs with a fabric that has French words on it. Should the words be readable when you're looking at the chair or when you sit?

Kitty: I vote to see the words when you're looking at the chair. It should be a fun conversation point. Make sure, if you don't speak French, that you know what it says. Or come up with your own humorous translation, such as, "He who sits in this chair pays for the wine!"

We want to use our third bedroom as an office or guest room but are having a hard time deciding which is more important. It's a very plain and not-too-large room with two average-size windows. We have beige carpet and very light beige walls. Can you suggest a room arrangement, furniture to use, and best colors to efficiently use the room in both capacities?

Kitty: I would think of the room primarily as an office because you will be using it far more often than the occasional guest will. But to meet both needs, you need to furnish the room with pieces that are multipurpose. I would start with a daybed. If you expect to have many guests, there are some wonderful styles available with trundles hidden underneath. There are so many classic styles available in catalogs in every price range from IKEA to Pottery Barn to Room and Board. I would also look for a desk with a companion or extension piece that could be a dresser or side table for guests.

I'd like to decorate my coffee table, but my husband likes to put his laptop computer there in the evenings and work while he watches TV. My table is about 3 feet square. I don't want stuff on the table to get in his way and make him feel unwelcome. Any thoughts on this?

Kitty: Three feet wide is not very large. So rather than a lot of little items, you're better off with a few larger-scale items. You could stack a few oversized coffee table books on the table, which he can use to raise up his computer. Or you could put a nice wooden box on the table for the *TV Guide* and the remote control. Or try a wonderful bowl of fruit or nuts. And then add a candle that he can move aside. One thing I'd stay away from is plants or something else that will get knocked over and make a mess.

1 Is your **water-based, nonyellowing polyurethane cloudy** when you first put it on a painted piece of furniture? **Don't panic.** That's how it's supposed to act. **It dries clear.**

2 Add interest and pattern to the back of bookshelves by installing cardboard cut to size and covered with wallpaper or even fabric.

3 Here's a great way to get ideas for furniture arrangement. At a party or family get-together, notice how people move your chairs and furniture around. Those configurations will give you clues about the most appealing setups for conversations.

4 I like to paint my wicker furniture. But not everyone wants such a radical change. You can easily freshen natural wicker with a coat of light brown liquid shoe polish.

5 To make your draped tables look less wimpy, place an old quilt or blanket underneath the tablecloth.

6 If you're curious about how things are constructed, you'll know at a glance if you can change them in some way. All you have to do is have a look at the sides, top, or bottom of a piece. Re-covering my dining room chairs, I realized that it couldn't be simpler! There are four screws holding the seat on, and all I had to do was bend down and peek under the seat.

7 Need more furniture with storage space in your room? Try this. Get a new plastic garbage can with a flat top and fill it with your sweaters or other winter wear, your Christmas decorations, or whatever. Put a round tabletop on it, and drape the whole thing with a round tablecloth.

Mirrors should ideally **reflect light,** either candlelight, lamp light, or sunlight—or **all of the above!**

lighting and mirrors

At first you might wonder why I've put lighting and mirrors together in one chapter. Maybe they don't seem to have too much in common. But really they do, when you consider that my very favorite way to use mirrors is to reflect natural light. If you look at it that way, mirrors actually become sources of light, and not just a way to check our makeup.

You may not even be aware of the lighting in your home, but I'll bet you know when you can't see to read because of a lack of appropriate lighting or you feel like you're in a showroom where there's too much glaring light. In this chapter, I'd like to tell you my best tips for decorating with lighting and mirrors and share the lighting and mirrors I use in my own home. Let's talk about lighting first.

Lighting

For rooms that are comfortable and functional you need both ambient light—the kind of light that surrounds you and illuminates the room in general—and task lighting—the kind of light that illuminates a certain area to help you work on a task. For the best lighting in a room, you'll likely need a few sources of ambient light and a few sources of task lighting. This principle is in contrast to the way many homes are built, where each room has a ceiling light stuck in the middle of it to light up the whole room. In my experience, this just doesn't work. One bright overhead light is never flattering, and it can never fulfill all of your lighting needs in a room. It's far better to get dimmer bulbs and have more lamps. Here are some ideas for bringing light into your life.

GET A DIMMER SWITCH. If you are stuck with an overhead light, such as in an apartment, install a dimmer switch. It's fairly easy to do. This way, you can keep the overhead light low, and then add your own lamps.

INSTALL TRACK LIGHTS. In apartments and often in lower-priced new construction, there's usually a standard chandelier hanging in the dining room. It's often inexpensive, ugly, and brass. But even worse than that, it dictates where you have to put your dining room table, limiting your flexibility. If you rent, I suggest you get the permission of the landlord to take the light down, store it carefully, and install track lighting in the same outlet. (You'll need to hire a licensed electrician to do this work.)

Installing track lighting in place of the chandelier opens up your options. Now you can put the table wherever you'd like it, whether that's in the center of the room or not. And there are some really great track lighting options these days, not just the cheap-looking silver canister lights you might remember from the 1970s.

Best of all, you can take the track lights with you when you move. A track lighting unit could be with you for life.

INSTALL RECESSED LIGHTING. If I had a room with just an overhead fixture and I could put in recessed lights, I would.

Ideally a licensed electrician would do this work, but it's a simple matter of cutting holes in the drywall of the ceiling, installing the lights, and running the wires inside the attic and down the wall to the switch. Be sure to stagger the lights throughout the room, rather than lining them up in rigid rows.

INVEST IN TASK LIGHTING. So far we've been talking about ambient, overall light. Ambient lighting is important, but you don't want all one type of light. People read, knit, and balance their check-

makes$ense

You can create the look of a unique, custom lampshade without paying designer prices. First, find a piece of wallpaper with a bold design you really like, such as sunflowers or an interesting geometric. Tape the paper to the inside of a paper lampshade, and then poke holes through the paper and the shade with a needle to outline the design. When you remove the wallpaper pattern, the light will shine through the holes and replicate the design.

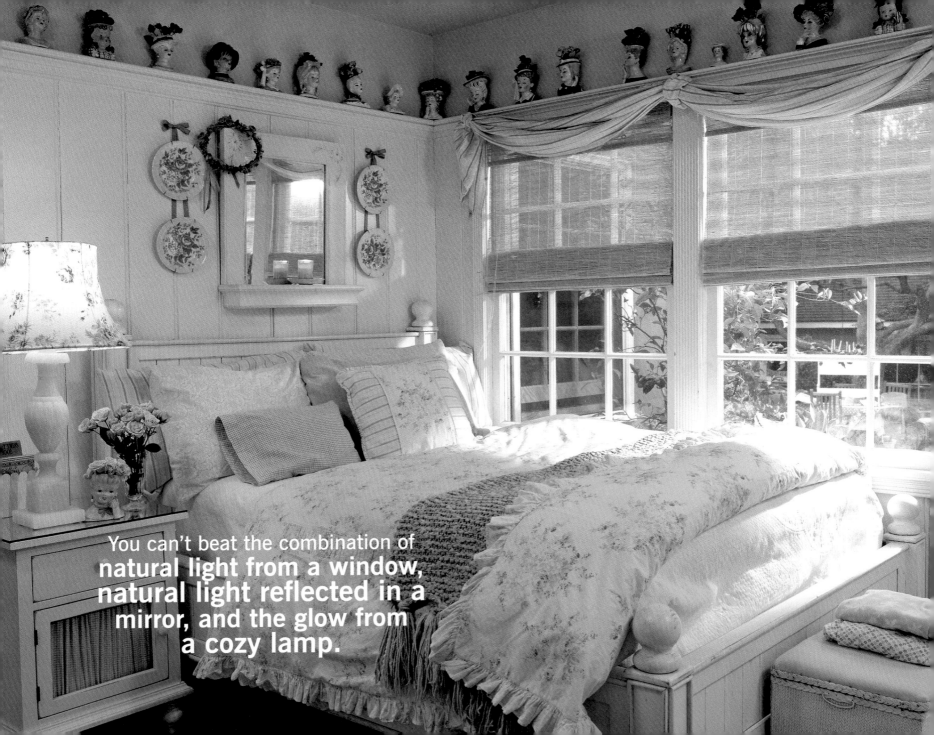

You can't beat the combination of **natural light from a window, natural light reflected in a mirror, and the glow from a cozy lamp.**

books—and they need light to see what they're doing. To figure out what kinds of task lighting you need in a room, think about what tasks you'll be doing there, then make sure you have enough light to do them. Often, we won't use rooms or areas of rooms because the light is not right.

Take some time to ponder any rooms that feel uncomfortable to you. Let's say you rarely use your dining room, or you can't wait to get out of there following a meal. Maybe the chandelier is too bright and could use a dimmer switch. Or is there a chair in your living room that you sit in to watch TV but never read in? Maybe that would be a great place for a table lamp.

MAKE A LAMP. Did you know you can make a lamp out of just about anything? I had one made out of a Buddha statue. And you don't have to drill into the item to make it into a lamp. You can use French wiring, where you put the item on a platform and run the wire behind it. You can buy a kit or have someone at a lighting fixture store do it.

You could make a French lamp from a jar full of buttons, an old bowling pin, or just about anything else.

CREATE INTEREST WITH LAMPSHADES. A lot of people take it for granted that they're going to get a white lampshade, but

Decorate Kitty's Way

❏ **Change your chandelier** to track lighting to create more flexibility in how you **arrange a room.** ❏ **Install mirrors** to make a room look larger and to **reflect natural light.** ❏ Having two matching lamps is not a decorating MUST.

Here are four unique lamp ideas: a **Buddha statue** wired into a French lamp, a **candle mold** made into a lamp, **a boring shade covered with strips of ribbon,** and another bland shade livened up with **glued-on buttons.**

black, red, or other color lampshades can make a difference. I especially like dark burgundy lampshades and black lampshades.

Black lampshades might be unusual, but they can add a lot of drama to a room. If you have a black lampshade, you'll notice the lamp more because things that are next to black are noticed more. So if you have a lamp you inherited that you're not very proud of, don't put the black lampshade on that lamp. Put it on a lamp you want to draw attention to.

Of course, covering lampshades to suit your room is fun. Later in this chapter, I show you how to paint a colorful chandelier and to cover lampshades. It couldn't be easier. I have one lampshade covered with buttons and another one covered in ribbons that are just strips looped around the shade and then tied around the rim at the top. (See "Hands-On Project: Lampshade Trim" on page 136.)

USE PINK BULBS. Here's a quick way to make everyone look younger. Replace your white lightbulbs with pink ones. The soft pink light gives people the rosy glow of youth.

Mirrors

Mirrors are great decorating tools, but they are rarely used to their best advantage. I think people don't generally give the placement of mirrors as much thought as they should. So here's how to:

MAKE A ROOM LOOK BIGGER. Mirrors make a room look bigger. If you have a narrow room, hang a mirror on one of the long walls and it will make the room feel wider.

ADD MORE LIGHT. You can make a mirror do double duty by hanging it opposite a light source, whether it's a window or a French door. The mirror reflects the light from the window back into the room.

For example, if you have a darkish room with just one window, put a mirror on the wall opposite the window to double the light in the room.

My daughter Brooke lives in a very small apartment with one bathroom. The bathroom is large, but it doesn't have a window or natural light source. Luckily enough, with the door open, the bathroom faces a large window. So by putting a very large, oversized, framed mirror in there, she captures the light from the window. When you first start out in an apartment, you might think: Why would I want a mirror this big? But by filling the whole area above the bathtub with a mirror reflecting a natural light source, you're bringing an unbelievable amount of light into that room. This is a very standard bathroom, but then you've got this very rich, textured wooden frame. This is something you could take with you anywhere. It would be a good first purchase in an apartment.

In addition to reflecting natural light, a mirror will also reflect

The **three mirrors** on these pages are all placed to **perform one of the most important tasks** a mirror can do: to **reflect outside light.**

artificial light. That could be why a lot of people put mirrors over their buffets, to reflect the candelabras. Place a mirror near a lamp to reflect the light, thus doubling the impact of the lamp.

REFLECT A VIEW. You may have a beautiful tree in blossom outside a certain window. You can't necessarily sit facing your garden all the time, but if the wall you're facing has a mirror on it that reflects the garden, that's a wonderful addition to your life.

ADD INTEREST TO A FURNITURE PIECE. Mirrors don't have to be hanging on a wall in order to add interest. A simple trick is to cover a dressing table or bedside table with a mirror. Instantly, that corner or surface is more interesting. I also favor using mirrors as mats for pictures. If the photo is old, you'll want the mirror to look old as well. (See "Hands-On Project: Aged Mirror" on page 137 to learn how to make a mirror look aged.)

My Home

You may be wondering how I use lights and mirrors in my own home. Let me show you.

LIVING ROOM: My living room is not gigantic, but I've been able to use many sources of lighting. A lot of thought went into each source of light. In the living room, I don't have matching lamps on either side of the couch. A lot of people feel they have to have matching lamps and side tables on either side of the sofa. I have neither. I'm not saying that's right or wrong. But that kind of symmetrical balance is not something I choose. I prefer more variety and flexibility. And besides, I didn't have two matching side tables or two matching lamps.

Over the couch I hung little sconces with little mirrors on either side of the painting. Those solved a problem I had struggled with for some time. This room tends to be on the dark side, and the windows are on the opposite side of the room. I didn't really want to put a large mirror over the couch, which would reflect back the natural light from the windows, because I wanted to put that painting there. I like the two shutters a lot, and I thought for a while about somehow incorporating mirrors into them.

Eventually, I got little mirror sconces for the spaces between the painting and the shutters. They are kind of small, and I think something round would be more interesting. But for now I've got them reflecting light back from the windows during the daytime and reflecting the candlelight at night.

I really like the painting over my couch, but that's not why I have a picture lamp shining on it. I have it there to bring ambient light to that side of the room. I'm not a huge fan of having a light over every painting. I don't want to feel like I'm living in a museum, but the picture light in this case helped me achieve my goal.

I also have a sofa table behind the sofa, but I didn't place a lamp there. That might seem like a natural place to put a light, but because I have a lamp to the left and to the right of the sofa, I didn't really want a third lamp lined up there.

I don't insist on matching lamps anywhere; however, on my mantel I have two matching Staffordshire dog lamps, which I have had for years. They are small, which makes them very flexible. I've had them on bookshelves and on other mantels in other rooms. I like the idea of having a light source on that long mantel to bring ambient light to that side of the room.

kitty's style and spirit

Remember the Benefits If you have children, think how much your decorating benefits them. When you're re-covering chairs, painting a wall, stopping a leaky faucet, changing the knobs in your kitchen, hanging your grandmother's plates on the walls, or placing a mirror opposite a light source, you're really caring for your family. These things can have a powerful effect.

Decorating is so much more than thinking, "I want to make it look perfect." You want your family and friends to want to spend time with you in your home.

I like **delightful** sources of light. Here we see a **cow-print shade;** a mirror-backed, leaded-glass window frame reflecting the outdoors; **a small button lampshade;** and a mirror reflecting **candlelight, outdoor light, and lamplight.**

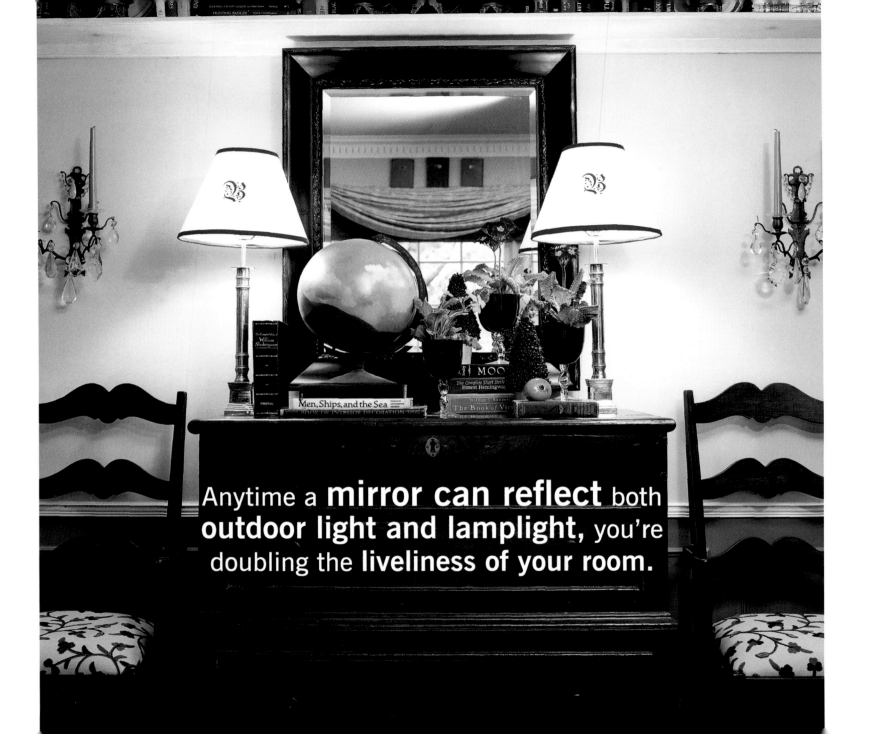

Anytime a **mirror can reflect** both **outdoor light and lamplight,** you're doubling the **liveliness of your room.**

I also like the idea of having a table lamp in a living room, to turn any chair into a reading chair. I use a red lampshade on my table lamp in my living room. That color is called *sang de beouf*, which is French for "blood of beef." I like that deep color, and I think oxblood, like celadon green, is a classic color that is always a good choice for long-term purchases like pottery or lamps. To me, it's almost a neutral.

In the left corner of the living room, I placed a light behind a plant. The light really helps the plant stand out at night rather than fading away into a dark corner. I think that hidden light sources like this give a room a cozy feeling. I've seen fancy, expensive houses that have lights hidden in the ceiling coves to shine light up to the ceiling and then back down into the room. But until I win the lottery, which is not likely because I don't buy tickets, I'll find other, creative ways to bring hidden, subtle light sources into my rooms.

One of the best things to do with an old picture frame is to put a mirror in it.

DINING ROOM: My dining room has a tendency to be dark so I didn't hesitate to add a mirror in this room. I painted an old picture frame black and got a beveled mirror installed in it. It was that simple. You can see that I've put into practice my belief about mirrors—place them where they reflect natural light. Indeed, the one window in this room is on the wall opposite this mirror.

I found the lamps that are on the blanket chest under the mirror in a catalog for a very reasonable price. I knew that I wanted

an ambient light source on the blanket chest, but I wanted it to be simple and tall. I like the look of vintage candlesticks. I like the silver look because the candlesticks tie in with the other silver things in the room. (And who would know they're not antique silver but an inexpensive alloy?)

I've had the sconces on either side of the mirror forever. They were used on the set for my television show. Before that they complemented an Italian chandelier that was in an English Tudor house, my most formal home. They might be a little too formal for this room, but it's nice to have a candlelight source. They certainly provide extra ambience when I'm entertaining, and I like the combination of electric light and candlelight.

color solutions

We know that pink lightbulbs cast a light that is flattering to human skin, giving it a rosy, healthy glow. If you don't have pink lightbulbs, you can line lampshades with pink or peach fabric or paper.

Hands-On Projects

I've really enjoyed making some lighting and mirror projects for my home. I'd like to share my tips for creating a colorful metal chandelier, lampshade trim, an aged mirror, and mirror decoupage.

HANDS-ON PROJECT: Colorful Metal Chandelier

If this chandelier, with metal flower petals that hold lightbulbs, looks vaguely familiar, that's because there are millions of them in the world, especially at flea markets. Most of these old lamps have wiring that's shot. Some have been converted to candleholders, with the wiring removed.

I wanted a colorful, fun, and whimsical chandelier for my bathroom to make me smile and liven up the room.

If you find an old, dilapidated chandelier at a yard sale or swap meet, even if it seems to work, take it to a lamp store to be rewired, just to be safe. Then, you can start painting and decorating. I'm listing the colors of paint I used, but you should choose the colors that fit your own sense of a good time.

WHAT YOU'LL NEED

* METAL CHANDELIER
* DROP CLOTHS OR OLD SHEETS
* PAINTER'S TAPE
* 1 CAN SAGE GREEN SPRAY PAINT
* SANDPAPER
* DAMP CLOTH
* 1 CAN HUNTER GREEN SPRAY PAINT
* NEWSPAPER
* 1 CAN YELLOW SPRAY PAINT
* 1 CAN APPLE RED SPRAY PAINT
* CRYSTALS, WIRE, AND FABRIC DECORATIONS (OPTIONAL)

Why have a basic light fixture when you can have a painted chandelier?

1. Assemble your materials outside or someplace where it's safe to use spray paint. Cover nearby objects with drop cloths or old sheets to protect them from the spray. If you can, hang the chandelier upside down from a tree limb, clothesline pole, or swing set. This makes it easier to paint.

2. Tape off the flower petals with painter's tape. You'll paint those later.

3. Use sandpaper to lightly rough up the surface of the chandelier. This makes the paint stick better than it would to a smooth surface. Wipe the chandelier off with a damp cloth.

4. Spray the stems and leaves with the sage green paint. Let the paint dry.

5. Standing at least 4 feet away, spray the chandelier with hunter green paint. To lightly "dust" it, use light, quick spurts so the sage green paint will still show through.

6. Let the paint dry completely, and then wrap the painted area with newspaper and secure it with painter's tape so that you can work on the flower petals. If you get too eager and don't let the paint dry, the newspaper will stick to the paint, and you'll get that look that tells you it's time to do it over again. Best to avoid that!

7. Remove the tape from the petals and spray the petals with yellow paint. Let the paint dry.

8. Lightly spray over the yellow paint with apple red paint. Use light spurts to hit the tips of the petals.

9. Spray the ceiling cap and chain with hunter green paint, followed by a light overcoat of apple red.

10. Hang crystals from the bottom if you want. I found a bunch of them with wires still attached at a swap meet. I also made a fabric sleeve to cover the chain. **A** A sleeve is just a long tube of fabric put over the chain before it's hardwired into the ceiling.

11. I covered small lampshades with leftover fabric from my curtains and glued lace around them. **B** Then I had my handyman hardwire the lamp into my bathroom ceiling. This colorful chandelier sure beats the old boring overhead light. ❖

This project is easy, easy, easy. I simply put lace trim on a standard-issue lampshade. It's the same lace I used on the chandelier lampshades in my bathroom. I bought the roll of lace for 77¢ at a thrift shop, left over from somebody's sewing box. The thin ribbon was left over from *my* sewing box from old projects of mine. The concept is to weave the ribbon into the lace, and then glue it onto the rim of a lampshade. It's a decorator look for under a dollar.

The trim gives the lampshade a custom look for pennies.

WHAT YOU'LL NEED

* LAMPSHADE
* LACE RIBBON (CHOOSE ONE WITH OPENINGS SUITABLE TO WEAVE RIBBON THROUGH)
* NARROW, SILKY RIBBON
* LARGE-EYE NEEDLE
* GLUE GUN

WHAT YOU'LL DO

1. Cut off enough ribbon and lace to go around the circumference of the lampshade, either on the bottom rim, the top rim, or both. Cut a little extra so you don't end up short. **A**

2. Thread a large-eye needle with the silky ribbon and weave it in and out of the lace ribbon.

3. When the lengths of silky and lace ribbon are woven together, glue them to the rim of the lampshade with hot glue from a glue gun. **B**

ANOTHER IDEA: Make a very attractive lampshade trim simply by twisting yarn. Take some fairly thick yarn a few feet in length and fold it in half. Secure one end to a doorknob, put it under something heavy to hold it in place, or have a friend hold it. Take your end and twist the two ends of yarn together until you've got quite a few twists. When it feels pretty tight, bring your end to the opposite end and fold the whole length in half again. Then, let go! It will turn into a lovely twisted border that you can glue onto a lampshade or use in some other fashion. Use different colors of yarn to create a trim that is perfectly coordinated to your décor. ❖

HANDS-ON PROJECT: Aged Mirror

This picture of my wonderful great-grandmother looked better matted with an aged mirror.

I like to use mirrors as mats for pictures and photos. It adds excitement, and if both the photo and mirror are old, it adds to the antique aura. But if you have some old photos, where do you get the old mirrors? Using my technique, you can actually age mirrors to make them look old. You simply cause the backing, which creates the mirror effect, to thin.

I wanted this look for a picture of my great-grandmother, but my mirror looked too new. With the aged photo on the aged mirror, the effect is quite charming. But don't wear your best clothes for this project. Trust me.

WHAT YOU'LL NEED

* MIRROR
* NEWSPAPER
* PLASTIC GLOVES
* LIQUID DRAIN CLEANER
* DISPOSABLE FOAM BRUSH
* OLD RAG
* SANDPAPER

WHAT YOU'LL DO

1. Take the mirror outside where the drain cleaner fumes won't choke you. Spread newspaper on your work surface because the drain cleaner will eat away at any surface it touches. Put on gloves to protect your hands.

2. Turn the mirror over and pour a little drain cleaner on the back of it. Using the foam brush, spread the cleaner around and let it sit there for a few minutes. Then wipe the cleaner off with an old rag.

3. Lightly sand the back of the mirror with sandpaper in an irregular manner. Don't try to get it even and consistent; you're trying for a randomly worn-out look.

4. Apply another layer of drain cleaner and repeat steps 2 and 3, checking the front of the mirror until you get the level of aging that's most pleasing to your eye. ❖

HANDS-ON PROJECT: Mirror Decoupage

I found a sepia-tone image of my mother holding a doll, and I was trying to think of a unique way to frame it so I could enjoy it often. I love the mirrored top to my dressing table, and the pretty and feminine vibe there, but I didn't want just another framed picture. So I came up with the idea of cutting out my mother's image and decoupaging it to the bottom corner of the silver-framed mirror I use to put on my makeup.

When I put on my makeup, I get to treasure the memory of my dear mother.

WHAT YOU'LL NEED

* MIRROR
* PHOTOGRAPH OF A LOVED ONE OR A COPY OF THE PHOTOGRAPH (CHOOSE A PHOTOGRAPH THAT YOU THINK CAN BE EASILY CUT FROM THE BACKGROUND)
* SCISSORS
* PICTURE FRAME WITH GLASS (THE GLASS SHOULD BE ABOUT THE SAME SIZE AS THE MIRROR)
* RUBBER CEMENT

WHAT YOU'LL DO

1. Clean the mirror thoroughly.

2. Cut the person out from the background of the photograph, carefully trimming around details. **A**

3. Apply rubber cement to the back of the cutout. **B**

4. Place the picture carefully on the front of the mirror. I put mine in the corner, rather than in the center, so I could still use the mirror at my table. **C**

5. Place the mirror inside the picture frame, under the glass, to protect it from dust. **D** ❖

I have cottage-style furnishings and am buying a house with a mirrored dining room wall, which is very formal. What can I do with this wall?

Kitty: A wall of glass can feel very cold and somewhat contemporary. But removing mirrors can be dangerous and costly. (And it can also bring 7 years of bad luck if you break one!) I would camouflage that length of mirror and try to soften the look.

You can soften it with fabric by adding very tightly gathered draperies, from ceiling to floor, on either side of the wall. You could staple them right to the top and bottom so it's almost like upholstering the walls, or you could gather them on a rod. It may take lots of material, so you may consider using sheets or check out the Country Curtains catalog (see chapter 13, Organizing, Tools, and Resources on page 309).

The least expensive fabric, which comes in very wide lengths, is natural burlap. A light burlap is a wonderful foil against a mirror because it adds texture along with warmth. A regular cotton fabric would give you warmth, but not texture.

Another interesting idea would be to hang a mirror over the mirror. I'd hang an oval, wooden mirror from the ceiling with a ribbon over a buffet. And then put lots of candles on the buffet. At night it would really look great, and all of the interest would go to the focal point of the oval mirror and not to the entire wall of mirrors.

Different types of artificial lighting— fluorescent, incandescent, and halogen— cast different wavelengths. How do those affect colors?

Kitty: That can be a real problem. There are so many options of light available, and you're right, they can really affect color. I recently put in a bunch of halogen lighting, and my lighting man made me change all of the incandescent lightbulbs in my recessed lights because he said they were fighting the halogens. The important thing is to have consistency throughout your house. Choose one type of artificial light and stick with it.

You may have noticed that some fluorescent lights give off a green tinge that makes warm colors (reds and oranges) seem dull. But other fluorescent lights have a pink tinge and enhance warm colors. Halogen and incandescent lights cast a yellowish light, which enhances warm colors and dulls down cool colors (blues and greens).

There isn't a strict rule of thumb for recessed lights. It **depends on the room,** but recessed lights are a **very efficient way** to update and **light a space.**

I want to put recessed lighting (high hats) in my living room. How do I plan the room out so I put the correct number of lights in, and where do I install them?

Kitty: There isn't a strict rule of thumb for recessed lights. It depends on the room, but recessed lights are a very efficient way to update and light a space. Eyeballs focus light straight onto an object. Wall washes are half-shields that you install to cause the light to flow to the wall in a wash.

Place the recessed lights in the ceiling approximately 3 to 4 feet apart, or even farther apart if you'd like. I think it's more interesting not to have strictly parallel lines of cans. You're not going for the tin soldier effect. Start with the most important spaces to be illuminated, such as a fireplace, and work out from there.

It's a good idea to use a wall wash to illuminate focal points in your room, such as a fireplace, wall hanging, or quilt. Say you want to illuminate the wonderful rocks on your fireplace. Install a wall wash in the ceiling 3 to 4 feet from the fireplace, with the light angled toward the fireplace. Then add the ambient light, which is used for illumination and not focused on a certain spot, a couple of feet behind the wall washer.

There's a lot to consider, so I recommend hiring an electrician to guide you in making your decisions, or making an appointment with a lighting fixture store and discussing the lighting layout when you shop for fixtures.

I want to put some sconces in my dining room, but I don't like the look of the cords hanging down. Other than tearing open the wall and installing the sconces so that they are controlled by a switch, do you have any suggestions on how to make them look better?

Kitty: A good electrician can hardwire them without making a lot of holes, but you will have to do some patching work. To avoid all that, find old sconces that were electrified, take the wiring out, and use them as candlestick holders.

If you're worried about dripping pillars, for $6.50 you can buy a little votive candleholder with a post attached that fits down into the candlestick holder. Or if you want to use pillars, use something called a *bobeche*, which is a ring around the bottom of the candle that catches drips. These two items take some of the worry out of using candles.

1 Don't rely on **overhead lighting.** If all the light comes from **above,** it can cast **un-flattering shadows.** Be sure to **use floor lamps, table lamps,** or wall sconces for additional **sources of light.**

2 Many people don't think to have a lamp on a breakfast bar or an island in the kitchen, but it gives the kitchen a warm glow, especially if you leave just a small lamp on at night to welcome someone home.

3 Do you have a wall of mirror or mirrored tiles that is looking a bit crummy? For a country look, cover the mirror with wood lattice. It will diffuse the mirror, masking the flaws. Lattice is easy to buy, easy to cut, and easy to carry.

4 Dramatize the large plants in your home by putting an upward-pointing light behind the pot. This adds a classy and romantic look at night. But don't use just any kind light. Use a special "grow light" that will help the plant to thrive.

5 For a unique autumn candleholder, surround a candle with whole walnuts in a glass vase.

6 Here's a diet tip I got from my friend, renowned New York designer Mario Buatta: To see yourself before you reach for a snack, put a panel of reflective material on the door of your refrigerator.

7 If you are thinking about a backsplash for your counters, consider mirror tiles, which will add a subtle sparkle to your kitchen. You can have them cut to any height you want, and you can cover the top with a piece of molding. Just clean as you would any mirror.

I like some symmetry on a mantel—two vases, for instance—as well as some asymmetry, such as three stacks of books and plates at different heights.

accessories

You might think of accessories as trimmings, garnishes, frills, add-ons, and extras. But actually accessories could be the starting point for your whole color scheme. My inspiration often comes from accessories, such as paintings, wall hangings, pillows, rugs, and other decorating touches.

If you have a framed needlework sampler, a handsome stained glass lamp, or an unforgettable tablecloth, you could have the start of your color scheme or decorating theme right under your nose.

In my home, both my dining room and my entryway were inspired by a painting of a woman on a ladder reaching up into an apple tree. All of the colors in those rooms came from that one painting, so you can either start decorating with accessories or finish decorating with them. You can get accessories to complement the colors and style of a room, or you can actually design an entire room to complement your favorite accessory.

How to Choose Accessories

People sometimes ask me to help them choose accessories for their home. I hesitate to do that—it's too personal. I think that any accessory you choose should have at least one of these three qualities:

1. *It should be something you really like.*
2. *It should be something you treasure.*
3. *It should solve a decorating problem.*

THINGS YOU LIKE: Choosing what you like for accessories is an obvious, but very good, start. Are you drawn to leaf motifs, exotic zoo animals, or lilacs in bloom? Perhaps there's a theme ripe for the picking. Are you partial to the simple lines of Shaker-style accessories, or do you prefer the graceful swoops of harp-back chairs? You're bound to have preferences.

I like round things. Anything round gets my attention—globes, orbs, billiard balls, bocce balls, or even a ball of rubber bands. There are certain shapes, colors, textures, and materials

Decorate Kitty's Way

❑ All the **accessories** in your home should be things you like or **things you treasure,** or they should solve a decorating dilemma. ❑ Use accessories in **odd numbers.** ❑ Spruce up leather-bound books with shoe polish. ❑ **Wooden boxes and bowls** make great accessory holders. ❑ Consider art an investment. ❑ Hang a collection of plates to create **instant pattern and design.**

Here's an example of accessories I treasure: a photo of my mother as a child holding a mirror, and the mirror itself.

that just speak to each of us. Do you head for the used furniture store while your best friend rushes for the Victorian gift shop next door? Listen to your instincts. If you can't keep your eye off an antique wicker-basket chair, clearly it's destined to become part of your home's accessories, even if your friend says, "Why would you want that old thing?"

THINGS YOU TREASURE: I admit this is only subtly different from choosing something you like. Here's an example: You may *like* a certain painting because it depicts a beautiful landscape and contains all the right colors for your room. But you may *treasure* a certain painting because your grandmother painted it.

Choosing things that you treasure as accessories is a great idea because it has to do with your heritage, and often these are things given to you so they're not going to cost any money. Certainly you

Plates, family photos, needlepoint, a red birdcage, and a cow-print lampshade—for me, **it doesn't get any better than this.**

have something you treasure. Maybe it's a silk scarf your grandmother wore, a watercolor from your favorite aunt, or a love letter from your father to your mother. Don't stash these things in your attic—come up with a way to use them as accessories.

Don't underestimate the suitability of soiled or broken treasures, either. A picture can be reframed, a stained doily can have its best edge peeking out from under a bowl, and a cracked teacup can still make a centerpiece in a corner cabinet.

THINGS THAT SOLVE A DECORATING PROBLEM: The right accessory, such as a vase of yellow flowers, could bring a bright color into a dark corner or direct the eye to a certain place. Another accessory, such as tall bamboo poles in a corner, could bring the eye up.

Keeping those three qualities in mind, be inventive with your accessories. Try new things. That's what's fun. Don't copy me. Free up your own mind. Nothing would please me more.

Talking Trendy

Accessories can also satisfy your need for certain colors or for trends. For accents, you can use colors that you might not want to live with all the time, such as reds that are too stimulating or yellows that would be anxiety producing, for accents. Or you might use accessories to add colors that are trendy. If bright yellow-green is the trend of the season, you don't want to buy a yellow-green sofa that might last for decades or paint your walls yellow-green because it might be hard to live with. But you can bring the trendy color into your home with pillows, vases, or even flowers.

(continued on page 151)

kitty's style and spirit

Be Yourself As you're leafing through this book, please don't put it down if you don't like the colors I use. The information I'm sharing with you will be applicable whether you love the same colors I do or not. A lot of the techniques I've used in my home work in any kind of a home. You can adapt the ideas to suit your own favorite colors and style. For example, I might show you how I put a decoupage map on my trunk, but you could decoupage shiny black paper, happy yellow daisy paper, or even gold leaf instead.

It's much more affordable to enjoy trendy **yellow-green with faux green apples** tied to branches **than to invest $3,000** in a yellow-green couch.

Flexible Art

My daughter Brooke and her husband are just starting out, and they don't have a big budget for art. So I had a friend of mine paint and texturize six canvases—two shades of green, two black, a cream, and a red.

These pieces are very contemporary, which they needed to be in order to work in this contemporary apartment. For instance, my sweet Norman Rockwell painting with the country chair and flowers and straw hat would not work here. But these modern pieces are fun. They can be hung together or apart, and the combination of colors can be changed to suit the holidays and seasons. And what's fun is not only the color and texture but the negative space around them.

I keep mentioning my preference for flexibility in your purchases. This is what I call flexible art!

These five painted canvases convey a certain feeling . . .

. . . which changes dramatically when a red canvas is added.

Shop at the Top

Some of the best advice I give is to "shop at the top." I don't care if it's for furniture, clothing, cars, or antiques. It doesn't matter if your budget is $100 or $10,000, shopping at the top works.

How do you shop at the top? Find the best stores for whatever you're shopping for. Go there and have a look around. Don't be intimidated! Just say, "I'm just looking. It's a beautiful store, and I've always been curious about what's inside." Or you might say something like, "I'm not quite in the market for such and such, but I may be in the near future, so can you tell me a little bit about this?" You don't have to tell them you don't have the money.

The idea is to gather ideas from the very best. Then when you see something similar at a less-expensive or secondhand store, you'll recognize the quality.

Notice that I say "shop at the top," not necessarily "buy at the top." You could, of course, and maybe you have all the money in the world. But how boring would that be? I think it's much more thrilling to find good pieces for a song.

So if you only have a Kmart budget, don't think that's the only place you can shop. If you've spent time at high-end stores, you might find yourself in Kmart one day and say,

"Gosh, that's the same type of lamp I saw at that very expensive store, except there it had a black lampshade." So you buy the lamp and a black lampshade and presto, just like that you've re-created an exclusive look on your not-so-exclusive budget.

Here's another way to shop at the top that doesn't actually involve stores. Check out open houses to see how they are decorated—the grander the house and neighborhood, the better. Those people can afford the finest architecture, the finest furnishings, and the finest of everything. What do they choose?

You can also drive by nice neighborhoods and houses to see how their homes' exteriors and landscaping are done. What colors are they painting their trim? What types of plants are in their gardens? What garden furniture do they have? Chances are they're paying professional designers to help come up with a look and to choose paint colors and plants. Go look at the best. It doesn't cost anything to look.

The concept of shopping at the top doesn't stop at decorating. This applies to other things like apartment-searching and clothes-shopping, too. I tell my children that even if they only have a small amount of money for rent, they shouldn't feel restricted to certain

I put in this very upscale frieze above my kitchen sink. Sure, this type of wallpaper costs $40 a yard or more, but how many yards do you think it took to cover this area? Not very many.

neighborhoods. Even the finest neighborhoods have guesthouses and garage apartments.

The same thing goes for clothing. If you've spent time looking at Saks Fifth Avenue or Neiman Marcus at the designer clothes, later when you're at a thrift store or secondhand store, you might recognize last year's Yves St. Laurent or you might think of a clever way to accessorize an outfit using knowledge you gained by shopping at the top.

While you're shopping at the top, don't be afraid to buy at the top if it suits your budget. Plus, you never know when you'll be at a high-end store that's having a sale!

Here's a perfect example of how shopping at the top paid off: My daughter and her husband were in the market for a table. They bought a very hip and elegant glass table through the local classifieds, but their eyes were already educated to quality before they got in their car to go see it. They knew the brand, and they had seen the same table in a colleague's home. In high-end retail, you might be able to trust the sales folk to help you select a very nice sofa with a long life span. But if you're looking in the newspaper or at used furniture stores, you'd best come armed with your own knowledge already in place.

This crystal chandelier was not very expensive, but it looks like what you'd find in a very extravagant home.

I saw shell-covered balls when I was snooping around a fancy gift shop. They were about $75 each. So I got some inexpensive shell necklaces, some Styrofoam balls, and my bottle of white glue and made it happen for myself for about $5.

If you visit a fancy house, you'll notice how a hanging ribbon is used to visually unite artwork.

The **blue and white pottery** on my red cupboard **mimic** the blue and white pottery in **a painting** on the opposite wall. This helps **tie the room together.**

My Home

Here is a sampling of the accessories I've chosen for my own home. I'm sure by the time you read this book, I'll have added a few more or changed the ones I have in some way.

Living Room

In my living room, I put a lot of thought into accessorizing the mantel and tabletops. In general, I find odd numbers of elements to be interesting, far better than the symmetry of even numbers. I do have the two large vases on the mantel, but the stacks of three books are a nice relief. You may be surprised to learn that I don't have family photos on the mantel. I prefer them in bedrooms, hallways, or on a side table in the living room—in a more intimate area where I can see them up close.

One of my favorite accessory finds is the fireplace screen in my living room. It's an inexpensive aluminum fireplace screen, but I loved the shape of the triangular top up against the brick. I loved the idea of faux bamboo, and so I had it painted to mimic bamboo, using a high-gloss paint and highlighting the little nodules with a darker tone. I'm really happy with it, particularly because it coordinates with the old tortoiseshell bamboo bookcase to the right of the fireplace.

In the summer, my fireplace gets a painted screen. **In the winter,** I use my metal screen and have **a fire almost every night.**

Another fireplace accessory that I love is an old French market basket that I found at a used furniture store for about $30. This is actually the type of shopping basket that Europeans use. But I liked the idea of a texturized piece on the left of my fireplace to hold small pieces of wood. And, of course, I take it to swap meets to carry my purchases. (See chapter 12, Flea Market Shopping with Kitty, on page 287.)

Another favorite living room accessory is my collection of old leather-bound books. It's hard to find leather-bound books, and they can be expensive. So if you ever find a set of leather-bound books for a good price, buy them. Or, if you have a bunch that you inherited and stored in an attic, dig them out and display them. In fact, I recently found a series of 30 black leather-bound books at my favorite used furniture store. The spines had faded almost to a gray, but the covers themselves were still a nice black. So I lightly polished the spines with black liquid shoe polish. Then I buffed them with a cloth to bring new life to the spines.

You can use this same technique on leather chairs and leather boxes as well. In fact, leather should be waxed or polished regularly to keep it supple.

The coffee table in my living room is not my favorite thing, which presented me with a decorating problem that I solved with an accessory. The coffee table worked great in my Santa Fe house, which had a very large living room. But you can't throw everything out and start from scratch, so the coffee table is now in my much-smaller living room. To make it work, I added a tray to the top, which helps to redefine and "intimatize" the table so it doesn't look quite so large.

Another favorite accessory is a set of old spools of thread, which I normally keep in my red Irish cupboard. The spools were

colorsolutions

You know I love plates. But if you have a difficult time finding plates in the right colors and vibes, try fabric. Just glue some cool fabric to the undersides of clear glass plates, and you'll have plates with exactly the look you want.

very inexpensive, but they add color and texture. I love the fact that the original thread is still on them. A lot of people wouldn't think of something as mundane as old wooden spools of thread next to treasured silver candlesticks. But it's visually interesting.

A very useful accessory in my living room is my set of three oval Asian wooden shoe boxes. I love the colors—muted green, red, and yellow—because they match my palette. Attractive wooden boxes or other types of vessels are so versatile. You can put stuff in them, display them on tables and mantels, stack them next to a chair to use as a side table, or separate them and use them in different rooms.

When you decorate with things you treasure, you can incorporate details of a loved one's life into your own life. When my dear dad died, I wanted to honor him and remember the best of him. So I took the buttons from his military uniform and hot-glued them onto a framed photo of him.

Dining Room

One of the accessories in my dining room is a three-part artwork. I'm a big believer in buying original art that you love. The first thing I bought with my first credit card was a signed Norman Rockwell lithograph that I could pay for over time. I think it cost $300 then, and it's probably worth a few thousand dollars now. The painting in my living room is a Fred Jessup that was a gift from my husband 30 years ago, and I still love it.

You might find it difficult to display your loved one's military uniform, but how about the buttons?

The tray on top of my coffee table creates an intimate spot on a table that is too big.

A set of vessels like these has almost unlimited uses.

Leather-bound books make great risers for pottery or small lamps or a tray on a table.

I got this whimsical three-part artwork, now hanging above the silk valance in my dining room, at an art show.

It's unusual to see books in a plate rack.

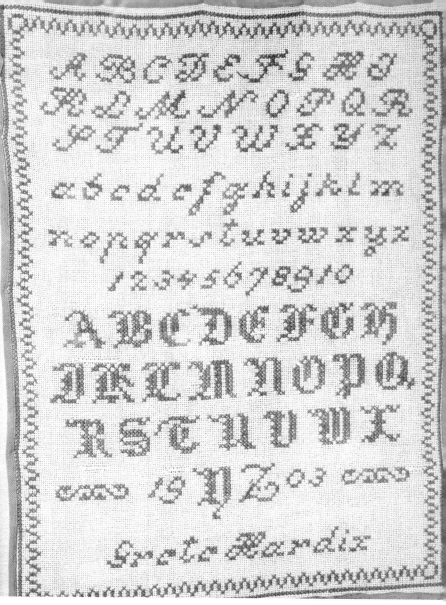

This red sampler coordinates well with the red plate rack in my dining room. I've been asked many times about this sampler, which was on the set of my TV show. So here it is for you to copy, if you wish.

Art is an investment. Even when you're young, you can always find some kind of an original that you can afford, such as a photograph. These are first-buy, lifelong purchases. I've always shopped at the top—and sometimes bought at the top—when it comes to paintings. But you can find inexpensive, original art at art fairs, auctions, and flea markets.

In my dining room, I wanted to put something in a strong red color on one wall. I found a plate rack at a flea market for less than $100 that I knew would work. It was originally Scandinavian blue, so I painted it red.

This large frame with several sections will handle a lot of smaller pieces and come off like one large art piece.

makes$ense

An inexpensive way to jazz up a tray and also display a favorite family heirloom like a piece of lace is to place the lace on the tray and then cover it with a piece of glass cut to fit the tray. So many of our meaningful keepsakes are hidden in closets, and they really should be seen and loved.

Rather than just putting the traditional plates in the plate rack, I used it as a place to hold small books. Books also serve as risers for some of the brass candlesticks on the bookshelves in the room, giving it a warm, cozy, library feel.

I have a cross-stitch sampler on the wall in my dining room. I found it years ago and had it framed, and it hung on the set of my TV show. Through the years, I've had many inquiries from viewers who wanted a pattern to make one for their own home. I can't provide that because it's an antique that was made long ago. But I can provide this super close-up photo of it. Hopefully you can reproduce it based on the photo.

Office

If you have dramatically colored walls, like I do in my red office, a large frame with several sections helps call attention to your wall color in an interesting manner. You get to enjoy the negative space inside the sections of the frame. It's a great idea for unifying smaller pieces that might get lost on a big wall.

Notice the mirror, which is framed with a plastic frame I got from the art store and painted with stripes of red and gold. It's accented with one of my thrift-store ties, which relates to the tie valance I have on the other side of the room. Anytime you can repeat the same vibe, color, or fabric in a room, it helps to subtly tie the elements of the room together.

My Bedroom

The majolica plates in my bedroom are from a collection I bought years ago. I chose them because they coordinated with the fabric on my sofas 25 years ago. The plates are really very fine, and they've hung in different rooms in my houses. I like the idea that they're a bas relief; they've got dimension to them. They look really good with my Chagall lithograph, so I like to keep them together.

I hang plates because it creates instant pattern and design. I like placing them in arrangements where there's an odd number, making a circle or a triangle. I often hang them with a rope or unite them with ribbon. Chances are you're going to have some kind of plates somewhere that you can hang.

Another great thing about decorating with plates is that they don't always necessarily have to match. You can have a collection of blue and white plates. Or you can have a collection of plates that are very fine. I have a collection of plates that my grandmother got as a wedding present that didn't match her other china. For 75 years they were beautifully protected and put away. They're too fine to cut food on, so hanging them is a way of using them.

I hang plates in almost every room of my house.

156 SPECIFICS

Birdie's Room

My daughter really wants understated simplicity in her room, so I hung a collection of simple plates there. The design on the plates stands out beautifully with the white background on the plates and the white wall. The green bow and grosgrain ribbon unites them, creating a visual line from the upper plate to the lower one and adding a bit of texture.

Another group of accessories in Birdie's room is my collection of lady-head vases. Why lady-head vases? They put a smile on my face. The obvious place to display them was on the natural ledge that happens to be in my daughter's room. But it's appropriate for a young girl's room because most of these vases tend to be young girls. The vases add whimsy and color to the room and draw your eye upward.

If you live in earthquake territory, like I do, you need to find a way to avoid breakage of pottery and crockery when the earth shakes a little. One of my tricks is to put pennies in the bottoms of vessels to make them bottom-heavy. This lowers their center of gravity and makes them less likely to fall off a shelf.

Other accessories for Birdie's room include clothes hangers with birds painted on them. These hangers were very, very inexpensive, about 99¢ for the single one and $3.99 for the triple. When I bought them, they were just dark brown. Then one day I asked an artist what she could do with them. She painted the leaves an off-white and then added color to the birds. You may not be a great artist, but it's easy to add detail with paint pens.

Lady-head vases, pink plates, and a hand-painted towel hook are all good accessories for a teenage girl's room.

Reincarnations

Just as I recommend buying flexible furniture, I also recommend flexible accessories. Here are some examples of pieces and accessories that have had several lives, in several settings, and will probably have several more in the future. I call these reincarnations.

The tapestry below was originally made for a piano seat, but I've reused it to line a serving tray, which I've then covered with glass. The dentil molding you see to the right was in a friend's house that was being torn down. Amazingly, it matched the molding already I my house. Likewise, the hall tree on the far right was salvaged from an old home but fits perfectly in mine. And finally, these colorful bocce balls worked hard in their previous life but now live a life of leisure, polished and relaxed, in my living room.

Hands-On Projects

I'd like to show you step by step how to make a few of my favorite accessories: a bow and ribbon picture hanger, a knitted throw, no-hassle tassel fringe, a knitted pillow, a framed chalkboard, and a canvas wicker-basket top.

HANDS-ON PROJECT: Bow and Ribbon Picture Hanger

It's a simple decorator's trick to visually tie two framed pieces together by hanging a ribbon, rope, or other material behind them. In my daughter Birdie's room, I hung a simple green ribbon behind two plates to help unify them and to add some texture and warmth. But for the two mirror-matted botanical prints in my bedroom, I wanted something more elaborate and special than a simple piece of ribbon. I was pondering my options when a friend gave me a large coffee-table book about Jackie Kennedy. On the cover, the former First Lady was wearing a dress with a large bow, and I realized that's exactly what I wanted for my two prints. And so I set out to create it.

I choose a variegated taffeta ribbon because the botanicals on the mirror mat are somewhat formal, kind of Old World. I love the way the ribbon looks when it's folded. In fact, my favorite part is the covered button in the bow, which draws your eye right to the center of the bow and forces you to notice the pretty folds.

You can use covered buttons in so many places. I've used them here in this hanging and on the pillows on my bed. They're so simple to make with a kit, but unless you knew such a kit were available you might not give it a try.

(continued)

The bow and ribbon accent really pulled these two mirror-framed prints together.

* BUTTON-COVERING KIT
* FABRIC OR RIBBON
* SCISSORS

1. Cut a circle out of fabric according to the guide on the back of the button-covering kit. Each size button requires a different size circle of fabric. **A**

2. Place the circle of fabric over the button cap and wrap the fabric over the teeth on the bottom of the cap.

3. Position the button backing on the bottom of the cap and use the little tool in the kit to push the backing on. **B** That's it!

4. To make the bow, fold five lengths of ribbons into loops, ends together, arranged in a circle to make a bow. Pin them together.

5. Sew the ribbon tails onto the back of the bow. The ribbons should extend one-third of the length of the artwork past the artwork. (For instance, if your artwork is 24 inches long, the tails should extend 8 inches beyond the artwork bottom.)

6. Sew the covered button onto the front of the bow. ❖

Knitted throws are no-brainers. I'm going to assume here that you already know how to do four things: cast on, cast off, knit, and purl. If you know those things, you can make a knitted throw and pillow for every room of your house.

The bigger your needles and the thicker your yarn, the more lush your throw will be and the faster it will get done. That suits me! You can start with thick yarn, or you can combine different strands of yarn together into a ball and knit with that. Mixing various yarns and ribbons is a specialty of mine. You might use a mohair, a knubby yarn, and maybe a ribbon. You could put together three, four, five, or more strands.

I usually make my throws about 36 inches wide and about 48 inches long.

You're done with your throw when you feel like being done. Cast off! Later, I'll tell you how to make the fringe to dress up your throw.

WHAT YOU'LL NEED

* LARGE KNITTING NEEDLES (SIZE 18 TO 20)
* THICK YARN (OR SEVERAL STRANDS ROLLED INTO 1 BALL)

WHAT YOU'LL DO

1. If you're using several different kinds of yarn to make a thicker strand, make a ball of yarn composed of several strands.

2. Cast on several stitches to see how many stitches it takes to make an inch. Multiply that by how many inches you want your throw to be, and that will determine how many stitches are in each row. Let's say it takes 4 stitches to equal an inch; then you would multiply that by how many inches you want your throw to end up. In my case, it would take 4 stitches per inch for 36 inches, or 144 stitches per row.

3. Now just knit a row and then purl a row, then knit a row, and so on. That combination is called a stockinette stitch, and it's the pattern most sweaters use. Knit and purl as many rows as it takes to

There is a hand-knitted throw, sometimes two, in every room in my house.

get the length you want. Because of the thick yarn, or several strands of yarn held together, the texture of the throw will be very interesting.

4. Once your throw is as long as you want it to be, cast off your stitches. ❖

It's very easy to add tassel fringe to each end of a knitted throw. To make your fringe plump, lavish, and wonderful, make each tassel at least 8 inches long. The longer they are, the more luxurious they look. Few things look cheesier than short, skimpy tassels.

You can use the same yarn you used in your throw, or use a different yarn, or a slightly different mix of yarns. This is a good place to use yarn you don't have enough of for a big project.

For your tassel fringe, add some differing colors of yarn, or even ribbon, for an extra kick.

WHAT YOU'LL NEED

* YARN (CHOOSE THICK YARN OR A COMBINATION OF YARNS AND RIBBONS TOGETHER)

* PIECE OF CARDBOARD OR A LARGE BOOK (USE ONE THAT'S A LITTLE LONGER IN LENGTH THAN YOU WANT YOUR TASSEL TO BE)

* SCISSORS

* KNITTED THROW

WHAT YOU'LL DO

1. Wind your yarn around and around a piece of cardboard or large book. The book or cardboard should be a bit longer than the length you want your tassels to end up because some of the tassels' length will be lost when you knot it onto the throw. So if you want your tassels to be 10 inches, for instance, wrap the yarn around something that's 12 inches long. Wrap the yarn around the cardboard or book as many times as the number of strands you want in your tassel. If you're using a ball of yarn with four strands in it, and you wrap it around the cardboard one time, you'll end up with eight strands of yarn in your tassel. Of course, we want ours much

more luxurious, so wrap it six or seven times. **A**

2. Cut through the bottom of the yarn to create strands that are folded at the top. **B**

3. On the corner of your knitted throw, pull apart the yarn to make an opening. **C**

4. Take the folded strands you have created on the cardboard and push the fold up through the opening in the throw. **D** This will create a loop. **E**

5. Pull the loose ends of the tassel through the loop and pull to create a knot. **F** and **G**

6. Trim the ends of the tassel as needed. **H**

7. Notice how plump it is. **I**

Add your next tassel at the other corner. Then add one at the center. Don't get a measuring tape to figure out where the center is. You just fold the throw in half, and there's your center. Keep folding the sections between tassels in half to find the center point, and add tassels until your fringe looks full and lush. You'll know when you have added enough because it will feel right. ❖

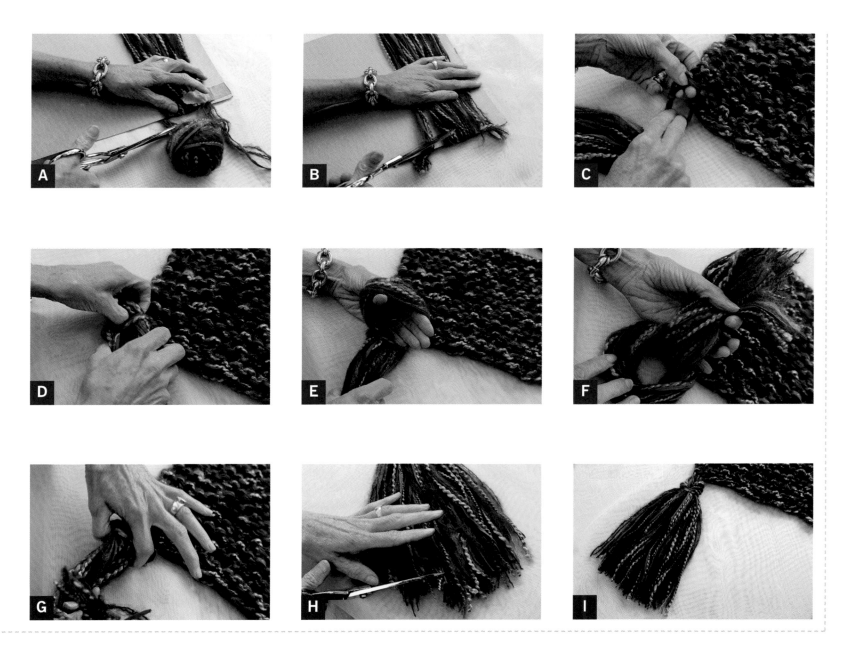

HANDS-ON PROJECT: Knitted Pillow

These pillows are so easy. They're made of a knitted cover that is slipped onto a standard 18-inch pillow. Rather than knitting a separate front and back piece for the pillow, I knitted one piece as wide as the pillow and twice as long. Then I folded it in half, sewed the two sides together with yarn and a needle, slipped it over the pillow, and sewed up the final edge.

This knitted pillow is too simple to be believed.

WHAT YOU'LL NEED

* PILLOW WITH PLAIN COTTON COVERING
* THICK YARN OR SEVERAL TYPES OF YARN TOGETHER IN ONE BALL
* LARGE KNITTING NEEDLES (SIZE 18 OR 20)
* LARGE-EYE SEWING NEEDLE

WHAT YOU'LL DO

1. Cast on your yarn and knit a row equal to the width of your pillow. You don't need measurements for this. You knit and hold it up to your pillow until it is the right width.

2. Then purl a row, then knit a row. To make your pillow more interesting, mix knits and purls in the same row. I know this is wild, but it gives the pillow more texture.

3. Knit and purl until your piece is as wide as your pillow and twice as long, then cast off.

4. Fold your knitted piece in half and hand-sew up the two sides, leaving one end open to create a pocket. Hand-sewing a knitted piece with yarn is very forgiving because the stitches don't show.

5. Insert your pillow into the knitted pocket and then sew up the final side. Lay your head down on the pillow and take a little nap. You've been working hard. ❖

I found an old painting at an auction. It wasn't a precious piece, and it was already timeworn when it came into my life. But it gave just the right vibe to a covered porch. A lot of people wouldn't think of putting an old painting outside, pointing out that it won't last forever outside in the elements. But I won't last forever either, and I'm having a good time. And besides, this is not a family heirloom, so what's the big deal?

When I moved to my current house, I decided the framed picture needed a new life, so I turned it into a chalkboard. It was a simple matter of stripping the paint off the frame (though not all the way because paint in crevices adds character) and spraying a piece of Masonite with chalkboard paint, which creates a chalkboard on any hard surface.

WHAT YOU'LL NEED

* OLD PICTURE FRAME
* CHEMICAL PAINT STRIPPER
* BRIWAX (PASTE WAX WITH TINT)
* SOFT CLOTHS
* PIECE OF MASONITE OR OTHER THIN, HARD SURFACE
* OLD CLOTHS OR TARP
* 1 CAN OF CHALKBOARD PAINT

WHAT YOU'LL DO

1. Strip the paint off the frame. I used a chemical stripper, but I didn't try to get every bit of the paint off. Leave some on for character.

2. Wax the frame with Briwax and soft cloths to give it a warm sheen. **A**

3. Set up your piece of Masonite or other thin material on old cloths or a tarp and

This somewhat battered framed painting hung outside on my covered porch. Now it found new purpose as a chalkboard in my red office.

spray it with the chalkboard paint. It's a good idea to do this outside and cover nearby things with old cloths or tarps to protect them from overspray. Follow the directions on the can and cover the front surface evenly. **B** and **C**

4. When the board is dry, install it in your frame, get out your chalk, and go to it!

ANOTHER IDEA: Put a mirror in it and hang it on the wall or lay it flat on a table as a tray-type centerpiece with candles on it. The mirror will reflect the flickering of the candlelight. ❖

A

B

C

I was so in love with the canvas-covered basket I got from an auction that I decided to cover a second one (shown on top here) myself.

The inspiration for this project came from an antique basket I got from an auction of items owned by very famous interior and set designer Tony Duquette. I believe the basket is French, and the lid of the basket is covered with canvas that was lashed on and painted. It makes a wonderful side table in my living room and provides storage as well.

I liked the basket so much that I made a new one myself. The basket that I used, though, is tightly woven together. That makes it more difficult to lash on the canvas top. I suggest using a basket with a looser weave, to make it easier to lash the needle through. It's best to get a basket with a flat top because then you can use it as a table.

I used twine to lash the canvas to the basket because I like the rustic look of it.

With a painted canvas top, your typical wicker basket is transformed into a whimsical yet sophisticated side table.

WHAT YOU'LL NEED

* WICKER BASKET WITH A FLAT, WOVEN LID
* PRE-PRIMED ARTIST'S CANVAS
* PENCIL
* SCISSORS
* STRAIGHT PINS
* TWINE
* LARGE-EYE SEWING NEEDLE
* PAINT
* SPONGE BRUSHES
* NONYELLOWING POLYURETHANE
* BRIWAX (PASTE WAX WITH TINT)
* SOFT CLOTHS

WHAT YOU'LL DO

1. Place the basket lid on top of the canvas and trace it with a pencil.

2. Add 2 inches for the hem and then cut it out. **A**

3. Fold the hem 2 inches under and iron or pin if needed to keep it fairly flat.

4. Place the canvas over the top of the lid, hem side down, and sew the cover down along the rim using the twine and the large-eye sewing needle. **B**

5. Paint the top using sponge brushes, giving it several light coats and letting them dry in between.

6. Coat the lid with several coats of polyurethane to protect for use as a coffee table. After it's all dry, wax it with Briwax and soft cloths. For mine, that made all the difference. Finally, set your bowl of bonbons on the basket top while you put your feet up and relax. But just for a while, then it's off to the next adventure. ❖

Got a collection of stuff? I find that displaying a collection vertically, as I did some of my red-handled utensils, shows it off best.

I have a collection of black-and-white photos. Will those look good on a gray wall?

Kitty: They will look good if the wall is a rich, warm gray with brown in it. It probably wouldn't work on a pale, cold gray wall with a lot of blue in it. Black-and-white photos can be cold. And gray can be cold. But the combination of the warm gray wall and the colder black-and-white photos would work. What would be even more dramatic, though, would be black-and-white photos on a red wall. I think that would be rich and wonderful.

I would like to make a picture out of a piece of fabric, but I can't find a frame that is big enough. Do you have any suggestions?

Kitty: One idea is to buy some do-it-yourself framing pieces. They come in all different widths and lengths to make your own custom frame. Also consider looking at a secondhand store for old mirror frames, which are sometimes enormous. If the mirror is broken or scratched, the store will usually sell it cheap.

When you do find a frame that will work, if you want to make the fabric for the picture stiffer, you can stiffen it up with a spray-on product called Stiffy. It's usually available at craft stores.

Is it possible to have too many collections or too many items in my collections?

Kitty: The last thing I'm going to tell someone who's passionate and has a lot of collections is, "You've got to stop collecting now." I think you can have endless collections. The idea is to gather all of the collectibles together but keep them from looking cluttered.

Let's say you collect old lunch pails. Rather than having some here and some there, gather them all together on one table or at least in one room. This maximizes the impact of your collection and makes it look organized and neat.

Sometimes the best way to display your items is vertically, if possible. You'll see this concept in retail stores. Vertical displays really make a statement. Let's say you have a bookcase and you want to display your collection of trophies. It's more interesting to place them in a line vertically on the shelves, rather than all on one shelf side by side.

Many years ago I saw a show where you covered an armoire with a wonderful paper and then aged it. I loved that piece and have always wanted to do that to an old secretary desk that I have. Could you tell me how to do it?

Kitty: That was one of my most popular segments, and it was done by Susan Kay Goans. She showed how to decoupage a chest with things like playing cards, cocktail napkins, and posters. You can write to Susan at PO Box 871026, Stone Mountain, GA 30087-9998, call her at (770) 979-8333, e-mail her at susan@designfaux.com, or visit her Web site at www.designfaux.com.

We built a New England farmhouse with a two-story barn and pool house that looks 150 years old. Do you have ideas how I can add character inside and out?

Kitty: Yes, I can think of lots of ideas. Rather than buying new things, scour salvage yards for old furnishings and construction materials. Reusing authentic interiors in clever ways will add personality. People can really sense when materials are old rather than newly minted. You can use old beams and windows as room dividers. Or remake old floors into great tables. Or hang old shutters on the walls inside your home.

If you don't have a demolition company nearby, put an ad in the local paper stating that you're looking for old materials.

Old shutters are a great way to add an aged look to a new house. I found these at a flea market.

What can I do to camouflage my ragged tabletop?

Kitty: My favorite way to "cure" a damaged tabletop is to put something interesting on it and then cover it with glass. Here are some ideas.

You could make what is sometimes called a yo-yo quilt, bubble quilt, balloon quilt, or pillow quilt. The quilt is basically little fabric bubbles, or balloons, that are flattened and stitched together. To make a yo-yo quilt, you first cut out round pieces of fabric. Any size will do. I used the rim of a cup for a template, and then I cut my pieces from that. Then thread a needle, tying a knot at the end of the thread, and sew a long basting stitch, by hand, around the circumference of a circle. When you finish stitching all the way around, pull the thread lightly so the fabric starts to gather and look like a little balloon.

Pull the thread as tightly as you can without it breaking, and tie a knot. If you put the stitched end of the balloon on the table and press down, you will have created a little circle of fabric with the raw edges, where you stitched, on the underside. Make as many of these as you like, and then hand-stitch them together, side by

A tabletop quilt requires only fabric cut into circles, a needle, and thread.

I made this little diamond-shaped quilt without a sewing machine, using scraps of material, with supplies that I carried around in my purse.

side, to create a quilt. You could stitch hundreds of them together and put them on a backing to make a bed quilt, or you could stitch together several dozen to cover a tabletop, like I did. I placed glass over mine to protect it.

Another way to hide a damaged table is to cover it with interesting paper—such as a piece of wallpaper, photographs, or documents—and top it with a piece of glass. Old letters from your grandparents, the deed to your house, or something that is sentimental in your family's history would all be interesting. If you're worried about the documents or photos getting damaged, make color copies of them. For example, my grandfather invented the wind

Black-and-white photos on a red background, covered with glass, turn this table into a conversation piece.

wing of a car, so it would be neat for me to group together a photograph of the wind wing of a car, a photograph of my grandfather, and a copy of the contract that says General Motors is going to order so many of them.

Or you could just use a pretty piece of fabric to cover a table. It could be anything from a lace doily to a piece of lace, an embroidery, or a cross-stitch. Start looking around when you're at thrift stores, flea markets, and rummage sales to see how many tabletop materials you can find.

I'm redecorating my family room. I painted the dreary wood paneling an off-white with a touch of yellow. We have French doors and many of my decorative items are blue and white transfer ware. Can you share any ideas for accent items?

Kitty: In general, accent items need to be personally chosen. However, since you asked for my input, I do have some ideas. (Are you surprised?) It sounds like you're going for a French country look. Shop for furniture or large accessory pieces in French blue-gray painted woods. Add some iron elements in the room, whether they're sconces, planters, a chandelier, or a baker's rack. Some large stone urns would be an asset as well.

One of my favorite reference books on the French country look is *Pierre Deux's French Country: A Style and Sourcebook.*

I love the look of old framed botanical prints, but they are very expensive in antique stores. How can I get that look without spending a lot of money?

Kitty: How to get the look without spending the bucks—this is my favorite type of question and my favorite type of quest!

Books are a great place to find botanical art. It might make book lovers cringe, but I've broken down art books with color photographs of flowers and framed them. Look for old books at yard sales, in used books stores, and at thrift stores.

1 If you have **old Pendleton plaid blankets** with holes or other flaws, **don't throw them out!** Pendletons make wonderful pillows or slipcovers.

2 When a favorite vase gets cracked, you don't necessarily have to toss it out. Instead, try this: Light a candle and drip some of the melted wax over the crack on the inside of the vase. When the wax dries, it should be strong enough to prevent the vase from leaking.

3 Finding accessories to coordinate with your room colors is not that difficult, especially if you take matters into your own hands. First, buy calico and fabric in colors you like, then rip the fabric into strips. Then, wrap the strips around Styrofoam balls, and wrap and wrap until the ball is covered. Use the balls to fill a wooden bowl for a custom look.

4 Here's how you can turn your sofa pillows into colorful holiday pillows: Button up a red flannel shirt, place the pillow inside, and fold the shirt around it. Tie the sleeves together and voilà! You have a holiday pillow.

5 Have a budding cowboy, or a den that needs a new lamp? Wind rope around and around the base of an old lamp, starting on the bottom, and hot-glue it every few rounds to hold it in place.

6 To add interest to a plain lampshade, glue macaroni bows to the inside of the shade. When you turn on the lamp, the shade will have a fascinating textural look.

7 A small wooden ladder leaning against a wall makes a perfect place to hang throws, quilts, and afghans.

8 Looking for a simple way to tack up important notes and favorite photos without a bulletin board? Fasten a number of clothespins to the wall, at eye level near your desk. The pins will hold your items and maybe make you smile.

9 A lovely way to **bring color** into a dull corner is with **fresh flowers in mason jars.** It gives a warm, **homey look,** costs next to nothing, and the wide-mouth jars hold a **bunch of blossoms.**

Rooms

My **blue-slipcovered** living room is dressed for summer. **How cool is that?**

living rooms and dining rooms

In this part of the book, let's go from room to room and discuss furnishing opportunities and challenges you and I might have, beginning with living rooms and dining rooms. At first thought, these might be thought of as formal rooms, reserved for company and special occasions. Heck with that. Let's use all our rooms! Who cares to live in a museum? But if our rooms are to be used, they must be comfortable, they must be welcoming, and they must be enticing, delicious, and alluring.

Living Rooms

When I say "living room," please think "living room or family room." Here's why: Some homes have a family room, others have a living room, and still others have both. But no matter what combination you have, these rooms perform generally the same function: We live in them! For that reason, and to make things simple, I'm just going to call them living rooms throughout.

The first question I ask in furnishing a living room is this: Would my guests feel comfortable taking their shoes off and putting their feet up? For me, the purpose of a living room is not to impress people or make a statement, but to create an environment that is comfortable, user friendly, uplifting, and conducive to people visiting with each other, reading, relaxing, or watching TV.

Making rooms comfortable guides every decorating decision that I make. For example, if you have an antique side table that you are worried about people setting drinks on, place a tray or large books on top of it to protect it, so people can be free to set their cups down. When people ask me if they can set something on a table or a floor, I say, "Honey, you can't hurt anything in here." I want my guests to feel comfortable. Nothing makes me happier

When houses are put up for sale, they are often painted all white.

Decorate Kitty's Way

❏ **Create conversation areas,** especially diagonally, when arranging furniture. ❏ Dining rooms **should be cozy,** so don't decorate to make the room look larger or to look understated and sparse. ❏ Include **multiple light sources** in your dining room. ❏ Use outdoor pieces indoors. ❏ Make **seasonal changes** in every room.

than when a guest takes off her shoes, tucks her feet under her, and wraps one of my knitted throws over her legs. And when Spot jumps up there to snuggle, that's as good as it gets.

Some homes have separate living rooms that were designed to be formal living rooms. These seem like throwbacks to parlors from the old days, a place to put the things you don't want your children touching, a place to sit up straight, and a place to be uncomfortable. What is the purpose of that? We don't have suitors visiting anymore. I know folks who go into those rooms only once a week to dust or worse yet only once a year, at Christmas! What a waste!

I like to give those living rooms something special that the family rooms don't have, so there's a reason to go in there more often than just at Christmas. I'm thinking of a fireplace, French doors that lead to the backyard, or a bridge table.

White walls don't work for me. I painstakingly removed years of white paint from this wall-to-wall mantel. **Now, the room glows.**

Arrange the seating in a living room to encourage interaction between people, as well as television watching.

Placing the Furniture

Walk into just about any living room in America, and I'll bet the focal point is an entertainment center, housing the TV, VCR, DVD player, and all the assorted cables, tapes, and discs. Never mind that the room might have another beautiful focal point, such as a fireplace, an alcove and window seat, or picture window. It's a good guess that all of the furniture in the living room is pointing toward the entertainment center.

Don't feel that you have to give your TV that much attention. Make your living room more interesting and keep the focus away from a looming, dark entertainment center. Instead of directing everything toward the TV, focus on conversation and arrange chairs and sofas in conversation groups. You can't visit with people who are sitting clear across the room. But neither can you visit with people sitting on the couch next to you, unless you're very friendly. Typically, to talk to people, you want to sit diagonally, and not too far away. Usually that means you have to pull furniture out away from the wall and into intimate seating arrangements. Arranging seating in a triangle is a good way to look at it; place a couch and a chair at right angles with a small table in between for a lamp and a place to set beverages. You can also direct traffic in this fashion, by placing the furniture so that people are not cutting across the room and interrupting whatever is going on in there.

One thing I find particularly interesting about decorating living rooms is the fact that the living room is usually the largest room in the house. So what color do you paint it? The lighter the walls, the larger the room is going to feel. But to make it comfortable, you want to make it cozy, so consider a color other than beige. Choose a paint color that is warm and inviting and that relates to the kitchen, which is likely to be nearby.

Talking about Trends

There will always be decorating trends for living rooms. But I encourage you to try not to be overly conscious of current thinking—of what's hot, what's in, what's a must-have this season.

A common trend I see in magazines is very understated living rooms, sometimes rooms of pure white with just a touch of one color. I think, oh, that's all well and good for someone who's right out of college and doesn't own one thing. But eventually people start collecting things. What are you going to do with your stuff to conform to the latest trend? Put it all in the attic?

I don't think sparse rooms reflect the way people really want to live. People prefer to be surrounded by things that they like and by things that are important to them.

But if you really, really need to be trendy, do it with temporary items, like plants. A few years ago, daisies were trendy, then it was roses, and as I'm writing this book it's orchids and tropical flowers. This is how I suggest adding the current vibes.

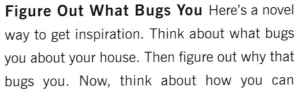

kitty's style and spirit

Figure Out What Bugs You Here's a novel way to get inspiration. Think about what bugs you about your house. Then figure out why that bugs you. Now, think about how you can creatively turn that into something that doesn't bug you. For example, could you paint it? Could you put fabric on it? Could you minimize it? Focus on what you can do with what you do have, rather than what you don't have.

Dining Rooms

Dining rooms are great places to add sophistication or to have fun. Because most people don't use them a lot, you can really break all the rules. So if you wanted to do something seemingly outrageous, like painting the dining room black, why not? Just make sure it's nicely lit! You don't want it to feel like a black hole.

If you dine often in your dining room, you'll want to focus mostly on how it looks in the nighttime. Dark walls, such as a deep burgundy, could work perfectly in a dining room. You would want to feel hugged and cozy in there, and not worry so much about the room looking larger.

Be sure to provide a number of light sources in your dining room. Many dining rooms have just one overhead light or chandelier, but there's nothing stopping you from putting lamps on a buffet table or installing wall sconces, either with electrical power or candlelight. One of my favorite approaches for a dining room is to have a mirror over a buffet table reflect the light of candles on the dining room table.

kitty's style and spirit

Be Open to Change From this moment forward, try to view all things that you have in your home—indeed, in your life—as subject to change. It's true that some things are more easily changed than others. The window seat in my dining room, for example, isn't as easily changed as the window seat cover.

I had fun with this dining room, playing up its **best features**—the window seat, French doors, and octagonal window.

My Home

My living room and dining room were white, white, white when I moved in. Very trendy, but not me. Here's how I made them my own.

My Living Room

My living room totally works for me. I don't have a family room, so my living room is used often and must serve many purposes. As I mentioned, I have washable slipcovers with a summer look and with a winter look. I have large, comfortable chairs; an ottoman; and children's chairs tucked under a large coffee table for extra seating. I have lots of light sources to give it a balanced feel. I have a wall of woodwork around my fireplace, which gives the room a more natural feeling. (Later in the chapter, I'll tell you how I got that look.) And I make sure I fill the room with living things: flowers, trees, and fruit. And of course I've got my umber walls, and the light blue ceiling to trick you subconsciously into thinking you're under nature's blue sky.

My living room is small, which limits the choices in furniture placement. Unlike many living rooms, this one is not centered on a TV. This living room is geared more toward creating a place for people to visit with each other. I set the chairs at angles toward each other and the couch.

My inspiration for the room came from the painting above the couch, which was a gift from my husband 30 years ago. The painting is dominated by red, which is my color. But it also has enough blue, green, and other colors to work with. Actually, the frame for the painting was originally gold. But it was way too gold for this room. So I painted it black. The black unites well with the octagonal table on the left side of the couch, which I

The **painting above the sofa** was the **starting point** for the whole room.

found at a used-furniture store and painted black with gold high-lights. (See "Hands-On Project: Painted Octagonal Table" on page 109.)

Notice the blue door on the left side in the painting? That's why I chose to put the blue shutters on either side of the painting. I bought those shutters just the way they are, and I like the chipping paint and the color. Don't think that outdoor pieces must be used outdoors. If you find a great piece of wrought iron, an old door, or a trellis, bring it inside.

I like to create a cohesive feeling in a room and house by repeating colors and details. Notice the blue and white pottery in the painting over my couch (see page 183). There's also blue and white pottery on the fireplace mantel, as well as on the red Irish cupboard directly opposite the painting. This subtly ties the room together. When you consider a painting to buy, you might think about how that could be a starting point for a room.

Concerning the frame of the painting on the mantel (see page 176), I realize it seems a little contemporary, but it still works in this room. I wish I could take credit for painting the stripes on the frame, but the painting came framed that way. I bought the painting at an antique show, but it's French in origin. It certainly draws your eye in. Even standing in the hallway, you notice the frame. But the frame doesn't fight with the image. It forces your eye to look into the center, at the painting itself.

Also, notice the width of the mantel. A long mantel like this is a decorating challenge. You want to be careful not to place accessories like little soldiers marching across. Vary the shapes and sizes of accessories.

I am fortunate to have a fireplace in my living room, which I change to suit the seasons. In winter, I have fires in my fireplace a lot, and I use a metal screen painted to look like bamboo. In summer, I cover the fireplace with a painted screen.

My Dining Room

Most people don't use their dining rooms on a daily basis. But I wanted to use my dining room in this house; in fact, I needed to use it. For one thing, I don't have a family room. And I have a very small kitchen. Because my dining room is adjacent to the kitchen, guests can spill out of the kitchen into the dining room. But the dining room would not get the use I envisioned unless I made choices in my furnishings to make it appealing and functional.

I added many colors and elements to transform the dining room from the white box it was into the warm room it is today. As I mentioned earlier, my starting point was the large painting of a woman on a ladder reaching for an apple. I used the painting as my inspiration for the colors in the room. I chose my favorite "elephant's breath" beige color for the upper walls and a hunter green for the lower walls.

This room gets its ambience from the library theme I chose. I had my handyman install bookshelves high on the wall around the perimeter of the room and on both sides of the bay window. You can buy wallpaper borders that mimic books along the ceiling line, but it's almost as easy to install real shelves and fill them with books, plates, and other accessories. I work here often, my daughter does her homework here, and our friends naturally gravitate here.

My dining room is really the heart of my home. I have coffee with family and friends here, do crafts, and entertain. So this room needs to be warm and wonderful.

See the big red apple on the **bookshelf** above the painting of a woman picking an apple? **That puts a smile on my face.**

To mix things up, I added plates to my **bookshelves** and books to my **plate rack.**

I pushed the wooden table up against the bay window rather than sticking it in the center of the room, directly under the light fixture. Now people don't have to walk around the table when going from the entryway to the kitchen and back.

Having the table against the bay window actually creates a nice place to sit. To be honest, I'd prefer a round table in this room, but this is the table I have and so I'm going to make the most of what I have. I "walk my talk." I won't put my life on hold until I find the perfect dining room table. It will come in its own time.

However, I did change my dining room chairs to suit the room. In my former house, which was a Santa Fe style, I had slipcovers made for my chairs in a festive green and red fabric. They worked okay in this room, but just okay. Then, not too long ago, I came across a remnant of the perfect crewel fabric for the chairs. I could not have found such a beautiful fabric if I had gone out searching for it. But I kept my eyes open, and it appeared. One of my more gratifying few days recently was re-covering those seats. (I show you exactly how I did that later in this chapter.)

A great bonus is that my crewel-covered dining room chairs coordinate well if I need to pull them into my living room for a large gathering. That's the benefit of having a color flow—you can pull things from other rooms and they work.

A Contemporary Living Room and Dining Room

I want to show you my daughter and son-in-law's apartment to illustrate the fact that I'm not trying to sell you on a certain style of decorating, but show you principles that you can use with your own style. As my children grow up and start their own adult lives, I'm very interested in the topics of apartments and furnishing rentals in ways that are personal and appealing.

It's important to realize that what works in apartments also works in homes. Decorating brings a sense of "you" to any place you live, whether it's a small rental or a large home that you own.

My son-in-law, Bryan, lived in this apartment before he and my daughter Brooke were married, and he wanted it to be modern and sleek and streamlined. He was also able to add some variety and texture without making it too cute or froufrou. When Bryan moved in, the fireplace wall was painted all white, which kept this focal point from standing out. With simple black paint on the fireplace, it now has the weight and sophistication it deserves. Get permission before you paint a rental, but most landlords are happy that you're taking an interest in upgrading the

Brooke's contemporary living room uses the same principles as my cozier living room to achieve balance and a flow.

property and will probably say yes (just be very neat when painting).

The black buffet on the far wall, which came from Pottery Barn, is a great place to store books, candles, and pottery and it keeps the streamlined approach going. The two high-back chairs add a bit of texture and warmth. There's a lot of black, and that can feel very cold, so adding the natural texture of wood balances the other side of the room. A TV cabinet also has a little bit of textural quality to it.

For the dining area, Bryan shifted a little in his sense of what is contemporary. He wanted a really neat glass table that he'd seen at a colleague's home, but in the meantime he borrowed a wooden trestle table from me that I wasn't using at the time. When I needed it back, Bryan found the glass table of his dreams in the local newspaper. He was so surprised that the glass table looked empty to him, and not appealing. He ended up getting a wooden table made to match mine. He loved the idea of adding the warmth of wood and the flexibility of a bench. When they move to a larger apartment or a house, this table can go in the kitchen, or on a patio, or in a workshop. And the glass table? It was perfect for a desk in the living room and proved how versatile a purchase it was.

The wooden table with a bench creates very flexible seating for a young couple starting out.

Hands-On Projects

Now I'd like to show you some of my favorite living room and dining room projects: my distressed fireplace wall, re-covered chair seats, and refinished corner cabinet.

HANDS-ON PROJECT: Distressed Fireplace Wall

When I first bought this house, the wall of woodwork around the fireplace had layer upon layer upon layer of white paint, and one of the first things I did was to strip it off with a chemical stripper.

I hired somebody to help me, and we worked for days, using a wire brush to get in the cracks and the crevices of the dentil molding under the mantel. You never really get every single bit off. When I got tired of the work, I said, "That's the end of that."

The wood was in good shape because it had been painted, and therefore protected, for so many years. But I wanted it to look old. So I decided to distress it by whipping it with my Chanel belt and garden cultivator.

We literally took out our frustrations at the end of the day by beating the wall. In some places, you can see we really went crazy. To the left of the fireplace, it looks like there have been worms eating holes in there, but really that was achieved by hitting it with the pronged end of a garden cultivator.

After I thought we'd beaten it quite enough, I waxed it with light brown Briwax (rather than adding a stain). Because the wood was very absorbent at this point, I put at least three coats of wax on there and buffed it to achieve a wonderful, warm patina. The pseudo wormholes are really noticeable because of the brown Briwax in the crevices.

WHAT YOU'LL NEED

* A WOODEN AREA OF A WALL OR PIECE OF FURNITURE
* GARDEN CULTIVATOR, PITCHFORK, OR SOME OTHER SHARP TOOL
* CHAIN (OR A CHANEL CHAIN BELT, IF YOU'VE GOT ONE LYING AROUND)
* BRIWAX (PASTE WAX WITH TINT)
* SOFT CLOTH

WHAT YOU'LL DO

1. Beat the wood with the sharp end of your tool and the chain. Hit it at an angle to get grooves, which are more interesting than simple holes. You want to make it look like it got dented over decades or centuries of wear. If you have any unresolved anger from your childhood—or even yesterday—think of that as you pound away. This is a good time to invite angry friends over for some free therapy.

2. When it looks beaten enough to you, rub Briwax into the wood with a soft cloth. If the wood is thirsty, you'll need several coats. By getting Briwax with a color to it, you'll be darkening the holes you've made, and your wood will have a nice glow.

3. Wax your wood with Briwax occasionally to nourish it. ❖

Any chair seat that is removable is re-coverable. Just flip the chair upside down. If you see four screws underneath that are holding the chair seat onto the chair frame itself, it can be re-covered. (I'll wait here while you jog into your dining room or kitchen and flip your chairs over to see what's going on under there.)

Covering chairs is so fun that even if you don't have chairs that can be re-covered, you might choose them for a fu-ture purchase so that you don't miss out on the excitement.

Generally speaking, the fabric that is on the chair seat is stapled on using a heavy-duty staple gun. In many cases, you can redo your chair seats without even re-moving the old fabric. It's like shingles on a roof. You can add a new layer on top of old layers. Sometimes, I've been able to put on two or three different layers. That's good because every time I move or paint my dining room, I redo my chair fabric.

If the fabric layers are too thick, how-ever, you should remove the old fabric. If there are too many layers or very thick fabric, it will be hard for your staples to hold the new fabric on, and for the screws to hold the seat to the frame.

You may also need to remove the original fabric if it shows through the new fabric. You can use the old fabric as the pattern or template for the new fabric.

My dining room chair seats started out in a blue needlepoint fabric. Later on, they got green slip-covers for my Santa Fe–style home. Now, they have a gorgeous Colonial crewel. What's next? Who knows what life will bring.

WHAT YOU'LL NEED

* CHAIR WITH PADDED SEAT THAT IS SCREWED ONTO THE FRAME
* SCREWDRIVER
* NEEDLE-NOSE PLIERS
* FABRIC FOR NEW COVER
* SCISSORS
* HEAVY-DUTY STAPLE GUN
* HAMMER

WHAT YOU'LL DO

1. Turn the chair over, unscrew the four screws holding it onto the frame, and remove the seat from the chair. **A**

2. Using your screwdriver and needle-nose pliers, pry up and pull out the staples that hold the fabric onto the seat. **B** and **C**

3. Lay the old seat fabric over your new fabric, with the wrong side of the old fabric against the right side of the new fabric, and use that for a template to cut out the new fabric. **D**

4. If your fabric has a pattern, such as stripes or a plaid, make sure the fabric is lined up correctly before you cut it so that it will be straight when it's done. **E**

5. With the new fabric still right side down, lay the chair seat on top. Staple one side, with one staple only, onto the center of one side of the frame. When stapling, lean over the gun and put your weight into it before squeezing the trigger. Hammer each staple after you're done to make it lie flat.

6. Staple the fabric, with one staple only, in the center of the opposite side of the frame, pulling the fabric snugly. There is an art to keeping the fabric pulled snugly enough so it's tight enough, but not so tight that you pull it out of shape.

7. Staple the fabric on the other two sides, using one staple each, onto the center of the frame. I make a big deal about this because you don't want to put a bunch of staples on one side, and then put a bunch of staples on the second side, and then the third side because if you do the fabric will not get installed evenly and your finished product will look lumpy.

8. Then, on each side, put a staple halfway between the corner of the seat and the staple in the center, easing the fabric evenly as you do. By positioning staples halfway between previous staples, you will eventually have evenly spaced staples all around, without using a ruler to space them out.

9. Leave the corners for last. They take the most care. Fold, gather, and staple the corners over the frame so that there is the least amount of creases showing. With careful easing of the fabric, you can do this. If you staple a corner and find the fabric on the top of the seat is bunched and overlapped, don't panic. Just take out those staples and do it again. I had to do that on my seats, so why not you?

10. When the new cover is stapled onto the chair, screw the seat back onto the frame. (The screws have to push through the fabric, so you'll have to apply some pressure.) Stand the chair upright and enjoy your handiwork. Sit your bottom in the chair and enjoy it all the more. ❖

HANDS-ON PROJECT: Refinished Corner Cabinet

It pays to think ahead about what you'd like in a room so that when providence strikes, you're ready. Before I saw this corner cabinet, I knew that I wanted a corner cabinet in my living room. When I saw the cabinet in a used-furniture store, I suspected that the size and the period would work. I measured the piece, took a Polaroid shot of it, and went home to ponder it.

I wouldn't have objected to the cabinet's timeworn paint-chipping-off look, but I didn't like the colors. I thought the

I knew I would be repainting this piece, so the bad paint job didn't bother me.

I chose the golden mustard color to go with a wooden Japanese shoebox in my living room and the blue to go with the old blue shutters on my wall.

The finished cabinet looks quite elegant in my living room.

$350 price was really, really good, and I believe they could have gotten twice as much for it. However, I didn't really study the cabinet because it was pushed against a wall. I had no idea until I got it home that it was so badly damaged. After I started working on it, I realized that it hadn't been painted in many years. The wood was very cracked and coated with layers of paint.

I decided I wanted to use buttermilk paint, which gives a very old-fashioned look, but is also hard to find. I got it from a catalog in Massachusetts, The Old-Fashioned Milk Paint Company, www.milkpaint.com (see chapter 13, Organizing, Tools, and Resources), and I chose a golden mustard color. I decided to paint the inside of the upper cabinet a contrasting blue color.

My inspiration for the gold color came from a wooden Japanese shoebox in my living room. And the inspiration for blue came from the light blue shutters hanging on the wall. You may wonder why I didn't choose red for the cabinet. Well, I already had a large red piece of furniture in that room—my Irish cabinet. And there's already a lot of black in that room.

Buttermilk paint is very opaque, so it doesn't cover all that easily. So I ended up putting as many as five coats of paint in some places to get the look I was after.

WHAT YOU'LL NEED

* OLD PIECE THAT NEEDS REPAINTING
* PAINT SCRAPER
* LIGHTWEIGHT SPACKLE
* SANDPAPER
* SOFT CLOTH
* STAIN-BLOCKING PRIMER, SUCH AS ZINSSER BULLS EYE 1-2-3 PRIMER
* PAINTBRUSHES
* PAINT
* BRIWAX (PASTE WAX WITH A LIGHT BROWN TINT)

WHAT YOU'LL DO

1. Put the piece in a place where you don't have to worry about dripping paint and where it's not too windy or dusty.

2. Scrape off loose paint with a paint scraper. Don't worry about getting all the paint off. Think instead of the history in this piece—every layer of paint and every nick is part of its charm. Embrace that.

3. Fill any obvious cracks with lightweight spackle. Once the spackle is dry, sand lightly.

4. Clean the surface with a soft, damp cloth.

5. Paint a layer of primer over the whole piece. This step costs a bit more and takes more time, but your color coat will be much more consistent with a good primer underneath.

6. When the primer is dry, apply the paint. Let the paint dry, and add a second coat.

7. Apply several coats Briwax (one of my favorite products in the whole world) with the soft cloth, really working it into the imperfections to give it an aged look.

8. Let each coat of Briwax dry for at least 20 minutes, and then buff to a soft glow. ❖

Do you have any ideas for dressing a fireplace mantel for spring?

Kitty: A fireplace mantel is a great spot to showcase the seasons, whether it's autumn colors and materials or Christmas greenery and motifs.

For spring, try tulips, daffodils, large branches such as forsythia, dogwood, or whatever is blooming in your part of the country. Light-colored baskets will make the room feel fresh as well. For early summer, you might consider a collection of children's toys, such as model cars, toy boats, small oars, and more.

My front door leads right into my living room. There is no entry hall, just a raised, tiled platform as wide as the front door and about 7 feet long. How can I make this feel more like an entryway?

Kitty: Place a very narrow (8 to 12 inches wide) console table along the wall. If you have a hard time finding one, go to a thrift store or an antique store and find a beautiful table and have someone saw it in half. Then attach it to the wall with brackets, with the cut side against the wall and two legs holding up the table. Or do without the legs altogether and use two old corbels to hold it up. Or do without the table altogether and secure a piece of glass on the corbels. The idea is to mimic a full-sized console table in a smaller space. Hang a mirror over it, and set a lamp on top.

Another way to create an entryway is with a small area rug that runs the length of the platform and has a design that contrasts with the carpeting in the room.

I have a 6-foot section of wall in my living room and dining room area that is between two tall windows. I stenciled a hydrangea plant in the center, about 2 feet high and 2 feet wide. What would you suggest to go on the wall over the plant?

Kitty: Would you consider a mirror? It would continue to give the feeling of depth that you've created with the stencil. Or perhaps three shelves would be perfect there, but not so large as to diminish the look of your stencil. I would say 3 feet wide at the most. Then, dress them with a small mirror, books, and plants.

How do I get a parchment look for my living room walls?

Kitty: Brown kraft paper can make an interesting look on a wall, particularly if you tear it rather than cut it. If you tear it in sections and overlap them when you adhere them to the wall, it can look like stone. Then cover it with several layers of nonyellowing, water-based matte polyurethane. It'll even be washable.

If you don't want to glue something to your walls, you can try a paint application. For example, parchment is beigy-brown tones over yellow. Start with a neutral color with quite a bit of yellow as your base color. Then apply a brown umber glaze and wipe it off with a rag.

I have a 1941 ranch house with a long living room. There's a fireplace at the west end and a television cabinet on the north wall. How can I create distinct areas for viewing and relaxing?

Kitty: Buy some graph paper and draw to scale the permanent items in the room—such as the fireplace, doors, and windows—and the large pieces like the entertainment center. Then take another piece of graph paper and cut out shapes to scale of your sofas, sectionals, upholstered chairs, and ottomans. Play with the arrangements, taking careful note of the doors to the outside and to other rooms. Don't be afraid to experiment with furniture on angles.

Don't let the windows intimidate you. Most TV viewing is at night, and there are endless window treatments to darken the room for nighttime viewing.

How can I create a tablescape on my living room coffee table? My house is Victorian in style.

Kitty: I'd stack some books with a Victorian glass or ceramic bowl. I like the idea of something alive, perhaps three African violets in a glass container or ceramic dish. You could also try a silver, glass, or wood tray with assorted heights of candles. Do you collect anything? Maybe place three medium to large collectibles on top of the books. Don't overdo it with little items, and stick to odd numbers.

Check out old issues of *Victoria* magazine for additional inspiration.

You can't beat books and flowers for dressing a living room table.

How can I mask an in-the-wall heater and air conditioner that are on the same wall in my living room? Can I put anything in front of them without interfering with function?

Kitty: How about using antique iron gates to hide the heater and air conditioner? The air could still flow through, and while it wouldn't totally mask the heater and air conditioner, it would catch the eye before it focused on the crowded wall beyond. Whatever you choose, don't place it too close to a heat source. Safety always comes first.

These antique gates would be perfect **non-combustible room dividers** to divert the eye from your heater/air conditioner.

I was thinking of painting my great room in a new color I've heard of called oxblood. I would like to accent it with white trim, white cabinets, and a large collection of blue and white china. But it's a very large space with my kitchen and living room together. Will that be wrong to use such a strong color?

Kitty: There's really no right or wrong. A color such as oxblood would work best in a room with a lot of light and with furniture upholstered in light neutrals. But it also depends on your metabolism (do you need to be calmed down or speeded up?), light exposure (facing south or facing north?), architecture (lots of windows, few windows?). I've seen houses with color combinations that you'd think would never work, but they do.

If you have a large room and you want to paint it an oxblood color, I think it could be beautiful. It's going to make the room look smaller, but maybe that's good. A lot of other colors coordinate with red, so it will be easy to find accessories and patterns to go with it.

I bought a 60-year-old house near Boston that I love, but the woodwork has been painted so many times I can barely see the detail. Can I strip off the paint?

Kitty: Stripping that much paint off of woodwork could be exhausting. If you put a chemical stripper on there and you started scraping, it would take you forever. So if there are so many layers of paint you can't see the design anymore and you can't stand to put one more layer of paint on it, one approach is to use a heat gun and melt the paint off. Some of the heat guns I like actually have a scraper built in so they melt the paint and then scrape it. It takes some getting used to, and you need to be sure to provide adequate ventilation. It's a lot of work, no doubt about it. (See "Hands-On Project: Distressed Fireplace Wall" on page 190 where I stripped paint off my fireplace wall.)

Another thing to consider is that the wood under the paint might not be worth that much work. It all depends on the era in which your house was built and the quality of the builder. Generally speaking, houses built before the late 1940s have better quality, tight-grain, old-growth lumber. The newer the house, the less likely it is to have woodwork worth a lot of labor to restore. In fact, much of the "woodwork" on most new homes is not really wood at all, but a composite of sawdust and plastic. So be sure your wood is worth all that work. Maybe you could strip a small section to see what's under the paint before you set out to do the whole thing.

I have a farmhouse table in my kitchen. I would like an idea for other possible uses for it in the living room area.

Kitty: I suggest you use your table as a base for your entertainment center. You will want to hide all the wires from the speakers, TV, and DVD player. How about skirting the table with fabric that has been gathered or pleated and applied around the edges with Velcro? Or staple those fabrics on and then cover the staples with ribbon or a welt. If you don't want to skirt it, perhaps you could place an old trunk or interesting wooden box under the table to store things and hide wires. That would be a nice look. Then you could hang an old wall cabinet with doors or drawers on the wall above the table and next to the TV.

If I paint the dining room red, can the adjacent family room be painted taupe?

Kitty: Absolutely! Find a great plaid or fabric that has at least those two colors in it to tie the two rooms together. You could use the fabric to re-cover your chairs, to use as a table runner, or to make pillows for your family room sofa. You might also find a rug with those colors.

I have a very tall and relatively narrow niche above a fireplace. It starts at eye level and extends about 14 feet up a double-story wall. The niche is only about 3 inches deep. My initial idea was to hang a tapestry, but we can't find one long enough. We have tried putting up two large paintings and two smaller tapestries, but they look silly. A mirror won't work with our decorating style.

Kitty: Wow, that's a real challenge. I'm trying to picture a niche that tall and the style of architecture your house might be. I like the idea of one long thing versus a collection. What about a rug of some sort, like a runner? It can be antique to modern, depending on your architecture. I think you're on the right track with tapes-try or a piece of antique fabric. Or perhaps you can buy a piece of woven tapestry by the yard and hang it from a beautiful brass or wood rod. Fringing the bottom would look good. My feeling is that your house is Old World, but if it's contemporary, you could hang something playful, such as a flag.

I live on Baja on the beach in a very open house with the kitchen, living room, and dining room all facing the sea. The main wall, which faces the ocean, was all white when I bought the place. I painted it terra cotta, but I wonder if I could have made a better choice because it contrasts so much with the ocean.

Kitty: The terra cotta may not be the right color for the setting. Let's say it's the daytime and you're sitting there and looking outside. Some people want to look at the water all the time and don't want to get distracted by the terra cotta color. Your eye's probably going straight to that color instead of the ocean. If you want the ocean to be noticed, the walls need to be a softer color. The terra cotta's probably too strong.

You might want a neutral—maybe a beige that has some blue in it. I wouldn't choose gray because on a gray day it could make the ocean or the wall look dirty. Your goal is to play up what's most important— and that's the view you have.

My house is English Tudor on the inside, and our living room has a medieval-looking fireplace. It's very bland looking, but it has an interesting shape—wide at the bottom and narrower at the top with a stucco hearth. We want to make our fireplace stand out. Our first thought was to have darker walls with a lighter fireplace. What do you think about that?

Kitty: Well, first of all, I wouldn't want there to be anything around the fireplace that looks artificial. The purpose of the fireplace is to add warmth. So I wouldn't want to see any weird colors. For me, I'd want to do something texturally interesting rather than adding interest with color alone.

I once troweled drywall mud and straw over a fireplace to give it some interest. In the old days, they used horsehair and straw to hold the mud together. Maybe you could even add some stones, not so much to

stand out, but to look like it had worn down over time. You want it to feel like the artisan who created it was particularly clever.

If you're going to add texture with stucco or drywall mud, you could "mud in" a large plate. Obviously, you wouldn't do this with a family heirloom. But you could secure it to the wall and then plaster in around it. I did that in one of my bedrooms.

Look at what I did to one of my fireplaces. I troweled straw into it. I realize it's a little odd, but I loved it.

I have a small house with a small living room. People have told me I'm limited to white walls because of the smallness. Is that true?

Kitty: Whoa! Those people are just afraid of color. I've always lived in small houses because I'm not a fan of big houses. I love living with color.

It's true that if you have a small room, the room will feel larger with a lighter color. But that doesn't mean the room has to be white. Would you like to have a cozy room? Would you like to walk into a room and feel like it's hugging you? I do. That's what I want.

Your home should reflect you and the people that live there. Only you can answer what's going to feel best for you. But I'll bet adding color to your walls will bring warmth and coziness to your living room, no matter the size.

I have a huge slate fireplace in my great room that has lots of colors in it, and we have some really crummy oak cabinets that we have to replace or paint. What would you suggest for wall color? Right now everything's white.

Kitty: This should be easy. Use the slate itself as your inspiration. See what beautiful colors nature has put together, and then pull those colors out for your paint color and upholstery. Look at the browns, beiges, grays, and whatever else is in that slate and ask yourself, "What makes that so beautiful?" And if you end up choosing some rich blue-grays or brown-grays for your walls, set them off with an off-white trim rather than beige.

1 **Framed menus** from a special restaurant make the **perfect artwork** for your dining room. Memories of **great meals** will certainly stimulate the **tastebuds.**

2 What do you do with paneling when you don't like it anymore? Instead of removing it, which can be a very big job, think of painting it. To give it a nautical look, glue nylon rope into the grooves, and then paint the whole thing white or a very pale blue.

3 Have a brick or lava rock fireplace that's looking dated? Here's my favorite trick for a low-cost update: Dilute a tan water-based paint with water (about 50/50) to create a wash. Sponge or brush it over the brick or stone, which will be very absorbent. You may need three to six coats to get a completely new look.

4 A wooden folding ladder, full of paint splashes and history, makes a compelling shelf unit when opened up in a corner. Stack books on some of the treads, plants on others.

You can encourage relaxation in
bedrooms by using soft colors and materials.
More stimulating colors, such as red and bright
yellow, **are best used in other rooms.**

bedrooms

Everyone needs a safe haven, a place to retreat from tiring days to relax, rejuvenate, and restore yourself. I believe that's what bedrooms are for. That said, though, there's one great divide when it comes to bedrooms—the age of the inhabitant. Is the bedroom for kids or for adults? You'll make different furnishing choices based on what's happening in the room. An adult's room is a relaxing refuge from the stresses of life, while a kid's room functions more like a mini living room, den, and study. Let's look at adults' bedrooms first and then focus on kids' bedrooms.

Adults' Bedrooms

Bedrooms are mostly used at night, so you want to design your room so that it works best for you when it's dark outside. You might want to have a bright, sunny bedroom for those dreary Sunday mornings, but consider what it is going to feel like at night when you're in there trying to sleep. I think it's good to have lots of things conducive to relaxing, such as a reading chair, light, magazine rack or bookcase, knitted throw, candles, and good pillows.

I suggest blue for bedrooms if you have a high metabolism and have a hard time relaxing at night. Blue is a cool color, though, so make sure that your room gets enough natural light before choosing blue.

You probably want to stay away from colors that cause anxiety or overstimulation, such as bright yellow or red, when decorating a bedroom. Where resting is the main activity, calming colors are the order of the day—or the night, as the case may be. You can have touches of stimulating colors in a bedroom, but you wouldn't

See how much less calming this room was before the blue paint job?

Decorate Kitty's Way

❑ Design bedrooms to **work best at night**—because that's when you use them! ❑ Consider collecting **individual pieces** of bedroom furniture instead of an entire matching set. It's almost impossible to use the pieces of a matching set in another room. ❑ Decorate kids' rooms with furniture that will **span years**. Use accessories for trends du jour. ❑ Build a **platform bed** to provide storage in tight quarters.

want a whole wall of bright pink or plum unless it were behind the bed. When furnishing your bedroom, give some thought to acquiring furniture that can be used in other rooms as you go along in life. I'm not a big fan of purchasing a whole bedroom set that matches because that cuts down on the flexibility of the pieces.

But many Americans do buy bedroom sets. It's probably the first thing a young couple buys. I don't want to bad-mouth bedroom sets. But if you fall in love with the bedroom set, be aware that it's almost impossible to break it up later on. Also, it's a pain to strip and refinish a set because you've got a lot of different pieces. It's just

The color blue encourages the brain to release **calming** chemicals. Do you feel yourself getting **sleepier and sleepier?**

too big of a project. So if you get tired of your bedroom set in 15 years and want to update it, you'll probably have to start from scratch. It's like a dining room set; you're married to that look.

So I recommend that you choose your bedroom furniture so that the pieces stand on their own. Rather than a long, narrow dresser that can only go in a bedroom, consider an armoire that would work in a library or living room, too. Choose side tables that could be used in a living room or den. A large mirror doesn't necessarily have to match the headboard, does it? Choose a mirror you like, and then it can be used later in any room in your house.

I have to admit that there's one benefit of buying a complete bedroom set. You can decide what you want all at one time, and you're done. Buying individual pieces means that it will take more time to find this or that piece. I enjoy the process of finding individual pieces that have the same vibe, but that's me.

This round, draped table fit here in my daughters' guesthouse in the past, but now I use it in my bedroom.

This mirror does not match this dresser. But that makes it easier to break these two pieces up. In fact, I used this mirror in the living room of a previous house—it was painted black back then!

Kids' Rooms

While adults spend mostly nighttime hours in their bedrooms, kids tend to spend more daytime hours in their rooms—playing, doing homework, having quiet time, and even having time-outs. Here are some thoughts on how to make choices for furnishing a child's room, including the size of bed, other furniture, and storage for toys.

Choose your child's "big boy/girl bed" carefully because it's going to serve them for years to come and might not be changed until their teenage years. The size of the bed is important. For girls, go larger. Girls tend to gather on the bed, no matter the age—if they're little girls, or teens, or they are in college—they are always on the bed, whether it's two or twelve of them, doing their nails, homework, or just giggling. With boys, go smaller. If there's more than one boy, they will never sit on the bed. Chances are they are going to be on the floor. It's also possible that you're going to have a desk, desk chair, and bookcases. Later on you might want have a sofa and maybe a couple of kids' chairs to sit on so they can play their video games and interact.

For corralling the toys, I don't think you can beat baskets. You

This ingenious room divider is crisscrossed with ribbon, which is a perfect place for a young person to tuck **photos and mementos.**

kitty's style and spirit

Keep Things in Perspective I've heard people say, "We don't know what's going to happen in 10 years' time," as an excuse not to move forward, not to do anything. So don't think of your projects as things that are necessarily going to last a lifetime. Instead, you should think, "If I get 3 years of enjoyment out of it, I can always change it. After all, I haven't spent a lot of money on it, it's been fun, and who knows what I'll be interested in experimenting with in 3 years' time?"

can also use boxes, but if there's a top, the kid will rarely put the top back on. You can even label the baskets, if you wish—some for dolls and doll clothes, others for LEGOs, and so on. Another good storage place is under the bed. A large drawer from an old dresser works well, if you attach wheels for easier movement and retrieval. If you choose a toy box, make sure it has good hinges that don't allow the lid to fall on a child's head. A toy box can have a future life, as well, when it's no longer used for toys if its design can grow with the child—a simple wooden toy box might be better than one painted with puppies or carved and decorated with ballet shoes. Place the toy box under a window, top it with a cushion, flank it on both sides with tall bookshelves, and you've got yourself a window seat.

It's also a great idea to have a child-sized table in their rooms to encourage them to play board games or card games. Reading is important, so it's best to have a good reading lamp not only on the desk but also near the bed. Some of these swing-arm lamps are great to attach to the wall.

Once, for an appearance on *The Oprah Winfrey Show*, I painted an entire breakfast room, from the chair rail down, with chalkboard paint. I tied the erasers in a bag and made a lip for the chalk. Another room I decorated for two little boys centered around the players on the Los Angeles Lakers basketball team (the boys' heroes). I did a lot of things with Lakers merchandise—I made bolsters out of sweatpants, I made throw pillows out of Lakers T-shirts, I had a very large men's tennis shoe that I made into a planter, and I fashioned a fabric basket hoop so they could throw Nerf balls from their bunk beds. Another time, I laminated a map to the headboard of the bed. I had other maps and globes around the room.

Kids grow and change quickly, so their rooms need flexibility. A kid might like Big Bird one year, then the Incredible Hulk the next. Rather than wallpapering the whole room in Big Bird wallpaper, install bulletin boards where they can tack up posters featuring the obsession of the moment.

makes$ense

Does your child love certain cartoon characters, but do you find commercial wallpaper too costly? You can create a large mural on a bedroom wall by using an overhead projector to project an image from a book onto the wall. Do this at night, and trace the image, then color it in during daylight hours. You can also do this on a fence outside.

I think it's important to get the child's input as you decorate his or her room. I overheard two women talking once about one woman's desire to decorate her teenage daughter's room. Her friend said, "Why would you do it now? The minute my daughter went off to college, I redid her room just the way I wanted it."

I felt great sadness for that child. It's important that your children's bedrooms reflect who they are so they can enjoy them. Both you and your child should put thought into what the child will be doing in the room, such as listening to music, collecting posters, playing with dolls, reading, or playing with LEGOs.

I find that involving a child in selection of the furniture is a good experience for both parent and child. You can teach the child how to plan, measure, and set priorities. You can help the child learn patience by not buying everything at once, and you can demonstrate how to do things thoughtfully and on a budget. Who knew furnishing a bedroom could be so educational?

Here's one thing to consider as your kids approach their teen years: Are there going to be kids of the opposite sex in the room? You can, under the guise of working with the child, help direct how the room is going to function. If you don't put extra chairs in there, everybody's going to have to be stuck sitting on the bed, which is not necessarily the best place. Place beanbag chairs and other sit-upons in your teen's room for friends to sit on.

I don't see how you can have **too many pillows.**

My Home

I have two bedrooms in my home, plus one in the guesthouse. I like to play around with colors and furniture whenever I move, so my bedrooms are not always green or always blue or always white. It's fun to try out new decorating schemes every few years, whether you relocate or stay in the same home. Perhaps you'll find some ideas here.

My Bedroom

Two of the greatest gifts I have ever given to myself are in my bedroom: the door to the garden and the fireplace. The bedroom was already quite nice when I moved in. It was fairly large, had beautiful hardwood floors, and had two closets (which was important to me with my hand-knitted sweater collection numbering more than 70).

But while the room had four windows, it didn't give me what I really wanted, which was access to my backyard. I love having a garden, and I want to be able to walk directly out of my room and enjoy it. So I did a very bold thing—I added an exterior Dutch door and two more windows on what had been a big blank wall.

The other mainstay in my life is a fire in the fireplace. I have a fire every single night (unless I'm traveling). I need to relax in the evening, and a fire does the trick. A lot of people would not consider adding a wood-burning fireplace, but it's not that big of a deal. I had mine raised up to be at eye level while I was in my bed. The molding around the top came from a friend's house that was being redone. It matches the molding in other rooms in the house. It was a big decision to add the fireplace, and I'm extremely happy with the final look.

Under the windows on either side of my fireplace, I added chests that I bought at Pottery Barn. They are simple in design, and I added padding and pillows to give them the feeling of window seats.

With the addition of an exterior door, my bedroom has been transformed.

See that blank wall? On the other side of that is my garden, dying to be seen.

I love being able **to go into my garden from my bedroom.** The Dutch door **lets views and sunlight in** but keeps Spot from running out.

Here are a few table tricks:

The tablecloth on this round, glass-topped table (above) looks fuller because **I have put an old quilt underneath.** And a mirror on any table or desk, as you see on my bedroom dressing table (at right), **adds light and excitement.**

Look what a simple piece of mirror did for the top of this side table.

The room also had a challenge—a very strange ceiling that looked too contemporary for this 1930s home. There wasn't any crown molding for added character, and the ceiling had an odd shape. Luckily, as I discussed in the chapter on ceilings, I was able to have an artist draw a beautiful conservatory-type mural up there, and I added a fun crystal lamp to replace the hanging lamp that had been there.

I painted this room a light celadon green. It's a calming color, yet not cold. It's a color I never tire of.

In furnishing the room, I took my own advice about not buying a complete bedroom set. Rather than having two bedside tables that match the headboard, dresser, bureau, and mirror, I've got a table that can be used anywhere.

My dressing table is also a very flexible piece. It started out its life as a desk, but I turned it into my dressing table by painting it white and adding a mirror top. So simple, and yet so beautiful.

For comfort as well as beauty, I re-covered my dressing table chair with terry cloth. It's quite wonderful to get out of the bath and sit on a terry cloth seat when you're putting your makeup on. When you see white sales, look for large bath towels to use. Or you could use the good part of a towel that was ripped or stained. That might be enough material for a chair seat.

My bed is just a simple, inexpensive four-poster bed, but I made it more special by adding decorative finials to the tops of the posts. You won't believe where I got those finials—in my attic! (See "Hands-On Project: Bedpost Finials" on page 222 to see what I did.)

Birdie's Room

My daughter's room is also quite pleasing. What her room had going for it was painted wood paneling going almost to the ceiling with a nice ledge of molding, and two windows. I had already put shades in the room, and so I didn't want the extra complication of curtains. I decided to make a simple valance to unite the two windows, held in the middle with a ring and cup hook. I found that the ledge at the top of the paneling was perfect for my collection of lady-head vases.

Together, Birdie and I picked out the white furniture for her room from Pottery Barn, including an old-fashioned mirror over the bed. To dress up Birdie's side table, we covered the top with a mirror.

Guest Room

What often happens with a guest room is that it ends up with furniture that doesn't really work anywhere else—furniture that's one step away from the garage or the thrift shop. In my guest room, I had to do the colors around the things that I had that I didn't have anywhere else to put—like the trunk that was hand-painted, the Hoosier cabinet that was hand-painted, and the sofa. Those were the only places I could find for them, so they all had to tie in together.

Being able to look out into the garden from this guest room was a real asset to that room. I didn't want to cover up the windows with heavy drapes, so I had red Roman shades made to be easily raised up for the view. I love the rich colors against the white walls. That gives the balance I needed between light and dark.

There was an alcove in the room that looked like it would be perfect for a bed. But the win-dows are kind of high, and so I pondered what to do with the space. Finally I hit on the idea of having a handyman build a platform to raise up the bed and provide storage underneath for my luggage and, in the drawers, my costume collection. Most houses in California have neither a finished attic nor a basement, so storage is usually an issue. In my case, my garage was converted into a workshop, so I have extra challenges for storage space. The bed is really just a mattress on the platform without a box spring. After all, box springs these days are really just a hard platform to raise up the mattress, so the need for a box spring was eliminated here. To get a really comfortable mattress, I took my son shopping with me and had him try out various mattresses. He's very picky when it comes to mattresses, so I knew that if he was happy with it, my guests would be happy.

After I had the platform built and installed the Roman shades, I thought it felt a bit like a romantic train compartment. To further that theme, I hung blue-and-white-checked curtains and a valance across the opening. To punch up the red in the curtains, I spray-painted a wicker chair to match. Until recently that chair was yellow, and before that, who knows? Spray-painting wicker chairs is one of my favorite ways to give a room a renewed lift.

As you've guessed, I did not paint my guest room yellow, as I quipped about in the color chapter when I mentioned that high-chroma yellow causes anxiety. A guest room painted yellow would limit the time your guests would want to stay. I'm a people person and like frequent guests, so I made my guest room as appealing as possible.

oneminutemakeovers
You may want to put your bed on an angle in the corner but wonder what to do with the negative space behind the bed. This is a perfect place for a corner cabinet that houses out-of-season clothing.

When your guest room is this cozy, **you get more guests, which I like.**

Hands-On Projects

It's very easy to make these accessories for a bedroom in your home. Here's how to make a lace-painted chest, striped chest, and bedpost finials.

HANDS-ON PROJECT: Lace-Painted Chest

It's hard to believe how easy this is to paint, especially considering how good it looks.

I use this pretty chest to store my jewelry. I like this lace-painting technique because it requires no special equipment nor does it require painting talent. And yet it looks like it took a lot of talent or a lot of money. A good artist could paint a chest like this. But you and I can let a piece of lace do the work for us. The design that ends up on the piece is actually the negative space on a piece of lace—the opening where paint can get through. I think it's too clever. Can you imagine this same painted lace treatment on a door? On a tabletop? On a trunk? Or maybe a bathroom cabinet?

WHAT YOU'LL NEED

* WOODEN TABLETOP CHEST OF DRAWERS OR OTHER SURFACE
* DROP CLOTH OR OLD SHEETS
* SANDPAPER
* CLOTH
* 1 CAN SPRAY PAINT PRIMER (IF YOU'RE PAINTING OVER A DARK COLOR)
* 1 CAN COLORED SPRAY PAINT
* INEXPENSIVE LACE, CUT INTO A SQUARE
* STRAIGHT PINS
* 1 CAN WHITE SPRAY PAINT

WHAT YOU'LL DO

1. Find an outdoor spot in which to paint, and cover nearby items with a drop cloth or old sheets. You could use a large box, like one an appliance came in with one side removed, as a painting chamber.

2. Remove the drawers from the frame and remove any knobs from the drawers.

3. Lightly sand each piece, and wipe clean with a damp cloth. Let dry.

4. If you're painting over a dark color, you may want to spray on a coat of primer. Let it dry. Spray the drawers, frame, and knobs with colored paint. Let them dry at least 1 hour. Replace the drawers in the frame.

5. Once you're sure the paint is really dry, secure a square of lace to the top of the chest with straight pins. **A** and **B**

6. Spray white paint over the lace, standing 1 to 2 feet away and using a continuous back-and-forth spraying motion. **C**

7. After a few minutes, carefully remove the lace and let the paint dry for 1 hour. **D** Repeat the lace-spraying step on knobs, sides, front, and back. When the paint is dry, replace the knobs. ❖

A

B

C

D

This is another chest I use for jewelry and other stuff. This box is an important part of my bedroom, but if you saw this box at a yard sale and it was painted black, cow print, or green with purple polka dots, you might miss out on its potential.

It's an art to see beyond the paint to the shape, size, and usefulness of an item. The next time you go to a swap meet or yard sale, practice looking at items that seem kind of tacky or awkward to try to imagine how they would look painted a different color. Seeing potential is a practiced talent, one that you can develop. In fact, you can start right here. Look at the photo of my green and white chest and imagine how it would look painted in your colors.

I'm a huge fan of stripes. The first thing to remember in painting stripes is that *half the stripes are already painted!* Whatever color is on the wall or object will make up half the stripes, and your second color will make the second half of the stripes.

Simple stripes give this chest a lively look.

WHAT YOU'LL NEED

* SMALL DESKTOP STORAGE CHEST
* DROP CLOTH OR OLD SHEETS
* SANDPAPER
* CLOTH
* 1 CAN WHITE SPRAY PAINT
* RULER
* PENCIL
* LOW-TACK PAINTER'S TAPE
* PAINTBRUSHES (SMALL AND MEDIUM SIZED)
* 1 QUART SEMIGLOSS WHITE PAINT
* 1 HALF-PINT COLORED PAINT

WHAT YOU'LL DO

1. Take your chest outside, and set yourself up in an area free of wind and dust. Cover nearby items with drop cloths or old sheets to protect them from overspray.

2. Remove drawers from the frame and remove knobs from the drawers. Lightly sand all surfaces and wipe clean with a damp cloth. Let dry.

3. Spray the frame and drawers with white paint. Let the paint dry according to the directions on the can, and then spray another coat.

4. Once the paint is dry, replace the drawers in the frame, leaving the knobs off for now. Measure the width of the box to determine the spacing for your stripes. I measured mine to be sure there would be white stripes on either outer edge of the box.

5. Use a ruler and a pencil to mark lines for the tape. I used ¾-inch painter's tape, so I put the first strip ¾ inch away from the side, then left a ¾-inch space and placed another strip of tape, and so on across the piece. You want the tape to go over the frame and the drawers.

Here's a really great painting secret—in my opinion one of the best tips in this book. The biggest problem with painting stripes is that the paint seeps under the tape and you don't get clean, sharp lines when the tape is removed. So here's what you do: Brush white paint (or whatever the background color is) over the tape and let it dry for 1 hour. **A** This will seal the edges so that your stripe color coat won't seep underneath. Few things could be more frustrating than spending all that time putting your tape down and then at the end, you've got blurs where the contrasting color seeped under the tape.

6. In a container, mix the white and colored paints. (I did this to make the teal lighter to match the color of the room. You might not need to take this step.)

7. Brush on the paint mixture in between the tape strips. Before the paint is totally dry, carefully pull the tape straight off. **B** You can use a small paintbrush for any touch-ups needed.

8. Paint the knobs with the paint mixture, and once the paint is totally dry (be patient), replace them. I added a circle of white in the center of each knob. ❖

This striping technique, where you seal the edges of the tape with your background paint before painting on the stripe color, also applies to big surfaces, like the wall in this dining room.

HANDS-ON PROJECT: Bedpost Finials

Not everybody is going to have something like this lying around, but it's the idea of adapting something that I like to stress. When I bought this bed, it was just a very standard four-poster bed that was very reasonably priced. But I thought the finials on top were cheesy.

I would have left them there, but then I found some hand-carved posts in the attic. The sentimentality of finding these in my attic, that they belonged to the house, made me feel that I should use them somehow.

I'm not sure how they were originally used—perhaps they were legs to a table or part of a bed. The idea is that you might find something like this at the swap meet and think, Where in the world would I ever use this? Well, here's one idea.

WHAT YOU'LL NEED

* OLD TABLE LEGS OR OTHER DECORATIVE POSTS
* HANDSAW
* PAINT
* NAILS OR SCREWS
* SPONGE BRUSH

WHAT YOU'LL DO

1. Decide how long you want your bedpost finials to be and measure that on your posts. Ideally, you would cut the posts at a natural place, rather than in the middle of a curve. **A**

2. Cut the posts with a handsaw. **B**

When I found some old posts in my attic, I wanted to incorporate them into my home in some way. They became finials to my bedposts.

3. Put a nail or screw partway into the end of the cut post. This will give you something to hold on to when you paint the post. Or you can insert the nail or screw into a piece of wood to keep the post upright.

4. With a sponge brush, apply several light coats of paint, letting the post dry in between coats. **C**

5. When the posts are dry, attch them to your bed. ❖

I want to use teal for my bedroom, but I've read that it's dated and out of fashion. Can I still use it?

Kitty: I'm never going to tell people to stay away from a color that they love. There's always a way to make it work. Teal may look dated, but it could look fresher and newer with contrasts of whites and neutrals. It depends on how it's put together. However, teal carpeting might feel dated. In 5 years' time, though, it might not feel dated as it's been "out" so long it might be "in" again!

My daughter has painted the walls of her room dark blue. She has Craftsman-style furniture and off-white carpeting, and that's as far as it goes. What else do you suggest? We need help quickly because I would like to finish her room before she's old enough to move out!

Kitty: To balance out the dark walls, you probably want the window treatments, moldings, and trim to be light, even white. White would be a good choice for bed coverings, too, because stains can be bleached out, unlike with a pattern or color. Also, eyelet lace and ruffles are so pretty and feminine (if that suits her personality, of course).

You could then add color with bulletin boards, clothes, souvenirs, etc. These things have a way of distracting the eye from the wall color.

No matter what you decide, make sure there is lots of good light in the room. If your main source of light is overhead lighting, create a cozy atmosphere with at least two table or floor lamps.

I plan to decorate my 3-year-old daughter's room. It has 9-foot ceilings, pale yellow walls, plantation shutters on two large windows, and pale Berber carpet. I want to use toile fabric on the two twin beds. Any suggestions on colors or other furniture?

Kitty: I don't think you can make a mistake getting painted white furniture for a little girl's room. I love the idea of toile because it's timeless and classic, and also French! For more ideas, I love the Ballard catalog (800-367-2775). You can get great ideas out of these, and both offer a range of price points.

White painted furniture is perfect for a girl's room. We turned to Pottery Barn for my daughter's room.

I have just redecorated my bedroom with a Mediterranean-style faux finish using a magic roller, where two different color paints are applied at the same time. I hung a large picture above the bed—it is long but not very wide. What can I put next to the picture to complete it?

Kitty: I am a huge fan of plates on walls. They are easy to find and come in endless colors, patterns, and sizes. I would consider putting three, at the minimum, on either side of your picture. You could do five on either side, three going vertically and two on either side of the center, depending on how much space you want to fill visually.

Another thought would be sconces. Iron would complement your Mediterranean look. This could be romantic with candles (you don't need to have them wired for electricity). Or, consider a combination of sconces and plates.

What can I do to refinish or disguise my cheap, black lacquer, Art Deco bedroom set? I really prefer Italian, French, or even a Gothic style.

Kitty: Now I hate to nag, but this is the point I make when I say that buying a bedroom set is risky. What if you tire of it? Unfortunately, to answer your question, there's no way to turn deco into gothic! It certainly can be painted, and I would definitely recommend spray-painting it. But I don't mean that you should buy 20 cans of spray paint. Rather, rent a professional sprayer from a good paint store. You could spray it off-white, and perhaps you could highlight any design features with a contrasting color (country green, for example).

Here I've used plates to fill up the wall around this rather narrow mirror.

I'm redecorating a bedroom and all I have so far is cherry wood furniture. I'd like to create a tropical-Tuscany feel. What color should I use on the walls?

Kitty: For a true tropical feel, consider a soft blue ceiling with a pale green on the walls. Also, I'd add a fan in the ceiling, with or without a light. Be sure to integrate something in bamboo or rattan. Don't forget tropical-looking plants, whether they be bromeliads, ferns, or palms. Sisal would be great underfoot.

My daughter is a fan of the *Lord of the Rings* books and movies, and she wants to paint her bedroom brown with gold trim. What do you think?

Kitty: How much does she want it? Does she want it 100 percent? What's really great is that she's expressing what she really wants. And if she believes in it 100 percent, I think it's great that she has an opinion and that she's done a lot of thinking. I'd say go for it, but you need to keep in mind that there are all different kinds of gold trim and different ways of applying it. You could stencil her name or a phrase

from those books with a sponged paint in gold so it's not too, too strong.

Keep in mind when you're choosing the brown that it's going to look darker on the walls than on the sample. So when you've got what you consider the perfect color, I suggest that you go the next shade lighter, unless the room has lots and lots of windows.

In a bedroom, if you want to have one wall a different color from the others, or have two walls a different color from the other two, how do you know which walls to do a different color?

Kitty: The different color wall should be the one with the focal point—for example, the wall with a bay window or fireplace. If there's no natural focal point, it should be the wall with the biggest piece of furniture—your goal is to anchor it. If you have a wall that's an odd color with no reason for it, it might look like you ran out of paint.

I wouldn't really try to make one wall a different color in every single room of your house. It can be a cool thing to do in a room, but if done in all rooms, it might feel gimmicky.

I have a master bedroom that's painted a khaki color, with big white plantation shutters, a four-poster bed with a whitewashed finish, and a large Georgian fireplace with a mantel. There's also a salmon-colored marble surround and hearth. Should I put salmon on the walls to tie in the fireplace? Or should I go with my first instinct and use pale blue-green? Which would work best?

Kitty: It sounds like you have a lot of really beautiful things going for your room. I like the idea of the blue-green because it's a complement to the pinkish salmon of the marble. One color is warm, and the other is cool.

My bedroom walls are light lavender and white stripes. I went for a romantic feel, but my husband says it reminds him of Victoria's Secret. I'm unsure of what color fabric to use to tone it down.

Kitty: Your husband dislikes a Victoria's Secret look? Anyway, I love the combination of purple, lilac, white, and green. You could find a duvet cover, painting, or pillow with those colors. Then add some plants to pick up the green.

I have a large antique quilt on the wall behind my bed, and it has a lot of different pastel colors and an edge of bright yellow. I wanted to do that room in yellow and blue. I've heard you say that bright yellow on the walls could cause anxiety. Do you think a soft blue on the walls would be good?

Kitty: If you think bright yellow will really complement the quilt, paint that color on the wall behind your bed where the quilt hangs. That way, you're not going to be seeing it from the bed. Then I'd paint the other walls a soft blue or off-white. I like one wall painted a different color, but only if there's a good reason for it.

One of my son's quirks is the need to view the covers of all of his magazines and video games at all times. He spreads them out, covering the floor and his bed. His room is not very large, and he has a large water bed, cabinet TV, small desk, chest of drawers, toy chest, and even a coin-operated candy machine crammed in there. One wall is taken up with sliding closet doors. Any ideas on where I can place magazines and video games where they can be easily seen?

Kitty: My first thought was to make the entire room a corkboard or bulletin board for him to pin up his magazines. You can purchase cork by the roll. You can even cover the sliding doors of his closet. I personally did this in my son's room years ago when he was young. (See "Hands-On Project: Cork Wall" on page 241.)

For the video games, shelving units are the only way to go in a smaller room. How about one of those revolving racks you see in the library that hold paperback books? They are designed so that you can quickly see the covers of the books. Videos and games would fit there. You could install very narrow shelves along the walls, and then hold the magazines and video boxes with bungee cords along the fronts.

A quilt rack is another way I've discovered to display magazines.

1 Give a solid-color **tailored bed skirt** a new look by layering a **fringed blanket** or **crocheted piece** on the top of the skirt so the color of the skirt **shows from behind.**

2 Add color and interest to a flea market headboard by laminating maps and trimming the border with rope or thick cord. This works for kids as well as adults. If you spent your honeymoon in Paris, France, or Paris, Texas, a map of that region will certainly bring back good memories.

3 Do you have your grandmother's old shawl tucked away in a safe place? You can liberate the shawl from the closet by draping it over a round table. Cover with a round of glass for protection.

4 Make great booster pillows for kids' beds by cutting the legs of men's sweatpants with a favorite team's logo on the side. Stuff the legs, tie the ends, and you've got a pillow.

5 For a clever addition to a child's room, get a plywood or fiberboard round the size of the child's table. Glue LEGOs on to completely cover one side. This is colorful and a good base for a LEGO project. Spray the other side with chalkboard paint and have some fat sticks of colored chalk on hand.

6 To jazz up a mirror on a dressing table, twist together strands of faux pearls and glue them around the frame.

7 If you put your family photos into a collage mat with multiple openings, personalize the display by writing clever comments and memories right on the mat. The display or words and photos will help you relive the moment much more vividly.

8 If you see old quilts with damage at garage sales, you can have pillows made from the good parts. They'll look stunning on your bed.

9 Add a splash of color to a kid's room by gluing alphabet blocks around a plain picture frame.

10 Place textured or **woven wallpaper** under glass on a **dresser top** to add visual interest and to **cover scratches.** Change the paper for **a new look.**

Touches of red in a kitchen help **stimulate the appetite.** Freshly baked **chocolate chip cookies** are good for that as well.

kitchens

If you want to remodel your kitchen, you're in good company. I've rarely met a person who was 100 percent happy with her kitchen. Unless you've got a fairly new house, it's likely that your kitchen could use some modernizing.

But kitchen remodeling is very expensive. When you take into account all the plumbing, cabinets, countertops, flooring, and appliances, you could easily spend $30,000 on just a modest remodel.

It's possible that you are not going to be remodeling your kitchen in the next year. But the good news is that I have lots of ideas to help you make changes in your kitchen that are affordable and fun and will give you and your family a lift. And you can get started right now.

The easiest and least expensive kitchen update is new paint. Most kitchen cabinets and countertops are in neutral colors, which means they won't fight visually with whatever color you choose for your walls. And when you decide on the new colors for your kitchen, think not just about your favorite colors but also about the physiological effects colors have on people.

Remember that, in general, greens make food taste more appetizing. Reds also add to appetite, actually stimulating the pituitary gland. Gray can be a good neutral color for a kitchen. Yellow is a color many people like because of its sunny disposition, but bright yellow can add to anxiety if you're exposed to it long enough. Blue actually detracts from the taste of food. You wouldn't want a totally blue room, but some blue is okay.

Another way to update your kitchen without spending a whole lot of money is to redo the tile on your counters and backsplash. I did that in a kitchen where the dated yellowish tile just didn't work for me.

Technically you *can* paint tile, but I don't think it looks very good. To me painted tile looks like the equivalent of painting a car with a roller and a brush. When I replaced my yellow tile, I mixed together tiles of various shades of green with wide white grout lines.

Another problem I had with that kitchen was the dark wooden cabinets. They just didn't work for me. So I painted them off-white. It's very easy to paint cabinet doors. I suggest taking off the doors to do it right. Then wash them down with TSP (trisodium phosphate, which is available at hardware stores). Prime them, then spray-paint them using a paint sprayer, which you can rent. I suggest an eggshell finish instead of high gloss. I kept the same hinges, but I got new knobs.

If you do come into a chunk of change and decide to splurge on a remodel, be sure to consider all your options. For instance,

Decorate Kitty's Way

❏ The quickest spruce-up in a kitchen is a fresh coat of paint—on the wall or on the cabinets. ❏ Remember that **tile countertops are timeless.** ❏ Consider white appliances, which seem to go well in any kitchen. ❏ Remove cabinet doors to **visually open up** the space or to showcase colorful dinnerware. ❏ Tear out cupboards to make room for freestanding hutches—a **small change with a big impact!**

in terms of countertops, don't you think granite is starting to look a little dated? A common mistake that people make when they redo their kitchens is to go for what's trendy at the moment. So there are a lot of new kitchens out there with huge expanses of granite countertops. Mark my words, in a few years they will look dated. Remember in the 1980s when everybody wanted whitewash? We had whitewashed floors and whitewashed woodwork and everybody wanted light, light, light. And then all of a sudden it just looked dated. What I'm seeing a lot of these days is soapstone, marble, and limestone. But often these can absorb stains or are easily scratched. I prefer tile, which is always a classic, or a combination of tile and butcher block. Every surface has advantages and disadvantages; be sure you know what's important to you when you decide on a countertop surface.

Actually, I was once able to design a kitchen from scratch, and I'm very proud of it. It had a giant island, brick floors, and black-and-white-checkerboard tile. I also designed my own refrigerator. I wanted to have a refrigerator that you could access from the front and the back, from the kitchen and the breakfast room. So I had a

This kitchen didn't work for me. The most cost-effective way I could transform it was to **replace** the tile countertops and **paint** the cabinets. It's hard to **imagine** those are the same cabinets.

commercial refrigerator company create it for me from my design.

In general, I think that the most interesting kitchens are those that don't look like they came out of a box. If you're going to have some glass in your upper cabinet doors, you don't want them all to have glass. I feel the same way about knobs and handles. A clean, uncluttered look without any handles or knobs is a contemporary look, but it doesn't add much personality. What makes it most interesting is if you use a combination of a knob and a handle, but in the same materials. For instance, let's say you like brass hardware. For a small knife drawer you might use a ½-inch round brass knob. For a larger drawer, you might use a larger knob, or two knobs, again in brass. For the

kitty's style and spirit

Find Your Own Style If you like my ideas, it's my wish that you adapt them to suit your own style. Yes, I'm giving you recipes in this book, but any good recipe is altered to suit the individual. Some people don't like chocolate, so they substitute peanut butter. Some people don't like tangerines, so they use oranges. These are basic recipes that I encourage you not to copy to the letter. Use your creativity and individual style to create a home that reflects who you are and what type of family life you have. The new trim on my kitchen curtain is red and white check. It would be wonderful if you thought of something different, something that you never thought of before, and then let me know.

Even a **tiny efficiency kitchen** can have **character.** Just add shelves, warm lampshades, plants, and wicker.

cabinets, maybe a handle with a 3- or 4-inch spread. It's good to have variations on the theme.

As for the color of your cabinets and appliances, don't be afraid to choose white. White is classic. Of course, I'm not suggesting an all-white, sterile look. But white cabinets and appliances make it easy to change your color scheme when you feel like it without having to do a whole new kitchen. You can always update and modernize by changing the countertops, or knobs, painting the walls, or getting new curtains. What I've found is that people who have chosen white cabinets are glad that they did over time. A dark stain or a whitewash can date a kitchen, but a white kitchen from the '20s is still good.

My Home

In my current house, the kitchen was the weak link, though you might not think so now. Whereas the rest of the house had moldings, hardwood floors, and special features like a bay window, the kitchen was nothing special. It's shaped like an alley, and when I bought it, it had cheap white cabinets on either side. I figure the cabinets, made of cheap fiberboard, had been added in the 1960s. Virtually nothing had been done to the kitchen since then, other than the addition of layers and layers of vinyl and linoleum flooring, which I would discover soon enough. But as you know, it's not what I *don't* have that gets my attention, it's what I *do* with what I *do* have.

My biggest need was a good space for my treasured O'Keefe & Merritt stove. My solution was to have my handyman tear out all the cabinets on one side. And why not? Just because someone at some point decided to put cabinets in a kitchen does not mean they are there for all eternity. When I tore out cabinets, I gained room for not only my stove but also my red table with the enamel top and my big green wooden hutch. The hutch replaced the cabinet storage I had lost.

Above the stove, I hung a red shelf with stuff from thrift shops, most notably my collection of red-handled utensils. All this gives my kitchen the old country look I love. Your own color scheme or style may differ greatly from mine, but you can still tear out cabinets to make room for individual cupboards and hutches you have collected and that you treasure.

Of course, storage needs being what they are, I needed to retain the cabinets on the other side of the kitchen. But I couldn't stand looking at those bland doors, especially because they are visible from the living room, entryway, and dining room. They were too, too boring. I figured I'd be better off having no upper doors at all rather than having ugly ones, so I took them off and threw them out. (Well, technically I used the doors in my unfinished attic as bridges between the ceiling rafters so I could store boxes up there.) With the doors removed, my lively red, yellow, and blue dishes shine through.

To make the doorless cabinets look more refined, I painted the back wall inside the cabinets the same "elephant's breath" color as my kitchen. I recommend this anytime you take off cabinet doors, or even if you have glass inserts in your doors. You can paint the back wall the same color as your kitchen (leaving the cabinet frames and shelves off-white or whatever color you prefer). You can also put patterned wallpaper back there.

If you are a renter, you can still make a boring kitchen more special by taking off the upper doors of your cabinets

kitty's style and spirit

Be Free I never want to think that I've got a decorating issue solved for good. Of course, it's okay to think that I've arrived at some stopping point so I can get on to the next thing. But I always have it in the back of my mind that I can revisit it later.

Even after you've finished a project, give yourself the freedom to go back and tweak it some more someday. For example, maybe put another coat of wax on it, or add another detail, or rearrange it.

Below is the kitchen as I found it. It almost looks like a hospital. **Very antiseptic.** And at left is the same kitchen after I gave it my touch. **Trust me, nothing expensive happened to this kitchen.**

COOKIE IN EACH HAND.

I took the boring doors off my upper cabinets, and now I get to enjoy my colorful dishes.

If you're going to have **open cabinets,** consider adding a **contrasting color or pattern on the wall behind the shelves.**

and letting the colors of your dishes lighten up your life. This makes the kitchen feel more like you. Store the doors carefully, so you can replace them when you move. Instead of painting the back wall of the cabinets, you could use double-sided tape or pushpins to install pieces of wallpaper or shelf paper for a more temporary solution.

My floor was a big problem. It was covered with new white vinyl that didn't reflect the quality of the rest of the house. As I mentioned earlier, I was pondering my options when I came across a house that was being torn down just a few blocks away. I stopped my car and asked the workers if I could have the old flooring. I loaded up, then had my handyman install it (after I painstak-

ingly pried up several layers of old flooring). I then painted the wood floor with black deck paint and sealed it with polyurethane.

I wanted to have a table under the large window, but the kitchen is so narrow that a typical kitchen table wouldn't do. Because I already had my vintage vinyl bar stools that work so well in many situations, I needed to find a table that would be bar height. In searching secondhand furniture stores, I just couldn't come up with a table.

Then it occurred to me that I'd seen rented cocktail tables at catered parties that would be the exact right shape and size for my needs. So I contacted my local party rental company and, sure enough, they had a cocktail-height table, 28 inches in diameter, that

they would sell to me for under $100. Meanwhile, I contacted a wholesale bar supply company, where I found a similar cocktail table new for about $175. I opted for the used one that I could get that very day. I knew the base wasn't particularly attractive, but I didn't care because it was sturdy and black and blended in with my black floor. The dimensions were perfect, and my bar stools can easily be pushed underneath or pulled out.

The final problem I had to solve was trying to make my kitchen a little bigger, which I did by incorporating the service porch area. I took out the door between the kitchen and porch and then moved the washer and dryer somewhere else. I had open shelves made for my newly empty space, and I painted the wall behind them in a lively red-and-white-checkerboard style, which I show you how to do later in this chapter. And finally, to make use of every inch of space, I turned all the walls in the porch area into a corkboard. In a small house, you have to be creative. Want cork on your walls? Read on to see how I did it.

I found this tall table by calling a rental company that supplies cocktail tables for **wedding receptions and other parties.**

Hands-On Projects

I created my cork wall and checkerboard pantry in just a few hours. And so can you!

HANDS-ON PROJECT: Cork Wall

I have a small house, so I need to make use of every nook and cranny. Because my refrigerator is already covered with family photos in magnetic frames, I needed somewhere else to pin up notes, invitations, coupons, and other things I don't want to tuck out of sight. But where to put it?

As I was pondering my small pantry area, I realized there were narrow spaces in between door frames and cabinet moldings, but none of them big enough for a standard bulletin board. I thought that if I glued cork to the wall space I did have, on the narrow strips above and around doors and shelves, I'd be creating exactly what I needed.

WHAT YOU'LL NEED

---

* ROLLED CORK (SHOP AROUND AND BUY THE THICKEST YOU CAN FIND)

* NEWSPAPER OR KRAFT PAPER

* TAPE

* PENCIL

* UTILITY KNIFE

* SPRAY ADHESIVE

* STAPLE GUN (OPTIONAL)

* GLUE GUN

* RIBBON

A cork wall tucked between the doors and ceiling in my pantry gives me **extra space for organizing** my life.

WHAT YOU'LL DO

1. Decide where you want to install your cork wall.

2. Make a template of the area you want to turn into a cork board. Place newspaper or kraft paper in the space that you want to cover, folding it over and taping it down around the moldings and around the light fixtures.  (If you try to skip the template step and simply press the cork into the narrow spaces and then cut it, it's going to crack. You can do that with fabric, and with paper, but you can't do that with cork.)

3. Lay the template on top of the sheet of cork and trace the pattern onto the cork with a pencil.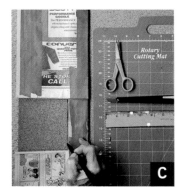

4. Cut the cork with a utility knife.

5. Spray the adhesive onto the wall and then carefully press your cut cork to the wall.

6. Put a few staples in the corners and top if desired.

7. Finally, to give your cork wall a finished look, use a glue gun to apply ribbon to frame the cork wall and cover the staples.  You can fold the ribbon on an angle to turn corners, smoothing it down with your fingers.  ❖

HANDS-ON PROJECT: Checkerboard Pantry

As you'll see by looking at my house, I like open cupboards in my kitchen. I like to see my dishes, crockery, and doodads. After all, if you're going to find treasures at flea markets, why not see them all the time? But that brings us to a challenge, which is making those shelves charming enough to hold our things.

I figured out an easy solution by painting a checkerboard on my pantry wall, behind the shelves. I did it by hand because I wanted the easygoing look.

WHAT YOU'LL NEED

* SANDPAPER
* CLOTH
* 1 QUART SEMIGLOSS WHITE PAINT
* BRUSH
* 2-INCH SPONGE BRUSH
* LARGE PAINTBRUSH OR SMALL ROLLER
* 1 QUART COLORED PAINT

WHAT YOU'LL DO

1. Clean out the pantry, tossing any spices or condiments you purchased prior to the Reagan era, and lightly sand the shelves. Wipe off any dust with a damp cloth and let the shelves dry completely.

2. I painted the shelves and wall behind them with two coats of semigloss white paint and let it dry following directions on the can. You might want yellow for your background, or light blue, or gold.

3. I recommend practicing your strokes a number of times on a large cardboard box to gain confidence. I wanted to achieve a "relaxed" look and found that it's better to concentrate more on continuous, consistent strokes than on spacing. I wanted the brush strokes to show, so I avoided having to go over the first coat/stroke. This meant that I dipped my brush into fresh paint after each vertical stroke.

4. Using a 2-inch sponge brush, paint vertical lines with your colored paint. Start at eye level and then work on the shelves above and below, eyeballing parallel stripes approximately $1\frac{3}{4}$ to $2\frac{1}{4}$ inches apart. Paint a line at either end of each section, then one in the middle, and then in the middle again. When all the vertical lines are complete, paint your horizontal lines. **A** and **B** Again I started at eye level and worked on the shelf above and the shelf below. ❖

I'd like to put a mural in my kitchen, but I'm not that refined of an artist. Is there something I can do to replicate a mural look?

Kitty: I used a lion mural wallpaper in my own kitchen. As you know, I like to shop at the top. So I suggest getting a mural of high quality, if possible. Spend an hour poring over walllpaper books at the paint store, and I think you'll be amazed at what you'll find.

I have dark oak cabinets in the kitchen with almond appliances. I want a more updated look, but I don't want to paint the oak. I thought about installing glass inserts in the upper cabinets. What do you think about adding decorative molding and antiquing it?

Kitty: I love the idea of adding glass in the upper cabinets. And there are so many interesting glasses you can use, like bubble glass, striped reed glass, and rose-tinted glass. When you start checking it out, the choices are actually overwhelming.

And why not consider changing the hardware as well? Have you seen the selection on www.myknobs.com? I've heard great things about that company.

As far as adding moldings, you might find the expense and bother prohibitive. As an alternative, consider painting the back wall inside of the glass-fronted cabinets a bright color like country blue, red, or yellow or wallpapering it in an interesting pattern.

I am crackling my kitchen cabinets, sponge painting my countertops, and applying wallpaper and border throughout my whole kitchen. There's already ceramic tile in between the cabinets. The drop ceiling has metal tracks, and I painted them and dry-brushed with bronze. My friends say it will be too busy, but I love busy. What do you think?

Kitty: Sounds a little busy to me! But if the wallpaper that you choose really ties in all these different techniques, it actually could have the effect of taming it and not really looking too busy at all.

I think that painting the tracks of the drop ceiling makes a lot of sense.

Do the major things first, like the cabinets. Sponge painting the countertops seems like risky business in terms of whether or not it will last. Why not tile your countertops instead?

I recently bought a 1920s bungalow. The kitchen has old, white metal cabinets, which I plan to replace with wooden cabinets, possibly white bead board or a light-colored wood. I need low-cost ideas for the backsplash, counters, and floor.

Kitty: I'm into classic old kitchens, and I'm actually looking for old kitchen cabinets to replace my cheesy 1960s cabinets. I suggest Formica counters and backsplash. For the floor, you can still buy natural linoleum by the roll or in 12 × 12-inch squares. Black-and-white checkerboard would be era appropriate.

We just purchased an 1800s farmhouse. Do you think it is better to go with maple or cherry cabinets, or maybe paint them and put a glaze over them to make them look old? I don't want the kitchen to look too trendy.

Kitty: I'd avoid maple and cherry. Kitchens in old houses were not very luxurious. Even if old manors were grand, the kitchens were plain. If you replace the cabinets, consider pine, perhaps waxed naturally. Or you could paint them. Nothing is more classi-cally country than painted cabinets. You didn't mention if the existing cabinets are original or if they were updated. If they were updated in the 1950s or so, chances are it's really going to be tough to make them look classic country. You may need to replace them. But paint some cabinets somewhere, for example, in the island or in a corner, to imitate a china cabinet.

You might consider putting an old cupboard in one corner that intentionally doesn't match your cabinets. This is a great country look. Don't forget to pay attention to the hardware. That alone can enhance the classic feel of old country.

Can you paint a laminate kitchen countertop? Is there a food-safe sealer to put on it?

Kitty: There are products that claim to cover laminates like Formica quite well. The key is really in the primer. I like to recommend Zinsser Bulls Eye 1-2-3 primer. It sticks to just about anything.

The only problem is that kitchen countertops are the most used and abused surfaces in the home. You're better off replacing the laminate.

To make a new kitchen look old, use old hutches like this in place of some cabinets.

My kitchen, breakfast nook, and family room are all combined toward the back of my house. My style is traditional, and I have wood floors, white cabinets with gold hardware in the kitchen, iron pieces, and a sage/olive green sofa in the family room. I would love to paint the walls of the breakfast nook a deep cranberry red. I also want to replace my countertop with a manufactured laminate. First of all, do you think the red will look okay if I have coordinating fabric to tie in the olive with the red? If so, can you recommend a color for the countertop and tile backsplash?

Kitty: I love the idea of the rich red in the breakfast room and feel confident that you can find a great fabric combining at least these two colors. Red is a very flattering color at night and feels very cozy to me.

Don't feel that your countertop has to relate in any way to the wall colors. Countertops need to be cost-effective and last (ideally) for many years. With white cabinets, you could go with white, such as a Corian, Surrell, or tile. If you wanted a pattern, perhaps a stone in the marble/granite category would blend well and still be practical and rich. Avoid pink or yellow-infused beiges. They will make your cabinets look dirty.

My French country kitchen is pale yellow with blue, red, and green accents. I have white cabinets. What color should I go with for the countertop?

Kitty: I love having butcher block somewhere. If it were me, I'd like to have a substantial area in wood. In traditional French country homes, one often sees a combination of tile and butcher block. If you choose tile, how about 4×4-inch white standard tiles with a soft gray grout (this is very French). Then perhaps on the backsplash you could introduce a simple border of French country tiles in a pattern or a solid color.

The success of a French country kitchen is achieved by combining many natural materials like wood, iron, and tiny patterned materials to give it a cozy look.

I love the look of formal draperies, oil paintings, and rugs in the kitchen. Is there anything wrong with this?

Kitty: I love the idea. Why not? Many of us think kitchens need to be spotless, sterile, and white. But that's not necessarily so. I did a shoot for my HGTV

show of a man who filled his kitchen with Oriental rugs over brick. His kitchen had a warmth and sophistication that was very appealing. You just vacuum the rugs in a kitchen like you would anywhere else.

Now if you had five young children who spilled a lot of food and drink, or if you were a gourmet chef and your kitchen got as much use as a commercial kitchen, then possibly rugs in the kitchen would not work for you. As for the formal draperies and artwork, you might choose otherwise if you had a lot of grease flying around your kitchen (like with a big wok operation). Fine silk draperies might be expensive to clean. On the other hand, you might have a wonderful exhaust fan that takes all this out of the air. Forget what's acceptable—if it works for you, do it!

I've been following your shows for years and have become a big fan of color. I've got a navy blue bedroom and a red dining room. I want to paint my large family room/kitchen some kind of green. Any suggestions on which shade I should choose?

Kitty: If it were me, I'd tend toward a sage green, one that's infused with gray rather than with yellow. In a family room and kitchen, you should consider a color that will be agreeable to most everybody. Greens or even blues that are gray-infused are easier on the eye, more classic, and more traditional than yellow-infused colors.

I've got all-white appliances, but now I wonder if I made a mistake. Nothing else in my kitchen is white. How can I make the appliances coordinate with the rest of my kitchen?

Kitty: You know, I don't think people even notice white appliances. I think they just fade into whatever color scheme you're using. So don't make yourself crazy about the white appliances. Think more about what you're going to do with your cabinets, countertops, and walls.

I don't feel the same way about black appliances. Black is stronger than white and really might not work in a country kitchen.

1 If the **handles in your drawers** are loose, don't replace them—just **tighten them.** Take the screws out, coat them one at a time with **white glue or fingernail polish,** and screw them back in.

2 Looking for a simple kitchen valance? Make a "rod" of rope or cord, and drape it with cloth napkins folded in half on the diagonal.

3 Do your drawers stick? You might get the feeling that your cabinets are old and worn out. But you can make your drawers work like new by rubbing a candle over the runners and contact points. The wax will bring your drawers back to their youthful vitality.

4 To create a virtual room divider, place a backless bookshelf between the two spaces, such as between a kitchen and dining area. Place books and accessories to face each area—cookbooks to face the kitchen, framed family photos toward the dining room.

5 Create a sparkling accessory of whichever color you want by stuffing a string of holiday tree lights into a large old magnum or vase. It creates a festive atmosphere on a bar.

6 Do you like plants in your kitchen? You can make a small clay pot way more interesting by gluing sphagnum moss onto the outside of the pot. Spray adhesive will do the trick. A colorful ribbon tied around the top adds a nice touch.

7 If you have a hanging pot rack, polish tarnished copper pots with lemon halves dipped in salt and display them on the rack.

8 Place a small lamp on a kitchen counter. If the shade is a warm color, it will add a coziness that your overhead lights can't touch.

9 Fill an old Coke crate with plastic utensils, cloth or paper napkins, and salt and pepper shakers. That way, you're always ready for outdoor dining or a picnic at the park.

To indicate whether the dishes in the dishwasher are clean or not, find a way to show that—either with a small chalkboard, a red towel hung from the handle, or red and green magnets.

10 You know that panel on the **front of the dishwasher?** It **can be more** than just a block of color to match your other appliances. **Here's what you do:** Take the panel off and spray it with chalkboard spray. Voilà! You have a place for **the whole family** to write their shopping needs.

What could be more simple—or more charming— than tacking a piece of picket fencing to a bathroom wall?

bathrooms

Perhaps more than any other room in the house, bathrooms need to function for your family. I'm all for good-looking bathrooms, but they must be user friendly first.

However, fads often influence what people choose, even when those fads take away from the functionality of a bathroom. Take pedestal sinks, which are a big fad right now. You can see why they're so popular—they're really architectural, beautiful, clean, and understated.

But they're not practical. People have towels, medicines, soaps, curling irons, hair products, and makeup that have to go somewhere. That somewhere isn't going to be under a pedestal sink. Plus it's a real struggle to keep the area under a pedestal sink clean.

The same principle applies to the trend of just having a sink bowl on top of a table. The negative space under the table can be stunning, and yet there isn't any room for stuff. And there's really nothing beautiful about a bathroom floor.

My prediction is that in 10 years people will be skirting their pedestal sinks to accommodate their storage needs.

So if I've convinced you to have a cabinet or some kind of storage space under the sink, what kind of cabinet should you have? Be creative and really put your personality into it.

I can understand why you don't want a boring cabinet. I think there's been a rebellion against the inexpensive home center cabinets that went into millions of houses. Many of these cabinets were very boxy and uninteresting. If you want the old-fashioned look that the pedestal sink style offers, consider turning an old bureau into a sink cabinet for that same antique look. That's unique, yet practical.

kitty's style and spirit

Be Productive When I'm doing my projects, I don't feel like I am wasting a second of my time. Whereas, if I'm doing a Sunday crossword puzzle, which gives me great pleasure, I think I'm wasting my time.

But when I'm reupholstering chairs, for instance, I'm not wasting my time because I'm going to have a result that I can sit on. Plus I'm able to do so many other things at once when I'm working on projects. So even if a project takes me a long time, while I'm working I can have conversations with friends, I'm getting exercise, I'm using my mind, chances are I'm hanging around my kids, I can be drinking a cup of coffee, and I can listen to music.

Here's what I think people will be doing with their pedestal sinks within 10 years.

When using an antique bureau for a sink cabinet, keep in mind that you'll need room for the sink to be cut into the top as well as for the plumbing. If the bureau has a top drawer, you'll lose use of that. So if there's no top drawer, all the better. Don't worry about the condition of the top. In fact, if the top is in bad shape, you'll get a better deal on it. You'll need to cover the top of the bureau anyway with some kind of material that will withstand water—tile, granite, and marble are good choices.

Another fad in bathrooms these days is to do away with medicine cabinets. A lot of people want to get away from medicine cabinets because they want to have larger mirrors instead. And often medicine cabinets seem to be somewhat dated. But consider the functionality of medicine cabinets. They're convenient, safe storage for medicines and toiletries that you need to keep out of reach of kids and pets.

If you'd like to have a medicine cabinet, but you don't like the look of medicine cabinets, there are some compromises. Some contemporary-looking medicine cabinets still fit within the studs, but the mirror and door are much larger. I've seen old-fashioned medicine cabinets where people have attached new, larger mirrors with nice frames to the old fronts.

When you're decorating your bathroom, colors can play differently because lighting in a small space can easily affect the overall look. Yellow—or any color that has a lot of yellow in it—is not a good color to have in the area where you're applying makeup. That's because yellow draws the color out of people's complexions. And you would tend to overcompensate for that by putting on more makeup, which you may not realize until you get outside in better light. This is less of a problem if your bathroom has a lot of natural light.

On the other hand, pink-infused colors such as peaches, corals, and salmons tend to be very flattering to complexions. That's probably why many spas and workout rooms have very soft, peachy pink, coral tones.

Decorate Kitty's Way

❑ **Vanity cabinets** are a must if you have storage needs in the bathroom. ❑ Use **pink-infused colors** to flatter complexions. ❑ Break all decorating rules when redoing a **small powder room**—just have fun! ❑ Use a tablecloth for an interesting shower curtain. ❑ **Hang a chandelier** in the bathroom—why not?

Powder Rooms

Now let me reverse myself on everything I've just said about bathrooms. When it comes to powder rooms, all these suggestions can be ignored. If you're lucky enough to have a powder room, that's a really good place to break lots of "rules" and really have fun. If you love pedestal sinks or if there are fads out there that you want to integrate into your house, a powder room is a great place to do it. You can have really dark, dramatic walls, which will make the space look even smaller. But so what? You can have walls of mirrors if you want. You're not going to be spending a lot of time in your powder room, so go for it.

My Home

My bathroom is an excellent example of making the most out of what you have. When I first bought this house, the bathroom looked almost institutional, with pink walls and floor and white fixtures. If I were building a bathroom from scratch, I probably wouldn't have chosen pink tile. But that's what I had, so I worked with it. I certainly wouldn't consider taking the tile out and replacing it, partly because it was in such beautiful condition. I'm grateful to the previous owners for their care of this house.

My starting point for the color scheme of this bathroom was the Laura Ashley curtain fabric. I repeated those pinks and greens in the striped wallpaper. So with these simple choices, I've set the tone for my bathroom.

One of the first things I did was put a skirt around the unattractive pedestal sink. I used the same fabric as I used for the curtains and I added a plaid trim for variety. This brought softness to the room and gave me storage space underneath the sink. I had a cord made of the same plaid fabric for the skirt closure. You don't really need anything to close off a pedestal sink skirt if it's held on with Velcro, but a cord like this finishes it off. You could use cording, ribbon, rope, or whatever you want.

Because I needed even more storage space, I added a small

Here's the hand I was dealt.

And here's what I made of it (opposite page).

wooden bureau next to the sink. It's not the perfect height, but it's okay. I also put a big mirror over the tub. I'm a big fan of big mirrors in bathrooms because bathrooms often are small and usually don't have enough natural light.

Along the ceiling line, I added dentil molding, which I got from a friend's house that was being remodeled. And, of course, I hung some plates in my bathroom. I have plates in every room in my house. I heard another decorator say that bathrooms should not have any food-oriented elements, not

colorsolutions

When checking out fabric to make pillows or curtains or skirts around a pedestal sink or anything else, check out the "wrong" side of the fabric. Sometimes the back of the fabric is more attractive than the front—it's often softer and more muted and may even have more character.

By taking the door off the cabinet, painting the inside green, and putting gold leaf on the outside trim, I turned something boring into something exciting.

Big mirrors in a bathroom are very bold, but they make sense for a small space without a lot of natural light.

My grandmother's **tablecloth got a new life** after 25 years in a linen closet.

plates, nor wallpaper with fruit images, and so on. I disagree. Plates in the bathroom feel just right to me.

A recent addition to my bathroom is a shower curtain made from my grandmother's tablecloth, which sat in a linen closet for maybe 25 years. It's very finely made, but it doesn't fit any of my tables. Because the sides of the tablecloth are already finished, and the bottom is already seamed, all I needed was a hem for the rod. So by putting in one seam and buying a $10 expandable rod, I've put it over my shower door, which is old and not very exciting. I've camouflaged that door and gotten a softer, slightly more formal look. And I'm using something that's dear to me. If I ever wanted to use it as a tablecloth again, I can always take the seam out with a seam ripper. For now it's being enjoyed, but not getting a lot of wear.

There were a few things about this bathroom that I wanted to change. One was a wooden cabinet built into the wall next to the sink. I just didn't like the look of it. Like the kitchen cabinet doors, this cabinet door was very plain. So I decided to take the door off and turn the wooden shelves into a display area for my collection of little silver things. I painted the inside of the cabinet green, and I put gold leaf around the outer trim. It was a fun project that really brought some richness into the room.

The other sore spot for me was the built-in soap dish above the sink. The dish was old and corroded, which is not unusual for a house of this age, but I didn't want to remove it and risk damaging

makes$ense

For a rustic look, replace your shower curtain rod with a length of wood the same diameter. You could also use a real branch from a real tree. This works with rods that are held up with brackets, rather than a system that uses a tension rod.

This soap dish was an eyesore until I gave it a decoupage finish.

the surrounding tile. I finally came up with the idea to decoupage it. After all, I don't really use it for a soap dish, but for a cup holder for my silver drinking cup. So a decoupage treatment would hold up fine. (See "Hands-On Project: Decoupage Soap Dish" on page 258.)

The crowning glory for my bathroom is the colorful metal chandelier with its covered lampshades and little crystals dangling down. (See "Hands-On Project: Colorful Metal Chandelier" on page 134 to see how I did it.)

My home has a small, second bathroom. Birdie's bathroom is possibly the smallest bathroom on the face of the earth. And it's extra challenging because it has two doors, one to the pantry, and one to her bedroom. I wanted to make it pretty and feminine but not overpoweringly so. That's why when I added a soft fabric ruffle to the walls (see page 260), I did it only on two walls, and let the other two walls give relief. The other thing I did for this bathroom was to create a skirt for the pedestal sink. This sink had metal legs holding it up and looked very dated. So the skirt adds color and femininity and also creates much-needed storage space. Then, all I really needed to do was to add nice accessories, like the bird-themed towel hooks, to make the space nice to be in.

Hands-On Projects

Even for such small rooms as bathrooms, I managed to make a few special projects. Here's how I made my decoupage soap dish, shaggy chic walls, and fabric-covered bins.

HANDS-ON PROJECT: Decoupage Soap Dish

The built-in chrome soap dish in my bathroom had been here 45 years—and it looked like it. Pitted. Corroded. Gross. Not pretty at all. I think every house of this age, built in the 1930s or 1940s, has such a soap dish. But they're very hard to replace without cracking the tile, and old tile is so hard to match. Unless you want to replace all the tile in your bathroom (which I do not!), you end up asking yourself, What to do? What to do?

I finally decided to paint the soap dish a rich green and then decoupage it using cutouts from two types of wrapping paper that picked up the spirit of the pinks and greens that dominate my bathroom. Then I covered it with layers and layers of water-based, nonyellowing polyurethane.

Of course, this solution wouldn't work if you use the dish for soap. If you are going to keep the dish wet all the time then the decoupage won't hold up.

WHAT YOU'LL NEED

* CLOTH
* MASKING TAPE
* WALL PAINT (YOU MIGHT WANT TO USE A PAINT THAT YOU USED IN THE BATHROOM ON THE TRIM OR CABINETS)
* 2-INCH BRUSH
* WRAPPING PAPER OR MAGAZINE IMAGES
* SCISSORS
* WHITE GLUE
* SPONGE BRUSH
* WATER-BASED, NONYELLOWING POLYURETHANE
* SANDPAPER

The vintage soap dish above my bathroom sink was not very exciting. But with a fun decoupage treatment, it's gorgeous. I keep my cup in here. If I wanted to use it as a soap dish, I'd put a small ceramic, plastic, or metal dish on the bottom to protect the surface from moisture.

WHAT YOU'LL DO

1. Clean the soap dish thoroughly with a damp cloth, and let it dry.

2. Use masking tape to protect the tile around the soap dish.

3. Paint one coat of your base color on the dish, and let it dry. Put on a second coat.

4. While the paint is drying, cut out the images you want to use for your decoupage.  Play around with where you want to place them on the dish.

5. Brush white glue onto the back of your images with a sponge brush  and set the images onto the painted soap dish, smoothing the edges carefully.  Let the glue dry thoroughly before proceeding.

6. With your sponge brush, cover the whole dish with several light layers of polyurethane, washing out your brush with water between coats.  (Bear in mind that water-based, nonyellowing polyurethane is cloudy when you first put it on.)

7. After seven layers or so, sand the dish lightly to take down any nubs or bubbles. And then apply several more layers for protection. ❖

You could call what I did to my daughter Birdie's bathroom walls a form of shaggy chic. I decorated with flattened layers of fabric, like gathered shaggy shingles. Or course, it's not for everyone. When a visitor wondered if the fabric shingles on the walls might get dirty, I said, "Well, I'm not frying bacon in there!" Birdie and I love it.

Birdie's bathroom is very small, with a tiny stall shower. Neither my daughter nor I wanted to use wallpaper. I wanted her walls to have some texture and to be a bit quirky. So I was looking through my fabric remnants and saw that I had some soft pieces in pinks and greens that matched the skirt around her sink. I thought of putting layers of pieces around the bathroom, but the colors were too vivid. But when I turned pieces over to the wrong side, I discovered they had the softness I wanted.

If this is too cutesy pootsey for you, consider other fabrics—washed denim, soft-backed vinyl, lace, muslin, ticking, or plaid wool. You could make a virtual valance above a window. Think what kind of spirit you want.

I didn't want all the shingles to be the same length, nor did I want the edges hard and cut. So I ripped widths of 8 to 10 inches wide, cut them in varying lengths, and washed them in the clothes washer. I didn't want cut edges, but I didn't want overly shaggy edges, so while they were damp I flattened them out and cut off the stray pieces. I continued to smooth them down as I worked because I didn't want them to stick out. For a different kind of edge, you could cut them with scissors or use pinking shears.

I stapled them to the wall, starting on the bottom. You can use heavy duty masking tape if you don't want to staple into your walls. I did two walls, deciding it would be claustrophobic to do all four walls. I did around the sink and windows and around the shower. This would be a perfect cover-up for walls with cracks or other imperfections.

At the very top, to cover the last row of staples, I glued on grosgrain ribbon with my glue gun. It was a fun project, and I made it up as I went along.

Originally, my daughter Birdie's bathroom lacked much interest. But this wall treatment of soft cotton shingles gave my daughter's bathroom a very unique, soft look.

WHAT YOU'LL NEED

* FABRIC (I USED COTTON)
* SCISSORS
* SEWING MACHINE OR NEEDLE AND THREAD
* STAPLE GUN
* GROSGRAIN RIBBON
* STARCH
* GLUE GUN

WHAT YOU'LL DO

1. Rip your fabric to the lengths you want for your shingles, perhaps 7 to 8 inches long and 1 to 2 feet wide. Varied lengths are more interesting, I think.

2. Wash the pieces and let them spin-dry, but do not put them in the dryer. They will be damp. Cut off loose threads.

3. Spread out the lengths of fabric and flatten them with your hands. Pinch and pleat each piece of fabric with ½-inch or 1-inch pleats and sew across the top of the fabric to hold the pleats in place. **A** If you don't have a sewing machine, you could sew the pleats down by hand. Don't try to make perfect pleats. They should be imperfect.

4. Then smooth the lengths out again and stack them up.

5. Starting at the bottom of the wall, staple on a layer of pleated shingles across the width of the wall.

6. Moving up, place the next layer so that the bottom edge covers the staples in your first layer, then staple that layer in place. The rows do not have to be the same length—in fact, it looks more interesting if the rows are staggered to create a more random look. **B** What's most important is to cover the staples in each row as you move up the wall. **C**

7. And so on up to the ceiling.

8. When you get done, you'll have just one row of staples visible, at the top of the wall near the ceiling. Spray the ribbon with starch to stiffen it and make it less likely to pucker when it comes in contact with the glue. Finish by hot-gluing a strip of ribbon across the top layer of staples near the ceiling. **D** ❖

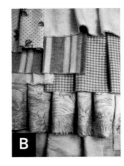

Covering waste bins with remnants of fabric you have on hand is an easy way to create something that is one-of-a-kind and custom made for your home. There's nothing to it. You make a template out of newspaper and then use that to cut the fabric. I used spray adhesive to glue the fabric on the can, and then I made the trim for the seam, the top rim, and bottom edge by simply folding lengths of fabric and gluing them on. Why fire up your sewing machine unless you absolutely have to? After that, I protected the whole thing with polyurethane.

Want that custom look for your bathroom bins? This is the project for you.

WHAT YOU'LL NEED

* PLAIN WASTE BIN
* NEWSPAPER
* PAINTER'S TAPE
* SCISSORS
* FABRIC
* REPOSITIONABLE SPRAY ADHESIVE
* WHITE GLUE
* WATER-BASED, NONYELLOWING POLYURETHANE
* SPONGE BRUSH

WHAT YOU'LL DO

1. Make a template for your waste bin using newspaper and tape. **A**

2. Use that template to cut your fabric. (I can't tell you how much fabric you'll need because waste bins come in all different sizes. If you wish, make your template, take it to the fabric store, lay it out on a piece of fabric, and buy that amount of fabric. Get a little extra for the trim. For more interest, especially with a plaid, you cut it on the bias.)

3. Using spray adhesive, glue the fabric to the bin.  It's helpful to tape one end on the bin and then work your way around the bin. I found that my regular spray adhesive stained the fabric, so I

1½ inches wide. Holding one end in each hand, fold the raw edges under.  Glue this strip to the side of the bin with white glue, pressing it flat as you do and holding it until the glue sets.

5. Repeat the process for the trim at the top and at the bottom.

ended up using repositionable spray adhesive, which did not stain the fabric. Experiment with your particular fabric to see if it stains.

4. Now make the trim. For the trim that will hide the seam along the side of the bin, cut a piece of fabric the distance of the bin from top to bottom, and about

6. The last step is to brush on several coats of nonyellowing polyurethane, letting each coat dry thoroughly before applying the next.

7. If you want, cover the inside with fabric, too, using the same template.  ❖

I need some help decorating my boys' bathroom. They are 7 and 10. The bathroom does not have any windows, so it needs all the help it can get to brighten it up. Ideas, please!

Kitty: How about a nautical theme? Find something that looks like a porthole. It could be a round mirror or even a real brass porthole. Hang it on the wall or even on top of the mirror over the sink. Paint the room a medium blue with white cabinets and trim. Hot-glue thick rope around the ceiling, doors, and floor for decoration. Striped towels and blue and white or red and white nautical accents would be great hanging on brass boat hooks or rods.

I have an antique bureau that I would like to turn into a bathroom vanity, but I just cringe when I think about cutting into this old piece. It's not a family piece, but I still don't like the idea of ruining it. Do you have any suggestions?

Kitty: If it really bothers you to cut into the top of an antique bureau, don't do it. Unless you find a piece that you're totally unattached to, you may not enjoy the results as much. Or, remove the top and put it in your attic. (Be aware that depending on how the piece is constructed, removing the top may damage it. Plus, if you remove the top, it will weaken the structure. The new top will have to be fastened on, not just placed on top.) Add a natural stone top with a porcelain sink, and enjoy it. If you ever decide you'd like to use the piece as a bureau again, you have the original top ready to go!

The bathrooms in our house have white Formica-type countertops. Is there a way to paint them, then maybe put wallpaper cutouts on and then waterproof it?

Kitty: Painting or decoupaging Formica countertops is probably not a great idea. In the long run it's just not going to hold up, particularly if it gets the standard amount of use. Replacing Formica shouldn't be terribly expensive. Check out the hundreds of patterns and colors available. Some are very beautiful. It's possible that an installer might be able to go right over the top of the old surface. That will be the least expensive way. Of course, you can always opt for tile, stone, or marble if your budget allows. But painting them is not the way to go. Sorry!

You once made a cover-up curtain for a storage area using a no-sew technique. I have a storage cabinet in my bathroom that is just crying out for such a treatment. Can you tell me how you did that?

Kitty: I actually have one in my kitchen. And I purposely removed the cabinet door to get this look. (Of course I don't have any small children in my house, and so I don't need cabinets that can be secured against small hands.) I just screwed a mini–curtain rod to the front of the cabinet. I didn't even need my handyman to do it! Then I just hung a crisp little curtain on the rod.

The medicine cabinets in our two bathrooms look terrible. They are old and corroded. I'd like to take them out completely and just hang nice mirrors on the wall. But where can we keep the stuff that goes in the medicine cabinet, like prescriptions?

Kitty: No problem with crummy medicine cabinets. Just replace them. No matter how old the house is, 90 percent of medicine cabinets are made to fit in between

framing studs. So they're easy to replace.

Medicine cabinets are easy to take out— just unscrew the two screws in the back that are holding your medicine cabinet into the wall. Then go to your local home improvement or bath supply store to buy a new medicine cabinet. You can often get a new one for as little as $30.

I like the look of this curtain much **better than a plain cabinet door.**

I'm trying to pick a paint color for the walls of my small, dark, second-floor bathroom. It has vintage 1960s pink tile from the floor to about chair-rail height and a gray border. What color do you suggest for the walls?

Kitty: Would you consider wallpaper? Perhaps a stripe to integrate the pink and gray? If you could find a combination of striped colors that pleases you, it would add zip as well as additional colors to play off of.

Wallpaper is a perfect way to **tie several colors together.**

1 **Silver and crystal** salt and pepper shakers without their lids make **sweet little vases** for fresh or dried flowers in a bathroom. Flea markets charge top dollar for shakers with their lids but next to nothing for **shakers missing their lids.**

2 Consider placing a small lamp on your bathroom counter, shelf, or cabinet. You'll want amber light for the most flattering and warm glow. You could find a glass shade or even a small Tiffany-type lamp.

3 If you have treasured linens that have been damaged in some way, salvage the remainder by using strips to embellish bath or guest towels. These may be your grandmother's linens that have been scorched or ripped, or perhaps a damaged piece that you found at swap meet for a song.

4 If you inherited card-table-sized lace tablecloths, as I did, you find they don't fit many tables. Use them in a new way by installing a tension rod across the lower part of a bathroom window then hanging the tablecloths over the rod on the diagonal. This is especially good in an apartment as no nail or screw holes are needed to create this treatment.

5 If you getting new carpeting in your bedroom, you'll notice that the carpeting under the bed is not worn. You can use that section to carpet your bathroom. First, you make a template by covering the bathroom floor with newspaper, cut and taped together to reflect the shape of the bathroom floor. Use that to cut the carpeting, which you can then tack to the floor with doubled-sided tape. The toughest part is around toilet. If you have enough gently worn carpeting available, cut two pieces, and keep the other one rolled up in the attic for when you need it.

The wall of the house creates **a sense of boundary,** and the bank of shrubs and the porch railing **create more coziness.**

outdoor decorating

No matter what part of the country you live in, whether it's an apartment in the city, a modest home in the suburbs, a mansion in the country, or something in between, you most likely love nature.

Think how we are affected by nature. At a gathering, the conversation often revolves around the weather. In winter, we wonder when spring is going to come. In spring, it's planting that's on our minds. In summer, we chat about how fast the grass is growing. And in autumn, we're dealing with the fallen leaves. Whatever the season, we crave nature, sunshine, and fresh air.

But the irony is we spend most of our time inside buildings, whether we're in school, at work, or at home. But I believe we're driven to find a balance between time spent indoors and time spent outside.

Creating an Outdoor Room

In this chapter, I'd like to help you to maximize whatever outdoor space you have, whether you own acres of land or rent an apartment with a tiny patio. When you're outside, you should feel connected to nature and all its beauty.

One of my favorite things to do is to create outdoor rooms. It's almost like adding an addition to your home, for a fraction of the cost. Very likely, you have the beginnings of an outdoor room already, such as a patio, a deck, or even just an inviting piece of grass. In order to create an outdoor room, you need three basic elements: a somewhat solid surface underneath (your "floor"), a sense of boundary (your "walls"), and something to cut the sun overhead (your "ceiling"). Let's talk about each in turn.

Your Outdoor "Floor"

If you have a patio or deck, the cement or wood creates a perfect floor for your outdoor room. It's easy to maintain, nice to look at, and comfortable to walk on. Both cement and wood can be dressed up, too, if you'd like. You can stain cement or wood to make it last longer and to change the color to suit your décor. The great thing is it's not permanent, especially with concrete. Nothing will be permanent unless you put the color right in the concrete when it's being mixed.

Here's something people don't often think of for their outdoor rooms: rugs. Concrete and wood can look—and feel—hard, and rugs soften that up. The simplest, most affordable rugs are indoor/outdoor Astroturf, which is made of a material called polypropylene or olefin. What's great about polypropylene is it's a synthetic fiber where the color is put into the fiber. It's

With a little effort, **a corner of the porch becomes a cozy outdoor retreat.** Notice how the colorful curtain lining inside the window **adds to the outdoor scene.**

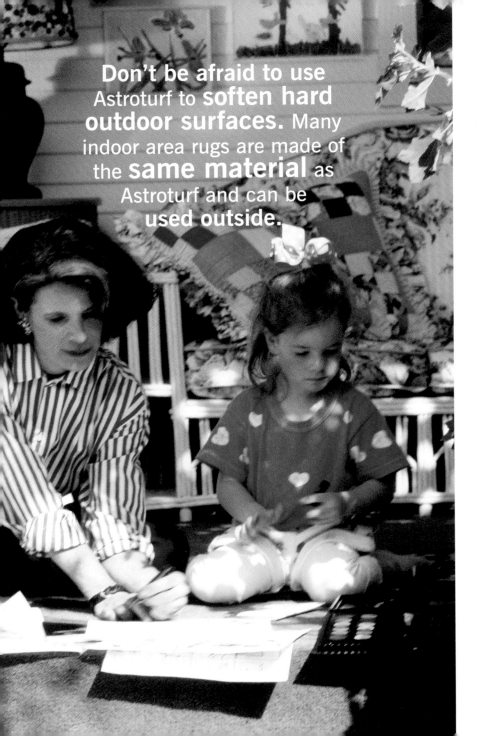

Don't be afraid to use Astroturf to **soften hard outdoor surfaces.** Many indoor area rugs are made of the **same material** as Astroturf and can be **used outside.**

not dyed later. So it's very moisture and fade resistant.

Many area rugs, even those used inside, are actually made of polypropylene. These rugs are affordable, and you can leave them out year-round in some areas. You can squirt them down with the hose, and if you spill something you can actually use bleach and it won't affect the color because the color is in the fiber.

A rug that you leave outside might not last for 20 years, but you might get tired of it by then, anyway. Indoor/outdoor rugs come in many colors and styles. You might even be able to find a polypropylene rug that looks like a Persian rug. If you see one that you might use in your family room or kitchen, it might also work outside.

If you don't have a patio or deck and you're starting with just a nice area of grass, it's a bit more complicated. Grass gets wet, it needs to be watered, and you don't necessarily want to set furniture on it. So you might want to build yourself a patio out of concrete, stone, broken concrete, or brick—or even build a deck.

Decorate Kitty's Way

❏ **Outdoor rooms** should have a "floor," "walls," and a "ceiling." ❏ **Stain concrete** or wood surfaces to match your outdoor theme. ❏ **Choose plants** to act as living "walls." ❏ Use broken-up concrete for **fences, benches, and pathways.** ❏ Drive through expensive neighborhoods for exterior ideas.

Your Outdoor "Walls"

The next element that you need to create your outdoor room is a sense of boundary. It's best to have at least one wall, which might be the back of the house or garage. Then you can add other elements to create a boundary on one or two of the other sides, such as a railing around your deck or a row of shrubs around your patio.

In the surfer's patio that I made on *The Oprah Winfrey Show,* we created the boundary with lattice, which is light and airy but gives some feeling of privacy. You can get that same sense of privacy by planting some shrubs or installing old iron gates. The idea is to create walls even if they don't go all the way up. Even outside, people want to feel like they're in a secluded (or defined) space.

If you choose plants to create your boundaries, there are a lot of foliage colors to choose from. In the 1990s, we saw a lot of gray-greens in gardens, a lot of herbs, and English garden foliage, such as lavender, thyme, and dusty miller. Now we're seeing more chartreuse colors in the foliage. I think the most interesting gardens have a variety of greens, from the gray-greens of herbs to the yellow-greens of tropical foliage.

There are so many options available. Consider hiring a landscaper for a consultation. I remember a landscape architect who came to my house and pointed out that my foliage had a lot of gray in it and so I might consider a house color with gray. I chose a color called gossamer, which was a brown with a lot of gray in it, and I had a pink door and a green roof. It sounds weird, but it wasn't. Personally, I want my house to have personality, but not to scream "over the top." His advice was sound, and it guided my paint color choices.

I decorated this small porch for a TV show. We created a feeling of boundary with a lattice screen and reinforced that with a roll-up shade.

Don't be afraid to add a mirror on a porch to reflect sunlight beyond.

I like a variety of greens in my garden—gray-greens, yellow-greens, dark greens—along with flowers. Here, my daughters enjoy the bench I made out of broken concrete.

Your Outdoor "Ceiling"

The last element you need for your outdoor room is a "ceiling" to shade you from the sun and protect you from the weather. You could install a lattice overhead or have vines overhead to filter the sun.

Awnings are also a nice way to create your outdoor ceiling, especially those that can be retracted in winter when you need as much light as you can get. Large market umbrellas are getting more affordable all the time, and they create a nice, cozy space underneath. For something more permanent, you can't beat an arbor overhead that gives the sense of a ceiling while letting the dappled sun filter through.

Outdoor Furniture

Wherever I've lived, I've always had quite a few pieces of furniture outside. One of my favorite pieces was a bench that I made out of broken concrete (see previous page). It was built into the side of a hill, so I wasn't able to take it with me.

I first observed broken concrete used for landscaping at my grandmother's house when I was a small girl. She used it to make fences. After I got married and got my first house, I discovered that I could use broken concrete to get the look of stone that I wanted, without the expense. I like the way a broken concrete patio or pathway gives you a solid base but still allows the earth to peek through.

You will need help to create something like this because chunks of concrete are very heavy. But it's especially worthwhile if you have a solid concrete patio or walkway that has outlived its purpose. Every time I looked at my bench, I thought of my grandmother.

If you happened to be driving around Mandeville Canyon in the Los Angeles area, you might see this house that I once owned. I had an artist trompe l'oeil the house numbers . . . and the three frisky pigs. They still make me smile.

I created this courtyard from broken concrete.

Can you imagine how this courtyard would look with solid concrete?
That's **way too much hardness.** This broken-concrete treatment gives
groundcovers or short grasses a chance to **break up the expanse.**

Yellow flowers planted in the front yard will help **friends find your house** easier.

Outdoor Colors

As with the inside of your house, the colors you use outside are important. Some colors of your home are pretty fixed and hard to change. If your house is brick or sided, you might be limited to painting the trim or changing the colors of the shutters and the doors.

Never underestimate the power of black on a house. If you want something on or around your house to stand out, paint something near it black. For example, if you like the brick around your house, having a black door will make the brick stand out more. The black door forces your eye to notice the rich color and texture of the brick. Conversely, if you don't like the brick of your house, having an off-white door and trim will bring less attention to the brick.

While we're talking about color, remember that the color yellow is always an attention grabber. This is especially good for the fronts of houses. Yellow flowers are a great choice.

What's nice about exteriors, especially in front of a house, is that you can find ideas by checking out what other people have done. You can drive, bike, or walk through neighborhoods and notice the landscaping, paint colors, shutters, light fixtures, and pathways. You can't just walk through people's living rooms to find ideas, but you can drive by their homes and see what they did.

Remember to shop at the top for outdoor ideas, too! Drive around the neighborhoods with the priciest homes. If you have a modest house with some Colonial or Spanish influences, go look at large, expensive Colonial or Spanish homes to see what the owners have done in terms of paint colors, ornaments, lamps, and landscaping.

Chances are that people who live in very expensive houses in the best part of town have hired highly trained and talented consultants, colorists, and designers to help make those decisions. By observing the exteriors created by those talented people, you glean the benefits of their wisdom without having to foot their bill.

My Home

Here are some clever ideas I've incorporated outside my home. My backyard is a private haven that I've created for myself. The garden path was inspired by a basket of old gardening tools I saw at a flea market. I thought they would look cool in a garden path. When I got home, I started to figure out how to do it. I had wanted to plant a lettuce and herb garden for some time. Trouble was, there was a lovely ficus tree growing in the only place where I could put my garden. Reluctantly, I had the tree removed. But to pay homage to it, I incorporated some of its curved branches into my pathway.

To make the pathway, I gathered leftover bricks, stones, and pieces of pottery from my house. I pressed those into the ground, along with some old garden tools. I even found some old, thick bottles that I knew wouldn't break. I'm delighted with the result.

Whenever I'm lucky enough to have a covered porch, I can hardly wait to turn it into an outdoor room. It instantly increases the places where I can sit and knit, where my kids and I can visit, where I can relax and read. Almost always, I use wicker furniture on a covered porch. But that's not all. I also use cushions and throw pillows, sometimes those made with old quilts. I have tables and lamps and rugs as well. I like to hang artwork and mirrors and have cut flowers. If you have a covered porch and you're willing to put some thought and time into it, there's no reason not to have a cozy outdoor room.

I am very fortunate to have a workshop in my backyard, which was fashioned out of the original garage to the house. But the door into the workshop was so bland. The previous owner was an architect, and so perhaps he enjoyed that sleek, unadorned look. But I like more ornamentation. So I found some solid, wood doors at a house that was being redone, and I had them installed on the wall outside the entrance to the workshop. And I had dentil molding installed above the door—the same type of molding that I

I saw a basket of old garden tools at a flea market, and that gave me inspiration for my **new garden path** through my lettuce patch. I also added bricks, stones, and broken pottery.

have inside my house. What a difference this has made! I love the look, and I love how it feels to go into my workshop.

People ask me if I'm afraid the doors will get ruined by the weather. Well, I guess if you lived in the tropics and it rained every day, you might have a problem. And there are no guarantees that stuff will last forever. To prepare the doors for outside weather, I filled the nail holes, used oil-based paint, and put on two coats of polyurethane. It won't last forever, but so what? It's not always about things lasting forever.

This probably won't come as a surprise to you, but I even have plates hung outside my home. The idea to hang plates outside came to me when I was pondering what to do about the stucco outside my new bedroom door. When I added the door to my garden, the new stucco didn't really match the old stucco the way I thought it should.

So one day I saw some big ceramic plates and I decided to hang them over my door. And why not? It takes my eye away from the stucco issue and gives me the good feeling that plates always give me.

kitty's style and spirit

Be a Free Thinker I think it's important that you forget about what others think and say about your décor. So often when you're in your early thirties, you're worried about what the Joneses are going to do. I'm here to tell you that the Joneses have messy homes every once in a while, too. And they have rooms that aren't quite perfect.

Inside your own walls, do what makes you happy, not what would make the Joneses happy.

Three plates hang outside my bedroom door. How uncommon!

I purchased a mirror for my backyard fence. The mirror is covered with cardboard on the back and has a vinyl picture frame molding around it. What can I do to prevent the cardboard from rotting off?

Kitty: I'd remove the cardboard entirely. It's only really holding the mirror in its frame, I suspect. So rather than protecting the cardboard, replace it with a weather-resistant material, such as aluminum or visquine (a heavy plastic-type material). Then seal the seams where the weather-resistant material has been added to the back of the frame with many coats of polyurethane.

How do you create a look of faux finish on the outside of a house?

Kitty: First of all, faux is a French word that translates as "fake." So faux finish is essentially using paint to make one thing look like something else. For instance, faux finishing would make flat walls look like stone, brick, or marble.

Some people use the term *faux finish* to describe textured walls or interesting paint colors or techniques. But to "faux" something

is to make it look like a totally different thing. I had my metal fireplace surround painted to look like marble. That's classic faux.

There are hundreds of books on this subject. But my favorite, by far, is *Paint Magic* by Jocasta Innes, who has been a mentor of mine. I've relied on this book for years, but it went out of print and for a while it was hard to come by. But this is truly your lucky day—the book has recently been reprinted.

Can you give me some advice on choosing colors for the outside of my house?

Kitty: Some of that decision depends on the neighborhood, but mostly it depends on the architecture of the house. I suggest you drive around all kinds of neighborhoods and observe what kinds of paint colors you see on homes that share your architecture.

Also consider the colors of the neighbors' houses. If you're thinking of a rich gray-brown, but your next-door neighbor's house and four others on the block are that color, that will affect your choice.

Plus, think about the impact you hope to have. Some people want their house to kind of blend in and fade away. Other people want to make a statement.

Here's an example of an exterior trompe l'oeil of shutters that I had painted outside my office window and above my garden.

Simple touches provide a country touch: shutters made of planks with clipped edges, and holes drilled along the top of a picket fence.

My home is stucco. So are all the other houses in my neighborhood. Most of my neighbors have very neutral, whitewashed looks. But I wanted something richer. Can you suggest an exterior color?

Kitty: If you have a tile roof, let that be your inspiration and guide. With a reddish roof, a gray-infused exterior would probably look off. It's better to go with a pink-infused color. But if you have a shingled roof, you might consider some kind of a gray. There are many interesting grays available. Then do something to kick up your trim, your front door, or your landscaping.

What can I do to make my house look country on the outside to match the country-themed inside? I live in Nevada and every house here has a stucco exterior.

Kitty: Without seeing a picture of the exterior, the first project I would suggest would be to put up shutters. But don't choose louvered shutters because that look is quite traditional. Have a carpenter make you some simple plank shutters. (Check issues of *Country Home* and *Country Living* magazines for inspiration.) Then add details like window boxes, wooden fences, and gates.

I live in a ranch-style house with a front porch the full width of the house. I have two twig chairs and a twig table on the porch, and I usually hang two ferns under the eves of the porch. But other than that, I am at a loss on ideas for decorating this space. Any ideas?

Kitty: Oh, my! You just painted a picture of one of the favorite houses that I owned some years ago. I'll tell you what I did: I set an old church pew on the porch for seating. I put dark green, country plank shutters on the windows. The front door was in the center, and I antiqued it by painting it a soft pink and gray and installed etched stained glass with a bird and tree scene in the door. On either side of the door, I planted two pink Cecil Brunner climbing roses, which I trained to grow up onto the roof, framing the door and softening the rectangular shape of the porch. For more seating, I had three groups of two wicker chairs, with a side table between them or a planter stand dripping with ivy and geraniums.

I loved my porch, and I miss it! Just talking about it makes me homesick for that house! Porch decorating is so much fun, so live a little! Porches are casual, so have your pieces reflect a more carefree lifestyle.

This is **one of the best porches** that I ever had.

My Victorian home is 114 years old. It's a two-story house, with gingerbread fish scales and scalloped trim. The roof is black shingles. Right now the home is gray with burgundy and white trim. I'm thinking of changing the outside to taupe and shades of purple, with black trim around the windows, white railings, and maybe a mauve color for the porch floor.

Kitty: I like everything but the mauve porch floor. I'd do black or gray on the porch floor; you have a lot of fantasy colors here. I like the idea of a black porch floor as an anchor.

If you wanted to consider another color for the ceiling of the porch, I'd recommend a soft, soft blue. And remember, if you think it's a soft, soft blue, when you put it up it's going to go darker, so start out very light.

1 **Add color to a lawn** by under-planting trees with **4-inch annuals** from the grocery store. You can **change them with the seasons,** depending on your climate, and give yourself and your family a **color lift.**

2 Concrete stain can give a walkway or patio a new look. I suggest Sherwin-Williams's H&C Concrete Stain. It comes in 17 colors.

3 Here's a good way to keep potted plants from leaking all over. Cut old sponges into squares, and cover drain holes in pots.

4 You know those shiny mirror balls that garden centers sell? You can get another interesting effect by placing a mirror in a metal frame on your porch or in your garden, perhaps hanging from a tree or a wall, to reflect the greenery and flowers.

5 Create a table for your patio by turning a large terra cotta pot upside down and adding a slate top.

6 Some stone birdbaths are so pretty it's a shame to waste them on birds (who probably don't have the design sense we have). Cover a gorgeous birdbath with a circle of glass and you have a perfect side table for a garden room.

7 You can update and refresh your outdoor furniture cushions by making slipcovers that tie over the old. Most outdoor chair pads are made to last more than one season, but often they don't look so good after a season outdoors. With slipcovers, you get fresh-looking cushions for a fraction of the cost of buying new ones.

Gathering Your Gear

The first thing I like to do at a flea market is **set a game plan** so I don't miss anything. I might go around the perimeter first or go **up and down the aisles.**

flea market shopping with kitty

I love flea markets, or swap meets as they're called in some parts of the country. I've found many of my favorite things at flea markets. My flea market pieces have such personality and really warm up my house. These items, such as old bookshelves, cabinets, knobs, lamps, and fabrics, have life in them; it's a history that you can feel. I love to shop this way. And so I thought you might like to join me on a flea market expedition to one of my favorite places, the antique flea market at the airport in Santa Monica, California.

In this chapter, I'm going to show you the types of things that catch my eye at flea markets and talk you through my purchasing decisions, as I consider the price and possible uses for each item.

Furniture Finds

During our day at the flea market, I found many great furniture pieces. I'll tell you about each of them in turn.

Metal Shelf Unit

At first glance, you might not see the potential in this metal shelf unit. You might look at the rust and the peeling paint and walk right on by. But when I saw it, it put a smile on my face. And whenever that happens, I stop and give it more thought. It's true that the paint makes the unit look dilapidated. I wouldn't leave it this way.

This unit has a lot going for it. It's not your basic table. It has a drawer, which is always nice, and a shelf. It's very classic and doesn't have a lot of ornamentation. It would be great in an office or you could use it in a kitchen, a bathroom, a baby's room, or even outside on a balcony, porch, or patio. You wouldn't have to worry about it being in the weather. You could stick it right in your garden, open the drawer, fill it with dirt, and plant petunias.

The simplest way to refurbish the shelf unit would be to spray

Think of where you could use this metal shelf: in a baby's room, an office, a kitchen, even in the garden.

Decorate Kitty's Way

❑ Recycle old furniture into **garden ornaments or planters.** ❑ Spruce up an **old ironing board** for a portable buffet server. ❑ Paint can work magic on things. To age a piece with paint, **paint a second color** over the base coat. When the second color is almost dry, wipe the edges and corners to reveal the base color.

it with rust-resistant paint. (It's always better to spray-paint metal because a paintbrush leaves marks. For the best job, stay at least a foot away when you spray.) Another idea is to remove the rust with a hand sander and polish it with iron polish or spray it with polyurethane. Then you can personalize it with paint.

This table has **potential.**

too fussy, you can use touch-up paints for enamel surfaces. To me, that just looks touched up, but you may have a greater tolerance for a badly distressed surface. If the top is not good at all, you could cover it with a piece of butcher block—for a price, that is! But this table looks pretty good, so I'd probably buy it.

Ironing Board

They don't make wooden ironing boards any more. You might look at one (see page 290) and think, I'm done with ironing. But maybe this ironing board could serve another purpose, maybe as a table.

Let's ask my favorite question: What does this ironing board have going for it? One of the things I like are the legs. It looks like it could be the span of a very contemporary building. I like the classic juxtaposition between the wood and metal. Because the ironing board folds up, you can store it. Forget about the padded top. That goes.

I think that this ironing board would be great in an entryway of a contemporary home, maybe sprayed with high-gloss black paint. You could get a piece of marble, granite, or stone cut for the top, to follow the shape of the board. I would probably wax the legs to highlight them. The fact that it folds up makes it useful for a picnic or if you're traveling around the country in an RV. You could set it out to

White Kitchen Table

This classic kitchen table reminds me of the table my grandmother had in her kitchen. I always loved that kitchen table, so much so that I bought one for myself not too long ago. Mine has a drawer, and the enamel top was in good shape. I needed only to paint the legs.

If you didn't know how to spiff up this white kitchen table, you might pass it by. To me, this is the type of old-fashioned kitchen table that one doesn't necessarily eat at, but works at. Can you imagine snapping peas at this table? Or cooling a tray of cookies? Like my table, this table has an enamel top with a drawer, like a forerunner to the islands we have in our kitchens today.

If you're considering buying a table like this, look at the enamel top carefully. I wouldn't buy a table like this if the enamel top were in poor shape. If the top isn't in good shape, though, and you're not

This looks familiar. Didn't Grandma have one of these in her kitchen? Look at this beauty in my kitchen.

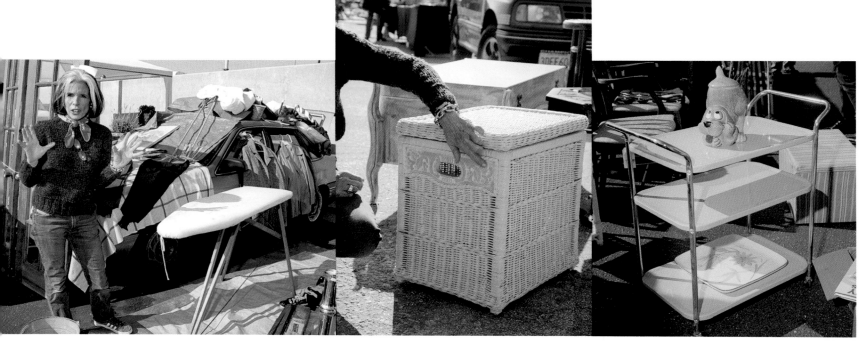

Ironing not your thing? How about turning this into a table?

You could change the color on this chest with one can of spray paint.

Can you see this cart in an office holding a printer?

serve snacks for visitors. Or you could use it in your kitchen, with two high stools, as a place to put your tea and crumpets for the morning. It's too high to be comfortable to sit around for a big meal, but it would be perfect when paired with a stool.

The proprietor was asking $35 for it, and I really wanted a deal. When he didn't come down on the price, I passed it by. Now I regret that. I thought about this ironing board for several days after the flea market. Not snapping it up is my one regret for the day.

White Wicker Chest

This small chest looks pretty basic, but let's see what it has going for it. It's a great size, large enough to be useful but small enough

to carry. It could be an ottoman, a hamper, a chest at the end of a bed, or storage for books. You could cover the top with fabric or glass and use it as a side table. You could highlight the designs on the sides with oil paint pens, or you could paint the whole thing white. A small chest like this would be good for people starting out.

Sure $45 might sound like a lot because you could buy something this size new for half that. But this is well made, tightly woven, and sturdy. Because of its clean design and classic look, it would look great in a lot of rooms.

Serving Cart

I like this little cart. In fact, I have a similar one in my workshop that I got at a secondhand store. This was probably made for a

You can **find** a place in almost any room for a **corner cabinet.**

kitchen and most likely used as a place to put the toaster or other small appliance. What this has going for it are the shelves, the wheels, and the fact that it's narrow, which means it can fit in more places. This cart certainly has possibilities.

This could be great in a small kitchen as an island, in a baby's room for diapers and supplies, in an office to hold your laptop or printer, or on a porch to serve tea and lemonade. This cart is in good condition, but if you were going to paint it, you'd want to mask off the chrome frame, legs, and wheels.

Corner Cabinet

I painted my corner cabinet with old-fashioned milk paint to give it an old-fashioned patina.

This corner cabinet reminds me of the one I bought recently for my living room. This is a little simpler, but it's in much better shape. I checked to see if it's put together well, if the joinery is holding up, and if the doors close properly. The cabinet is fine structurally, but it could use some embellishment. I'd paint the outside one color and inside another color. I painted the cabinet I bought a dark golden milk paint on the outside and a rich blue on the inside. Mine had rustic old knobs, but this one is nicer so I think it could benefit from newer knobs.

Wood Desk

This desk would make a good dressing table, like the one I have in my bedroom. You could easily paint it. I think the knobs are too masculine, so I would replace them.

You could have a mirror cut for the top. Simply make a template of the desktop out of newspaper. Then take the template to a mirror store and have them cut the mirror and polish the edges. Be very, very careful bringing it home and installing it on your desk. Some people place little felt dots on the corners underneath the mirror to keep it from sliding around.

An old desk is perfect for a dressing table.

I might paint a desk like this, but I wouldn't want it to look new. So a good trick would be to paint a second color on top, and then when it's 80 percent dry, wipe some off the edges and corners to reveal the base coat. That will make it look like it aged over time.

Wicker Basket

This wicker basket reminds me very much of one I bought at an auction years ago. I liked it because the top had been covered with canvas and painted dark green. This made it perfect for a side table. I store my extra set of slipcovers inside. (See "Hands-On Project: Canvas Wicker-Basket Top" on page 166.)

This wicker basket can do more than hold stuff.

I painted this old desk in my bedroom white and topped it with a mirror I had cut to fit.

A standard wicker basket takes on new sophistication with a painted canvas top.

Accessory Possibilities

As I walked around the flea market, I saw lots of accessory possibilities. Sometimes you have to get creative and imagine a piece cleaned up, painted, and used in a different way. The ability to imagine things used in other ways is an ability you can develop.

Bocce Balls

One of the first things I saw at the flea market was this plastic bin of bocce balls. I was instantly attracted to them. I like anything round, and round objects are hard to find.

The proprietor was asking $25 for the whole set of bocce balls. Any time you can get a set of something, that's good. One is nice, but a set is best. I love the bocce balls' primary colors. I imagined I could assemble the bocce balls in a bowl or basket. Or I could make them into bookends if I added a base so they wouldn't move. Or I could stack them and create a lamp. I thought that at Christmastime I could mix them with holiday ornaments in a bowl.

I was immediately drawn to these bocce balls at the flea market. Waxing brought out a better glow than I had imagined.

This old wooden ruler served a noble purpose and deserves to be saved and used in a new way.

I wanted the set, but I wanted a deal. So I asked, "Is $25 the very, very, very best you can do?" And he sold 'em to me for $20.

Large Folding Ruler

Old rulers are worth a second look. This ruler is old, it's nice wood, and it has a personality. It's timeworn, with a nice patina on it. The print on it is better than that on brand-new rulers. When you compare this with what you get nowadays, the quality is clear.

This ruler has performed a noble function, which in my opinion makes it worth protecting. And it can still be used today. In a masculine room, it would add a nice vibe. You could secure it to a desktop and use it to measure.

This could also be the start of a wooden measuring instrument collection. It would be easy to collect old ways of measuring, including rulers that are circular, linear, folding, American, and European. You could have a wall of them for a young boy's bedroom, which would still work as he got older and graduated from grade school, to high school, to college. They could work in a man's workshop, a hobby room, or a sewing room. You could use this ruler for decorative storage by nailing brads into it to hold spools of ribbon.

Iron Filigree

I'm always attracted to metal pieces. They can be delicate, or they can be masculine. They can really epitomize a period. Every period in architecture has a distinctive design. If you have a Spanish house, heavy ironwork is very appropriate. But French and Craftsman styles also have a lot of metal. From the simplest to the ornate, iron pieces can reinforce an architectural style or set a tone. Even in an apartment, they can add architectural interest.

What's so great about a metal grate? You can use it on a dining room table as a trivet. You can put a plant on it to protect a table from moisture. You can really notice the ornamentation of an iron piece when it's flat. Or you could hang it on a wall or lean it against a wall, because part of the charm is to be able to see through it.

The downside is that iron pieces are generally heavy, which can make them difficult to hang. For the average do-it-yourselfer, it could be very dangerous. You need to secure them carefully so they don't fall and bop someone on the head.

This iron piece would be great above a window in a library.

Solder a ring to a metal gate to make a **plant holder.**

Iron provides instant architectural interest. A simple iron grate on a wall adds sophistication.

Cabinet Knobs

These reproduction knobs (bottom left photo) are $4 to $6 each, which isn't dirt cheap. But they're painted metal. And even if they're not antiques, they're unique. You don't have to buy enough for your whole kitchen. You might want to just put them on your drawers or on a cabinet.

Don't discount knobs like these if you live in an apartment. You can install them, and then you can take them with you when you move. Keep the old ones in a drawer and screw them back in when you leave.

If you had two very, very large knobs with screws attached to them, you could put them on the top corners of a window and drape a piece of fabric over them, like I did with my dining room window.

I bought three red knobs for my green kitchen cabinet. Three isn't going to break the bank. The cabinet was fine before; it had standard, round knobs. New knobs added a little bit of personality and a little red on that side of the room.

What could be more appealing than a basket full of knobs shaped like cherries?

Just a few cherry knobs added a nice touch to my green kitchen cupboard.

Old Lighting Fixtures

These brass lighting fixtures cost $25 for the pair. Their style could be French or Colonial. But I don't look at them as lighting fixtures. I would take out the wiring and make them candleholders. They could go on a mantel, on either side of a picture, or they would be very sweet in a powder room. You could highlight the metal with an oil paint pen. These I would call very shabby chic.

Take the wires out of these sconces to make candleholders.

Japanese Rice Scoops

Look at these old wooden rice scoops. The proprietor said these are 160 to 170 years old. I don't know about that, but for $10 each, who cares? They can be used to hold pens, pencils, or brushes. This is an example of decorating with antiques, especially when you're starting out. You might not be able to afford a Queen Anne desk, but you can buy some Japanese boxes.

These **old rice scoops** would work in a **masculine office.**

This old bark cloth has many uses.

See these cane chairs? They need bark cloth!

Bark Cloth Draperies

These old draperies are made of bark cloth. This type of cloth is fashioned after cloth made in the tropics from the soft inner bark of trees, before fabrics were woven.

The draperies weren't cheap at $20 per panel, but they are from the 1930s and 1940s, and they really don't make drapes like this anymore. They're pretty indestructible. These are in great shape. This type of fabric is great for upholstery. These could be used around a dressing table, even though they aren't really very feminine, because they're already pre-pleated. Draperies can be good purchases because they give you a lot of fabric to work with. If they're old and musty, you can put them in the dryer with a fabric softener sheet or hang them on the line to air out.

Just a few minutes later, I came across these classic cane chairs, which were in really good shape. But something's not right with them. In my mind, these pinkish flowery seats are all wrong. You know what would be perfect on these chairs? The bark cloth we just saw.

colorsolutions

If your wicker baskets are looking a little drab, you can whitewash them instantly by adding a coat of white liquid shoe polish.

Globe

I like globes. They have that vibe of the classroom, of learning, of being young and finding out about the world. They make me think of our planet and of traveling. Globes have that nice round shape that I like so much. You could buy a globe like this for a few bucks and paint it. What could be simpler than painting a globe? How about a glossy black orb? You could even decoupage it. You would bring shape and color into a corner, onto a side table, or onto a buffet.

Does this globe make you think of fourth grade?

Colored Bottles

Colored bottles like those shown on the opposite page could be the start of a collection. They're generally not that expensive, and they're great vessels for flowers on a table, inside or out. An artist I know hung blue bottles on a tree to capture light. If you've already started a collection of bottles, put them in a window so the light shines through them.

I found this globe already painted at an art show in a park. I'm a big fan of buying original art like this.

Colored bottles always make me **stop and look.**

With the flowered quilt in the background, some shoppers may not have seen the potential in these hinged doors. But look what my friend Carolyn did with them!

French Doors

The proprietors said they found these old doors up in an attic. These doors are very old and a little pricey at $180. But look how classic they are. Can you see the solid brass hinges and "L" brackets? They've been painted over, so I wondered how the doors would look with the paint gone and the brass polished.

You know, for someone starting out, these doors would be a good first piece to decorate with antiques. They are narrow, which means they are flexible enough to fit in a lot of places. They could cozy up a corner, act as a mini–room divider, or make a wonderful headboard. Wouldn't these be great in a bedroom with lace panels? I'd love them with mirrors for a bedroom or dressing room.

kitty's style and spirit

Be Creative I use action verbs to describe my designing process. If you're looking at a room, think about how you can combine, minimize, magnify, amplify, rearrange, adapt, modify, reverse, substitute. For example, if you have an entertainment center that is too big to move and you don't have anyone to move it because it's snowing outside, how are you going to alter it? How can you combine it with something?

The doors were so fabulous, I talked my friend Carolyn Pisano into buying them for her daughter's bedroom. Carolyn didn't really see the doors' potential, so I talked her through it. She found a $5 lace tablecloth at the swap meet (talked down from $10). Carolyn cut curtain panels from the tablecloth for the doors and also for a table runner. She hemmed the curtain panels and attached them to the top and bottom of each door with small curtain rods. She scraped the paint off the hardware, but I thought the brass finish looked dull. I removed the brackets, and I polished them with standard brass cleaner and lots of elbow grease. It took 3 hours to get the shine, but it was definitely worth the effort. Then I waxed the doors with Briwax. I'm amazed at how good they look. This has got to be the buy of the day.

We bought this antique lace tablecloth for $5.

Paned Windows

Old wooden windows look good in any setting, leaning up against the wall or hanging on the wall. You could use these for photos of a family vacation and have mats cut to fit. Funny thing is, you probably would never use these as windows again. Old windows are too leaky and rattle too much for our modern lifestyles. But they are fun as antiques to add interest inside. They're especially great if they have stained or etched glass.

Coca-Cola Box

We all need more places to store stuff. This old box is no longer used for delivering bottles of Coke, but it can have a new life in your home. I'd love to see this filled with paintbrushes and pens or sitting on a picnic table and holding condiments, paper napkins, and silverware.

Old windows look most interesting when the paint's chipping off.

This old box could have a new use.

Medicine Chest

This wooden medicine chest was taken out of an old house. It could be a storage cabinet in a workshop or a spice cabinet in a kitchen. You could install it during a remodel. I measured the back, and it's exactly the right size to put between studs that are 16 inches apart. This is heavy and made of tight-grain wood. They don't make them like this anymore.

You could install this medicine chest in a garage between wall studs.

Metal Gates

You might see these old metal gates and think wistfully of a large old estate. And you might recall that you don't have a large old estate. Forget that. These old gates would look great on a balcony. They would give a sense of privacy yet let the wind blow through. They're heavy enough so they wouldn't fall over in the breeze.

Old gates add architectural interest to an outdoor room.

Chandelier

Metal chandeliers are very popular right now, which means people are paying more for them. If you get one at a flea market, get it rewired before you start working with it. Otherwise, if you painted it first, it could get banged up when the electrician is working with it. Or you could just take the wiring out and put candles in instead.

I have two chandeliers. One is in my bathroom (see "Hands-On Project: Colorful Metal Chandelier" on page 134). The other one was very inexpensive, and I bought it to hang on a chain outside above a table.

I added many special touches to my bathroom chandelier— the paint pen touches, the covered shades, the chain sleeve, and the fun crystals on the bottom.

Look at all of these **lamps!**

oneminutemakeovers

Who says curtain rods have to be boring or expensive? You can use flea market golf clubs, croquet or polo mallets, or even fishing rods instead.

If you wanted the chandelier to be rusty and look old, you could do a painted rust treatment. Or if you wanted to make it more sophisticated, you could use paint pens to highlight the leaves and flowers. When you hang it, decide if you want the chain to look new or old. It would really detract from all your hard work if you painted the chandelier black with added gold trim and then you hung it on a brand-new chrome chain. It would kill the whole look. Paint the chain black instead.

If you don't want to look at the chain at all, you could cover it with a chandelier sleeve. Obviously, a chandelier sleeve needs to be put on before you hardwire it to the ceiling because you can't slip it on later.

Old Tiles

I tend to find lots of tiles, both old and new, at flea markets. You might like them but wonder what you can do with a small amount, not enough for a whole countertop or table-top. Tile is scrubbable, which makes it good to use both inside and outside. If you have only one beautiful tile, you could use it as a trivet. You could glue pieces of bamboo, molding, or

trim around the edges to finish them off. But tile is really meant to accent a larger object and is often set inside something else. A pretty tile could be the centerpiece of a mosaic. You wouldn't want to break the tile, but you could put other broken pieces around it and then use the mosaic on top of a table that would be outside.

It's a major project, but if you were redoing your fireplace, you could set a bunch of tiles into the wet plaster. I once put a plate into wet plaster in my bedroom. Obviously, you wouldn't do that with a precious piece.

The ideal place for a few tiles is on a wooden or metal tray. Many trays already have lips to cover the tiles' raw edges. If the tiles don't perfectly fill up the whole tray, you can buy thinner tiles to put around the edges as a border. Glue the tiles down with hot glue. Or try a product often called All-in-One, which is both a grout and an adhesive. First you put a thin layer of the material on the bottom of the tray to secure the tiles. After it's dried completely, you use the same product to grout in between the tiles. Or you can use your glue gun to glue the tiles down, and then add grout. If the tray is going to be used outside, sanded grout would be a good choice. The thicker the grout lines, the better sanded grout holds up.

How often have you walked past appealing old tiles without any idea how to use them?

Flea Market Fundamentals

Follow my tips to have your most successful flea market adventure ever.

- Bring a cart or basket with wheels to carry your treasures.

- Bring bungee cords instead of rope or cord and scissors to strap treasures in or on your cart.

This French shopping basket holds firewood in between its flea market duties.

- It's always a good idea to bring a tape measure. You might want to measure a piece of furniture to see if it will fit in your space.

- If you're shopping for something specific, such as antique draperies for windows or fabric to cover chair seats, bring the dimensions with you.

- Bring photos of something you're trying to match or coordinate with. Conversely, bring a Polaroid or digital camera to take shots of something you might want to consider buying but aren't ready to. Chances are the item will sell that day, but you might get lucky and find it at next week's flea market. Get business cards and contact info for later.

- Bring lots of dollar bills. It's easier if vendors don't have to make change.

- Don't be afraid to bargain over prices. Most vendors are prepared to bargain. In fact, they expect it. But a lot of shoppers are shy about it. Safe things to ask are, "Would you be willing to take . . .?" or

I got these $25 bocce balls for $20.

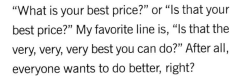

Don't be afraid to touch things at a flea market. I saw this gateleg table and thought it would be much more interesting upside down.

So I flipped it. It folds up, so it's easy to transport.

You could top it with marble or glass.

"What is your best price?" or "Is that your best price?" My favorite line is, "Is that the very, very, very best you can do?" After all, everyone wants to do better, right?

- Arrive early. The sharp people and the dealers (who will resell the stuff they buy) always get there first thing in the morning.

- Stay late. You're going to get the biggest bargains at the end of the day, es-pecially on large items that vendors don't want to load back up and haul away.

- If you're looking for bigger things, have a truck ready to take large pieces home. Don't expect the seller to be available or even willing to help schlep it.

- If you buy something that's not easy to carry around the flea market with you as you continue shopping, ask the vendor to put a "sold" sign on the item. You can come back to pick it up when you're ready to leave.

- Even if you don't have a specific pur-chase in mind, go to flea markets that specialize in antiques to educate your eye, and ask tons of questions. Every-one is in a talkative mood at a flea market.

A clean, organized, well-equipped work area makes the pleasure I get from doing projects, such as the lace-painted chest, even **more pleasurable.**

organizing, tools, and resources

When you do a lot of projects, you come to know the best products and tools and the ways to organize them. Where would I be without my staple gun? Lost, that's where. Or my paint pens? What a painful thought. And if I couldn't turn to the Country Curtains catalog, my life would be poorer for it. In this chapter, I'd like to share with you the products I love, the tools I cherish, and the systems I've developed to keep them all in order.

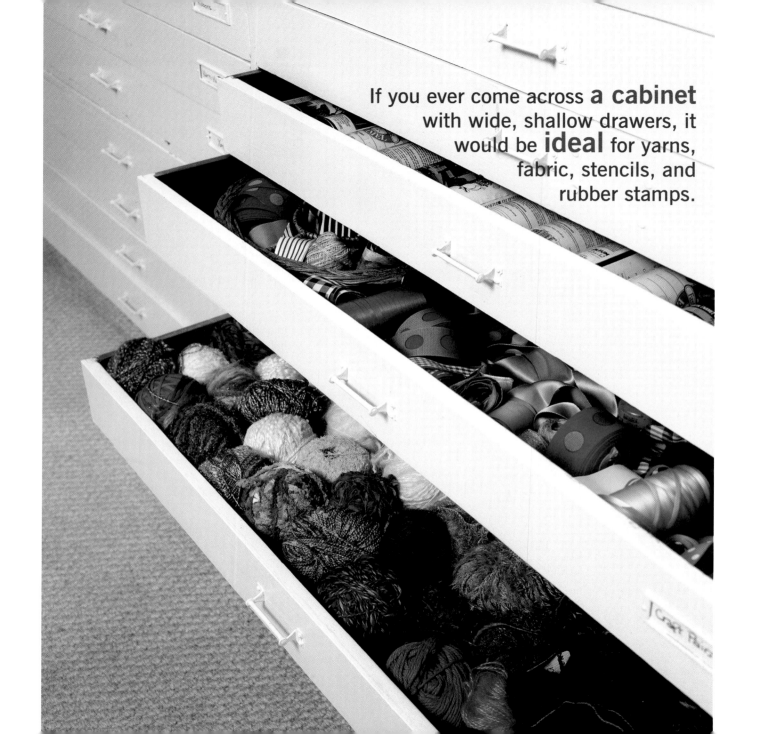

If you ever come across **a cabinet** with wide, shallow drawers, it would be **ideal** for yarns, fabric, stencils, and rubber stamps.

Organizing

When you adopt a hands-on approach to making your home beautiful and comfortable, you start collecting a lot of supplies and tools, such as buttons, fabric, glue guns, knitting needles, paint pens, rubber stamps, stencils, and on and on. Unless you organize these things well, you'll find yourself getting frustrated when you can't find what you're looking for.

With some time and energy, you can arrange your items to put them at your fingertips when you are inspired and need them.

Here are some ideas that I've come up with for organizing my things. I'm not saying these are the best ways for you to organize. But perhaps you will be encouraged by these ideas to create your own solutions.

Old wooden drawers, crates, and boxes are perfect for keeping paints, paint pens, and knitting supplies organized and easy to carry around.

Tools

To be handy around the house, you need tools. Without the right tools on hand, you'll find yourself stymied or the projects you attempt will be so difficult that you'll get discouraged and give up. Here are some of the tools I like to have on hand.

CHISEL: I have a lot of fun with my chisel. Have you ever pried up old flooring? I have.

GLUE GUN: Oh, how I love my glue gun. I've used it for so many projects. Just plug it in, and you've got hot glue in minutes.

HAMMER: Buy a hammer with a claw for removing nails.

HEAVY-DUTY STAPLE GUN: This is a tool I could not live without. Don't get a cheap one. You might pay $20 or more for a good one, but they pay for themselves in one upholstery project.

NEEDLE-NOSE PLIERS: A must-have tool. Imagine how torturous it would be to pull up staples from the bottom of a chair without pliers. You'd never attempt to re-cover another chair without a pair of needle-noses.

OIL PAINT PENS: Oil paint pens are beyond wonderful. They are a true color, and not a

You might have to pay $15 to $20 for a sea sponge, but I think they're well worth it.

watered-down felt pen. Get one in every color! (Gold is the most popular.)

SCREWDRIVERS: Make sure that you have both straight-head and Phillips-head screwdrivers.

SEA SPONGE: For any type of sponged paint treatment, you'll want a natural sea sponge. They are heads above synthetic sponges for getting a natural look.

oneminutemakeovers

Ever think of placing a bookcase on its side? Depending on its height and width, you could end up with a sofa table or a low bench with compartments for boots, perfect for the back porch.

Resources

Here's something you might not know: When I'm doing TV shows, I'm often prohibited from mentioning any products or resources by name. If I like Elmer's glue, for instance, I'm only allowed to refer to it as white glue. I guess that's so no other advertisers feel left out.

But now that I've written my own book, I can finally mention some of my favorite products and resources. Here's a sampling.

Books and Magazines

PAINT MAGIC BY JOCASTA INNES: I recommend this book more than any other. I idolize Jocasta, and I was able to go to England to shoot a show in her workshop. I also shot with her in San Francisco. Her book *Paint Magic* has been reissued by Frances Lincoln. Check out her Web site, www.jocastainnesdesign.com.

PAINTED FURNITURE PATTERNS BY JOCASTA INNES: This is another favorite book of mine. Unfortunately, it's out of print, but check on www.amazon.com because they often have out-of-print books. The book was originally published by Penguin USA.

COUNTRY LIVING: This is one of my very favorite magazines. The editors understand cozy and comfortable homes. They are able to incorporate old things in new and useful ways. You can reach them at www.countryliving.com.

VERANDA: This is also another very good magazine, with beautiful photographs. You can reach them at www.veranda.com.

Supplies

BRIWAX: This is one of my most favorite products. It's made of natural beeswax and carnauba wax and will help to protect furniture and other pieces and give them a warm glow. It comes in a variety of colors. You can find it in the furniture polish section or paint department of a good hardware store.

I keep mentioning this product, but I swear I don't own stock in the company nor do I work undercover in their public relations department. I just want you to get the same glow on your furniture that I enjoy.

www.briwax.com
(800) 683-6945

CHAROLETTE FORD TRUNKS: This is my favorite resource for restoring old trunks. You'll find how-to books and videos, plus a large assortment of replacement parts and supplies like leather handles, hinges, and other hardware.

www.charolettefordtrunks.com
(800) 553-2649
PO Box 495, Dumas, TX 79029

Invaluable Resources: Handymen

I'm handy, and perhaps you're handy. But even handy people like you and me need help from time to time. I don't claim to be an expert on everything, and I don't like doing certain things. I'm intimidated by electricity. I don't have a problem sawing, but I don't have a table saw. I don't care for hanging wallpaper, and I'm not a good plumber. For me to get these things done in my house, I need a handyman or handywoman I can count on, and I don't hesitate to call one.

HOW TO FIND A HANDYMAN

Having a good handyman is wonderful. But finding one takes some care. The best way is by word of mouth, by getting a reference from someone you know who has used this person and can vouch for him or her.

Another good way to find a handyman is through real estate agents. A lot of time real estate agents know handymen because they will often need small thing fixed in houses for sale.

Consider asking the shop teacher at your local high school for a recommendation. Chances are good he can recommend a handyman. Or check with your local hardware store. They might even keep a list of good people or contractors who buy supplies on a regular basis. For instance, there is a place around me that sells stone. They have a list of installers they know and trust.

I recommend a company called Case Handyman, which I learned about when I did *The Oprah Winfrey Show*. The franchise is in certain parts of the country, and they all are bonded. In other areas of the country, there's another franchise called Handyman Connection, which employs part-time tradesmen.

When I wanted my handyman to install these curtain rod holders, I had several tasks for him to do, to make the best use of his trip to my house.

Think twice before you call a handyman from a newspaper ad. At the very least, ask for *and call* several local references before you let that person come over. I think it's still a risk, so proceed cautiously.

HOW TO WORK WITH A HANDYMAN

The best way to work with a handyman is to wait until you have a list of at least five or six things to do. Maybe you want your screen fixed, have a drawer that sticks, bought new carpeting and need the bottoms of your doors planed, and need some electrical work done. What you need is a jack-of-more-than-one-trade handyman.

Gather your list and offer it to the handyman. You're likely to get a better deal that way; if he charges by the hour, often there's a minimum charge. And sometimes a handyman can do a lot in an hour.

For example, the last time my handyman came over he brought the wood to repair my corner cabinet, and he picked up hardware to install my curtain rod holders. When he was here, I had him cut four curtain rods, install the hardware, and fix something in the guesthouse.

CLAIRE MURRAY RUGS: This is a great resource for hooked rugs and kits.

www.clairemurray.com

(800) 252-4733

PO Box 390, Ascutney, VT 05030

COUNTRY CURTAINS: I swear by this company, where I buy a lot of my curtains from catalogs or online. The company is located in Stockbridge, Massachusetts, and has been in business since 1956. I've done a shoot there, so I've met the folks. Their curtains are affordable, and they'll help you figure out all different kinds of options. They're great about sending samples, and you can buy extra fabric for making matching pillows.

www.countrycurtains.com

(800) 456-0321

GINGERBREAD TRIM COMPANY: I did a show once on putting up faux beams, and I got a lot of inquiries afterward from interested viewers. The beams are made of Styrofoam, so they're light, but they look like the real thing. The company also has columns, arches, signs, and much more.

www.gingerbreadonline.com

(941) 743-8556

PO Box 496200, Port Charlotte, FL 33980

THE OLD-FASHIONED MILK PAINT COMPANY: Whenever you want the look of an old-fashioned finish, you can't beat milk

paint. It's made with real milk, or buttermilk, and often has natural pigments from the earth. I prefer the premixed type, rather than the kind you have to mix from powder. The colors are generally delicious looking.

www.milkpaint.com

(866) 350-6455

436 Main Street, Groton, MA 01450

PAINT PENS: Throughout this book, I've gone on and on about paint pens. Let me continue here. As you may know, working with oil paint can be a hassle, mainly because of the mineral spirits or turpentine that's required for cleaning up. Paint pens are easier to use, so there's little or no cleanup.

I love paint pens for highlighting furniture, lamps, accessories, and anything else I can think of.

Uchida

www.uchida.com

(800) 541-5877

3535 Del Amo Boulevard, Torrance, CA 90503

RESTORATION HARDWARE: These stores and the catalog and online operation have mushroomed in the past few years, and it's not hard to see why. People are looking for the old-fashioned look for their homes, and Restoration Hardware is the place to find everything from bathtubs to cabinet knobs to lamps and furniture.

www.restorationhardware.com

(800) 762-1005

Here's my idea of a **good time:** a cozy porch, a collection of **paint pens,** and an object that needs **some details highlighted.**

SOLATUBE: We all need more light in our homes, it seems, but adding windows or a big skylight is sometimes impossible. Solatubes are round, cylinder-type skylights, usually about 12 inches around, that are easy to install to reflect light from the roof and channel it into your room.

www.solatube.com

(800) 966-7652

2210 Oak Ridge Way, Vista, CA 92081

SQUEEEEEK NO MORE: If you have squeaky floors, this ingenious repair kit works right through carpeting and hardwood floors to provide instant squeak relief. All you need is a power drill. Many people must have squeaky floors because I get a lot of letters and e-mails asking me for the name of this product.

www.squeaknomore.com

(800) 459-8428

ZINSSER BULLS EYE 1-2-3 PRIMER: This is a paint primer that really works well. So often, you need to prime something before you paint it. But if you don't use a good primer that really covers well, all efforts might be wasted.

I've had very good luck with Zinsser, but I've also used a product called KILZ with great results.

www.zinsser.com

(732) 469-8100

173 Belmont Drive, Somerset, NJ 08875

or

www.kilz.com

(866) 774-6371

3135 Old Highway M

Imperial, MO 63052

Kitty's Story

I was raised on a little island south of Detroit, called Grosse Isle, which is French for "large island." I was the oldest of three children. Because of family circumstances, including my mother's death when I was 7, I spent a great deal of time with my grandparents.

My father's mother and father lived on our little island in a beautiful English Tudor house right on the water. I considered it a mansion when I was young, though when I look back I realize it wasn't so big. I spent a lot of time there, and it was my refuge.

My grandfather's father came from Ireland; my grandfather was a self-made man and was in the real estate business. They had their house designed and built on a large piece of land. It was a real landmark house on Grosse Isle. My grandmother was very proud of the furnishings in the house, especially her antiques that she had purchased over the years at auctions.

My mother's mother and father lived in a big, traditional house in Grosse Pointe, Michigan. It's a two-story brick house I remember very well. My maternal grandmother grew up with antiques, unlike my fraternal grandmother, and so she didn't value them. She had a few key pieces, but most of the furniture in her house was new. She found antiques to be stuffy and boring.

A Handy Grandmother, A Dandy Grandmother

My father's mother was a handy woman. She taught me how to knit. She was a passionate gardener. She introduced me to the cultural arts, the opera, and the symphony. She also loved to make jams and jellies. My grandmother enjoyed having me around because she had raised sons and never had a daughter. She was very matter-of-fact, and she believed that education was of paramount importance. She was very gracious and generous with her sons and grandchildren, and she offered to pay for 4 years of college or boarding school for every one of her grandchildren.

My other grandmother, my mother's mother, was raised with a silver spoon in her mouth. She wasn't at all handy. She never ironed or cleaned, but she was full of love, deeply Christian, and she spoiled me.

I loved my grandmother and made pillows out of her needlepoint seat covers.

The antiques in this grandmother's house had come down through generations. Unlike my father's family, she was from a family of all females. She had five sisters, and none of them ever worked in any way. The time I spent at her house was very different than the time I spent at my other grandmother's house. I could count on this grandmother to always buy me beautiful clothes. She had no interest in ever providing anything basic, only the "gravy."

I guess you could say that one of my grandmothers was meat and potatoes and the other was the dessert. I had the best of both worlds. Nevertheless, being a motherless child, I felt at a young age that I couldn't depend on anybody. Perhaps this contributed to who I would become later on—a woman who can make things happen for herself and her family.

Retail Detail

I was sent off to boarding school for high school: all girls, all nuns. The boarding school was filled with antiques and fine things, and my eye became more educated. After I turned 14, every Christmas and summer I commuted to work with my dad to the beautiful, fine department store in downtown Detroit where he was an executive. I was on the teen panel and the college board, and I worked in the department that catered to young women. These young women came in to buy their fall wardrobes of sweaters, kilts, and blazers.

The store was like Saks with furniture. Being surrounded with clever displays, color, scale, and balance was an education in interior design and merchandising. One summer I was assigned to the fabric department (although not a sewer myself, not then, not now), and they set me up with a desk in the front of the department as an "expert." People asked me for sewing advice, such as how to coordinate a pattern for a dress with various fabrics.

I majored in marketing and retailing at Michigan State, hoping to follow in my father's footsteps as an executive, merchandise coordinator, or buyer at a fine retail store. Even at college I worked part-time at a retail store. This time it was a men's clothing store, where I learned a lot about men's striped ties, and Shetland V-necked sweaters, and even measured a few inseams of football players.

European Adventure

After graduating from college, I sold most of my clothes, stocks, and even my car and moved to Europe. I had a finite amount of dollars, and after about 4 months I ran out of money and needed to get a job. My first job, with a fresh bachelor's of science degree, was as a chambermaid in Switzerland, for which I made $100 a month. Of course, room and board were included, and we had 3 hours off every day to ski.

I spent more than 3 years in Europe and traveled to many countries. I worked in several different countries over the years, and I liked spending enough time in a country to get a sense of the spirit of the people. These travels also exposed me to architecture, art, clothing, and interior design.

When I left Europe, I moved to California. I worked as an assistant buyer and fashion coordinator for Robinson's department store. I've never told my children about this, but one of the most interesting jobs I ever got was something I applied for on a dare—as a clothing designer for Frederick's of Hollywood. I had an interview with Mr. Frederick. I took the job because he offered me so much money I couldn't think of a way to turn him down. In retrospect, it was an amazing learning experience because I got to get inside the heads of a lot of people I'd never come in contact with. For instance, I once got a letter that said, "Please rush my order. My marriage is on the rocks." I realized that it takes many different kinds of people to make the world go round. Everyone lives and thinks differently. I kept my eyes open, and I noticed what people were drawn to and what they weren't drawn to—even if it was a product as delicate as lingerie.

The Ugly, Ugly House

When I got married and my husband and I bought our first home, real estate prices were through the roof. I didn't know much about interior design, but I knew that houses were sold by the square foot and so I chose to buy the biggest house we could afford. It was really, really ugly. Adults cried when they saw this project. My family members were vocal about their disappointment.

But at this time in my life, I started to realize that I have no fear, but that I do have great curiosity. It was in this house that I started to develop my signature philosophy: It's not what you *don't* have, it's what you *do* with what you *do* have.

For example, the backyard was large, but it was almost completely covered with poured concrete. I had a finite budget and much work to do on this house. I knew the concrete needed to be removed. But how to do it? So I found a man advertising in the newspaper with a jackhammer, and the two of us broke up and took out the concrete.

When I learned that I had to pay by the pound to have the concrete hauled to the dump, I decided to reuse it. I recalled my grandmother's garden in Michigan; the walls surrounding it were made of stacked concrete. So I set my broken concrete pieces in sand and then planted ground cover in between.

I studied home magazines and took classes at UCLA on interior design, and I found out where to buy fabric and wallpaper cheaply. At the end of 1 year, I had redone the house, and my husband and I decided to put it on the market. The Realtors who had sold us the house were so amazed at the transformation they asked us if they could take photographs to use in their company ads.

The ad said something like, "We turned the ugly duckling into a golden goose." It had photographs of various rooms in the house and of our family.

Value of House Doubled

In 1 year's time, we had doubled the value of our house and sold it in no time at all. And I was off and running. The real estate ad that featured our makeover came to the attention of a local designer in Los Angeles. She called and asked if I would work as her assistant.

At the same time, my husband and I used the profits we had made on our first house to buy a second house—this time an English Tudor.

I remodeled my first house so attractively, on a budget, that we doubled the value of the house in one year.

This house had much better bones than the first house. At least I had resources and a notebook full of talented tradesmen to help me.

It was ironic that I was working on our new home on my small budget and helping my friend Gabrielle in huge, very high budget projects in multimillion-dollar homes, offices filled with museum-quality antiques, and even a design project for a Gulf Stream airplane.

Shopping at the top and helping Gabrielle to spend other people's money was an education, but it didn't really get my juices going like working on my own projects did. Few things were more exciting for me than trying to come up with a look that I desired with the money, or lack of money, that was available to me.

My husband and I lived in that second house for a few years, again doubling our money and eventually selling it to actress Shelley Long for our asking price in 1 week's time. Our next house was a totally different style, a typical California ranch house, but the attraction was its huge backyard. It was at this point that I really got into gardening. I read gardening books like cookbooks and went to every garden show I could.

It was in this house that I was first an "owner-builder," as a contractor for my own kitchen remodel, which can be seen in Chris Madden's book, *Kitchens*. Our third child was born when we lived in this house, and I remember being 7 or 8 months pregnant just as

I designed this beautiful kitchen for my family. It was featured in Chris Madden's book on **kitchens**. Here I am with my daughters Brooke (left) and Bridget (better known as Birdie). My son Bo was off playing with friends.

they were putting the finishing touches on the brick floor of my new kitchen. (However, as I say in the chapter on floors and kitchens, hard brick on that kitchen floor turned out to be very hard on the legs.) I remember sealing the brick floor with Thompson's Water Sealer and covering my nose to protect myself from the fumes. My friend Sandy Hill came by the day that I was working on the floor and was shocked that I would be doing such a project when I was about to deliver a baby. (Women do crazy things when they're about to deliver!)

News That Would Change My Life

Three months later, after my daughter Bridget was born, Sandy called with news. She anchored a network news show in Los Angeles and then hosted *Good Morning America* in New York with David Hartman. She had done a pilot for ABC that was being called *The Home Show,* created in response to research showing that an information-oriented alternative to game shows and soap operas would do well. The executive producer, Woody Fraser, who had been involved in the evolution of *Good Morning America* and is known as Mr. TV in the industry for his reputation with live television, thought that the show needed experts to contribute on a regular basis. Sandy recommended some experts, including me!

I spoke with Woody and invited him to my home. I was not much of a fan of television in general, and certainly not daytime TV, so I couldn't envision what he wanted to create. I showed him around my house, and I said that just talking about interior design would be boring on camera unless you actually showed things being done. I suggested that it might be a good idea to actually purchase a house and have it redone during the course of the show's

season. Woody ended up staying almost 5 hours as we brainstormed together. At that time, I had no idea that I was interviewing for a job or creating a career for myself.

A few weeks later I got another call from Woody's office asking that I come to a television studio to do a demo on camera. I was so excited driving to the station that day in my Peugeot station wagon stuffed to the gills with baskets. I was going to do a 7-minute segment on clever ways to use baskets in your house, including hanging them on your walls, using them to house cookbooks, placing very large ones next to your fireplace to hold wood, and even using them for coffee tables.

After I arrived at the studio, I had my makeup professionally done for the first time in my life, and I was introduced to Rob Weller, who was hosting the show along with Sandy. Nobody ever explained that there would be so many cameras going at once, or that a green light on a camera didn't mean go, that red meant go. I had no idea where to look, so I ignored the cameras totally and focused on getting my information across.

After my time was up, Woody Fraser told me that I looked great on camera and that he would be sending this tape to New York. Over coffee, he told me that he had purchased a small Craftsman bungalow in the San Fernando Valley, and he was in the process of figuring out what my budget would be to redo this house for the show.

When I auditioned for *The Home Show*, the producers decided I looked okay on camera.

It was amazing and overwhelming all at once. I didn't even know that I was looking for a job and here I had one, based on my idea, assuming that New York executives would approve. They did.

My Career Had Begun

My career began on January 11, 1987, my first day on camera. It was my daughter Brooke's 11th birthday, and ever since then, 11 has been my lucky number.

We took just 13 weeks to redo the house because we weren't sure the show would be renewed after the season was up. Six and a half years later, I was still part of that show, lasting for its entire duration. Hosts came and went, but a certain core of experts, specifically crafts expert Carol Duvall and I, remained for the entire run.

At the end of *The Home Show,* Home and Garden Television began. The first day that HGTV went on the air, again in January, my show, *Kitty Bartholomew: You're Home,* was up and running. Again I was on the ground level, this time of an entire network.

A few years later, I decided to put my ideas and decorating philosophy into a book, and you're holding the fruits of that labor—and of my entire decorating career—in your hands right now. Enjoy!

—Kitty Bartholomew

Photography Credits

© Bart Bartholomew: pages 17, 21 (right), 47 (right), 116 (right), 234, 235 (left), 272, 273, 274 (top), 275, 281, 322

© Kitty Bartholomew: pages xiii, 13 (right), 28 (center), 30 (top), 50 (bottom left), 75, 77 (right), 178, 194 (center), 201, 206, 212 (bottom), 233 (right), 237 (right), 254, 260 (top)

Courtesy of Kitty Bartholomew: page 323

© Sharon Cavanagh: pages ix, x, xii, 4, 5, 6, 12, 18, 19, 20 (left), 21 (left), 22, 25, 26 (bottom left, right), 27, 28 (left, right), 29, 32, 33, 36 (bottom), 39, 40, 41 (center, right), 47 (left), 49, 50 (top left), 51, 52, 53, 54, 55, 56, 57, 58, 59, 60, 65, 70, 73, 76, 77 (left), 79 (bottom left, top right, bottom right), 80, 82, 83, 85, 86, 87, 89, 91, 93, 97, 98, 99, 101 (right), 103 (right), 104 (left, bottom right), 106 (center), 107, 108, 109, 110, 111, 112, 113, 114, 115, 117, 121, 122, 126 (bottom left, bottom right), 128, 129, 130, 131 (top center, bottom), 132, 133, 134, 135, 136 (left, center), 138, 141, 142, 144, 145 (left), 146, 147, 149 (top left, right), 150, 151, 153 (top right), 154, 155,

Photographer Sharon Cavanagh shoots Kitty through the kitchen window.

156 (right), 157, 158, 159, 160, 161, 162, 163, 164, 165, 166, 167, 168, 169, 170, 172, 181, 182 (left), 184, 186, 187, 188, 189, 191, 193, 194 (left, right), 198, 203, 208 (right), 209, 210, 213, 214, 215, 219, 220, 221 (left, center), 222, 223, 227, 228, 229, 230, 235 (right), 236, 237 (left), 238, 239, 240, 241, 242, 243, 245, 248, 249, 252, 255, 256, 257, 258, 259, 260 (bottom), 261, 262, 263, 265, 266, 267, 269, 274 (bottom), 276, 277 (left), 278 (left), 279, 280, 283, 286, 288, 289, 290, 291, 292 (top left, top right, bottom right), 293, 294, 295 (bottom left, bottom right), 296, 297, 298, 299, 300, 301, 302, 303, 304, 305, 306, 307, 309, 311 (left), 312 (top), 313, 314, 319, 326

© Vicki Clabaugh: pages 10, 131 (top right), 137, 277 (right), 325

Grey Crawford/Reprinted by permission of *Country Living*, a publication of Hearst Magazines, a unit of Hearst Corporation: pages 2, 20 (right), 31, 72, 103 (left), 156 (left), 211, 250

© Mark Lohman: pages ii, v, vi, vii, viii, 8, 13 (left), 15, 23, 24, 26 (top left), 30 (bottom), 34, 43 (right), 46, 48, 50 (right), 66, 67, 71, 74, 79 (top left), 81, 94, 101 (left), 102, 105, 106 (left, right), 118, 125, 126 (top), 127, 131 (left), 145 (right), 148, 153 (bottom left, bottom right), 173, 175, 176, 177, 179, 180, 183, 185, 204, 207, 208 (left), 212 (top), 216, 217, 218, 233 (left), 268, 278 (right), 285, 308, 310, 312 (bottom)

© Kathy Price-Robinson: pages 41 (left), 45, 78, 136 (right), 149 (bottom left), 153 (top left), 311 (top right, bottom right), 315

Rodale Images: page 7 (bottom)

Mitch Mandel/Rodale Images: page 7 (top)

© Jeremy Samuelson: pages 1, 11, 43 (left), 69, 100, 104 (top right), 182 (right), 197, 221 (right), 224, 270, 271, 292 (bottom left), 295 (top), 316, 318

© Mark Tanner: pages 35, 36 (top), 37, 38, 61, 62, 64, 88, 90, 116 (left), 120, 139, 171, 196, 199, 200, 202, 225, 226, 244, 246, 247, 264, 282

Acknowledgments

I would like to acknowledge Bill Schmidt, wherever you are, as being the first person to get my creative juices going. I'd like to thank Gabrielle Davis, an amazing designer and teacher, with whom I worked on very high-end projects. You educated my eye to shopping at the top, the designer world, the finest antique stores, and big budgets. I am grateful to Sandy Hill, the first host of *The Home Show*, whose phone call opened the door to the career in television that I wasn't even seeking but which fit me like a glove. Sandy opened the door to Woody Fraser, who started *Good Morning America* and who took chances with unknown people like me. You were pivotal in my career. Thank you. I want to thank George Merlis and Albert Fisher, the first producers of my HGTV show. George, with whom I also worked on *The Home Show*, makes my heart glad when he refers to me as the "Julia Child of Decorating," and Albert is so beautifully gentle; step by step both of them helped me build a career. Vicki Clabaugh flew down from Vachon Island, Washington, so many times to give me invaluable "hands-on" physical and moral support. My thanks to you. And finally, I want to thank Kathy Price-Robinson; without her, this book would not have happened. She's been after me for 15 years to write a book, and I regularly declined because I can't type and I can't sit still for very long. But Kathy was persistent, and she made this whole wonderful project happen. I am grateful to her in so many ways. *Her* total dedication to reproducing *my* spirit on the printed page drives her every word. She's been the guiding force, and my collaboration with her has been one of the great gifts of my lifetime. I have come to love her as a sister. —Kitty

I want to thank Kitty for her beautiful spirit. What a joy it is to work with such a generous and humble soul. And what a trooper!

She is definitely a gift from god, and my fervent wish is that this collaboration lasts for many, many years—I know the friendship will. I would also like to thank four teachers who made a difference in my life: my second-grade teacher, Mrs. Phillips, who taught me how to write a capital K and set me on a life of letters; my 11th-grade psychology teacher, Mr. Summerland, who told me—a shy and depressed teenager—that I would someday do something great and that I should come back to his class and share my story; my community college journalism teacher, whose name I can't recall, who gave me an A+ on a paper and told me that if I didn't become a great writer, it would be because of his lack of skills as a teacher and not from any lack of talent on my part; and finally, my longtime *Los Angeles Times* editor, Dick Barnes, who taught me how to perfect my craft using that tough type of editing where the editor gives guidance and then insists that the writer fix the article herself. To teachers everywhere, I want you to know that you change lives. —Kathy

We are also both grateful for the talents of Ted Weinstein, our gracious literary agent, and our capable and encouraging editors at Rodale, Karen Bolesta, Ellen Phillips, Jennifer Reich, and Karen Neely, as well as our hardworking and inspired art director Patricia Field. Our thanks go to George Garma for helping to style many of the shots, and to Sunday Hendrickson, who also styled many shots. And we are indebted to our photographers, most notably Sharon Cavanagh, who worked her tail off for this book, as well as the talents of Bart Bartholomew, Grey Crawford, Mark Lohman, and Jeremy Samuelson.

The generosity of these people is, in Kitty's words, "beyond wonderful." —Kitty and Kathy

Index

G

P

Paint
  aging technique with, <u>288</u>
  choosing finish for, <u>4</u>, <u>11</u>
  color
    Ask Kitty about, 35–38
    for ceilings, 42, <u>42</u>, <u>44</u>, 48, 51, 52, 62
    climate influencing, 38
    for exterior of house, 276, 279, 280
    lighting influencing, 35
    for moldings and trim, 36, **36**
    for porch, 282
    testing, 37
    for walls, 25, 35, 37, 38, 168, 181, 198,
      200–201, 202, 206, 223, 225–26, 253,
      254, 266
  milk, 195, 315
  for parchment look, 197
  primer for, 317
  storing leftover, <u>18</u>
  stripping, 199
Painted cane chair, Hands-On Project for,
  114–15, **114**, **115**
Painted faux finishes, 21, 37
Painted floor canvas, **47**
  Hands-On Project for, 54–56, **54, 55, 56**
Painted Furniture Patterns (Innes), 116, 313
Painted octagonal table, Hands-On Project
  for, 109, **109**
Painting
  aging technique with, 118
  bedroom set, 224
  books on, 37, 116, 279, 313
  ceiling fan blades, 64
  countertops, 244, 245, 264
  doors, 72, **72**
  faux (*see* Painted faux finishes)

fireplace, 203
front doors, 72–73
kitchen cabinets, 232
paneling, 203
sponge
  common mistakes in, 31
  Hands-On Project for, 31–32, **31, 32**
  tiles, 232
Paintings, inspiration from, 25, 30, 35, **38**,
  183, 185
Paint Magic (Innes), 37, 116, 279, 313
Paint pens, 312, 315
Paint samples, on popsicle sticks, <u>12</u>
Paint Wise (Innes), 116
Paneling, painting, 203
Pantry. *See also* Cabinets, kitchen
  checkerboard, Hands-On Project for, 243,
    243
  in Kitty's home, **239**, 240
Parchment look, for walls, 197
Pathway, garden, of Kitty's home, 277,
  277
Patios, 270, 271
Pedestal sinks, 251, 252, **252**, 254, 257
Pendleton blankets, uses for, 172
Photos
  aged mirror mat for, 137, **137**
  black-and-white, wall color for, 168
  in collage mat, 229
  locations for, 151
Picture frames. *See* Frames, picture
Picture hanger, bow and ribbon, Hands-On
  Project for, 159–60, **159, 160**
Picture lamp, 130
Picture mats, mirrors as, 129
Pictures, aged mirror mat for, 137, **137**
*Pierre Deux's French Country: A Style and
  Sourcebook*, 171

Pillow(s), **211**, 228, 229
  holiday, 172
  knitted, Hands-On Project for, 164, **164**
  made from quilts, 107
  from Pendleton blankets, 172
Pink
  in bathrooms, 253, <u>253</u>
  for ceilings, 42, <u>42</u>
  lightbulbs, 10, 127, <u>133</u>
  mood effects of, 9–10
Plants
  decorating pot for, 248
  decorating with, 181, 197
  lighting for, 141
  in outdoor rooms, <u>271</u>, 272
  preventing leaks from, 283
  for softening window view, 70, **70**, 88
Plate rack, in Kitty's home, **154**, 155, **187**
Plates
  collections of, <u>144</u>, 156, **156**
  for decorating walls, 224, **224**
  fabric-covered, <u>152</u>
  in Kitty's home, 156, **156**, 157, **157**, 254,
    257, 278, **278**
Plexiglas, for covering artwork, <u>10</u>
Pliers, needle-nose, 312
Polyurethane, 121
Popsicle sticks, paint samples on, <u>12</u>
Porch(es), **272–73**
  canvas rug for, 65
  colors for, 282
  decorating, 281
  of Kitty's home, 277, **281**
Pots, kitchen, polishing, 249
Pots, plant
  decorating, 248
  as outdoor table, 283
Pottery, protecting, from earthquakes, 157